ADVANCE PRAISE FOR

When the Church Was Young

"Too many Catholics take their ancient roots for granted and fail to study the Fathers of the Church, whose writings are essential bricks in the house of our faith. This book is wonderful in making accessible the building blocks of Catholic doctrine, and it holds them together with clear depictions of the lives and histories of the saints, scholars, and scoundrels who lived in the young days of the Church. What a great study guide for the individual, study group or classroom!"

—Fr. Mitch Pacwa, S.J., author of *The Holy Land: An Armchair Pilgrimage*

"Dr. D'Ambrosio has for years held pilgrims spellbound as he speaks about the Fathers. How good it is to have his spell bound between the covers of a book. His love for our Fathers is true, deep, and beautiful. In these pages he shares that love as only a master teacher can."

—Mike Aquilina, author of *Good Pope, Bad Pope*

"The dawn of the Church is an absolutely fascinating time, but most people don't know much about it, and many myths have been woven around it. Marcellino D'Ambrosio has done us all a favor by providing a clear, readable, and eye-opening look at what really happened in this crucial part of the Church's life."

—Jimmy Akin, author of *The Fathers Know Best*

"Marcellino D'Ambrosio brings ecclesiastical history to life with a clarity and vitality seldom achieved in this field. I've read many books on early Church history and can affirm without hesitation that, for a popular audience, this one ranks at the top of the list because of its straightforward prose, rich yet accessible content, thoroughness, and honest presentation of the facts."

—Patrick Madrid, radio host and author of *Envoy for Christ*

"*When the Church Was Young* is gripping, compelling, and fast-moving. Honestly, it's hard to believe it's about a bunch of old dead guys—I found myself wanting to learn more in the three-hundred-page adventure with this book than I have since college. Homeschooling moms, converts, people who like to read: Take note. You'll want to buy this book (because, no, I'm not letting you borrow mine)."

—Sarah Reinhard, author of *A Catholic Mother's Companion to Pregnancy*

"In providing such an accessible and engaging account of the Church Fathers—the frontiersmen of Christianity—Dr. D'Ambrosio has accomplished the rare feat of combining scholarship with readability. Christians of all traditions can trace their faith to these pioneers; their story is our story."

—Professor David Alton, House of Lords

When the Church Was Young

Voices of the Early Fathers

MARCELLINO D'AMBROSIO

franciscan
media
Cincinnati, Ohio

Unless otherwise noted, Scripture passages have been taken from the *Revised Standard Version*, Catholic edition. Copyright ©1946, 1952, 1971 by the Division of Christian Education of the National Council of the Churches of Christ in the USA. Used by permission. All rights reserved.

Quotes are taken from the English translation of the *Catechism of the Catholic Church* for the United States of America (indicated as *CCC*), 2nd ed. Copyright 1997 by United States Catholic Conference—Libreria Editrice Vaticana.

Cover and book design by Mark Sullivan
Cover image: St Apollinaris, St Sebastian, St Demetrius, St Polycarp and St Vincent, detail from the Saints Procession, mosaic, south wall, lower level, Basilica of Sant'Apollinare Nuovo (UNESCO World Heritage List, 1996), Ravenna, Emilia-Romagna. Italy, 6th century. / De Agostini Picture Library / A. Dagli Orti / The Bridgeman Art Library

LIBRARY OF CONGRESS CATALOGING-IN-PUBLICATION DATA
D'Ambrosio, Marcellino.
When the church was young : voices of the early fathers / Marcellino D'Ambrosio.
pages cm
ISBN 978-1-61636-777-0 (alk. paper)
1. Fathers of the church. I. Title.
BR67.D325 2014
270.1—dc23
2014016012

ISBN 978-1-61636-777-0

Published by Franciscan Media
28 W. Liberty St.
Cincinnati, OH 45202
www.FranciscanMedia.org

Printed in the United States of America.
Printed on acid-free paper.
20 21 22 12 11 10

CONTENTS

When a new star appeared over Bethlehem, the sleepy little town was occupied territory. Sixty years earlier, a foreign army had marched through the region claiming Palestine as a Roman province.

Rome's engineers were busy building new buildings, and its legions were conquering new territories. But Rome herself was no longer new. She had grown old and decrepit. The republic of Cicero had degenerated into the despotism of Caesar. Tyrant after tyrant had seized power at the price of much bloodshed. Devotion to family, hard work, and frugality had been replaced by an addiction to pleasure and power. A welfare state based on conquest and slave labor bought the loyalty of the mob with free bread and gladiator games. The people were all too ready to trade their liberty for creature comforts.

Into this depressing situation, the Gospel of Jesus Christ introduced a quiet excitement and a new hope that continued to grow, despite all the efforts to stamp it out. It began as a spark in Galilee, was fanned into flame on Pentecost, and within a decade or two reached the very gates of Caesar's capital, which then became the new center of Christian life and mission.

The story didn't end with the apostles. Paul and most of the twelve had been executed by the corrupt old empire, which saw them as an alarming threat. When the last apostle died, probably around A.D. 100, the new way of life, the new hope of the Christians, had barely penetrated society.

So much was left undone. There was no New Testament yet. True, there were some letters by Peter, Paul, and John written to one community or another. Also, by this time, there existed some collections of words and stories from the life of Jesus and the Church of the first generation. And there were other writings too, including one with some rather disturbing visions. But which of all these writings truly represent the teaching of Jesus and the apostles? If authentic, how authoritative are they? Should they be regarded as inspired Scripture, on the same level as Moses and Isaiah? And, by the way, was Jesus truly God, or was he just the greatest of the prophets? Was he fully human, or did he just appear in human form? Some of Paul's writings are hard to understand. What did Paul intend? What did Jesus himself intend?

The leaders who answered these questions picked up the ball from the apostles and carried it all the way through the years of the Church's infancy. They came to be called "the Church Fathers" much as the creators of the new American republic came to be known as the "Founding Fathers."

Fathers are those who beget life. And while physical life is a marvel, spiritual life, which comes from intimate knowledge of God, is a yet more wonderful thing. The Fathers begat this life primarily through their teaching. The Word of God, the teaching of Christ and the apostles, was likened by them to seed, which bestows life. But they also likened it to bread, which sustains life. Like good fathers, they were not only begetters, but providers. They not only sowed the apostolic seed, they provided nourishment, counsel, and discipline with an eye toward bringing the infant Church to maturity.

There were many teachers in the early Church whose teaching perished with them and whose names have been forgotten. The early Christian teachers who came to be called "the Fathers" are those who put their teaching into writing and so are able to teach us still. And we urgently need their teaching. The cynical, tired world today is remarkably like the worn-out Roman society of their day. The questions they responded to are our questions, and their problems are our problems. Their voices, resonating with the youthful energy of the early Church, need to be heard again today.

That is the reason for this book. The Church in their day was endangered from within through division and compromise. And it was endangered from without through persecution and moral seduction. Sound familiar? The Fathers' witness was key to the unity and vitality of the Church back then. But their witness is also key to the restoration of unity and vitality right now.

This book is not meant to be a textbook introduction or an encyclopedic handbook. Excellent versions of these exist, and I highly recommend them. This book, on the other hand, is intended to acquaint the reader with the colorful personalities and the seething passion of those who are our common ancestors and to share a few gems from the treasure of their precious teaching, which is our common patrimony.

And when I say "our," I mean the entire Christian family. Long before the schism between East and West, Protestant and Catholic, long before the words *catholic*, *orthodox*, and *evangelical* referred to communities distinct and separated from other each other, the Fathers of the Church gloried in the one faith of the united Body of Christ, which can be none other than evangelical, catholic, and orthodox.

It is time to rediscover our common inheritance. By returning to the days when the Church was young and exploring our roots together, we will experience new growth that will produce new fruit, new unity, and great joy.

Many years ago, when I fell in love with Christ and was eager to explore the heritage of his Church, I had the good fortune to meet a Trappist monk. He had left New Melleray Abbey for a season to serve as a spiritual guide to young men such as me. This priest, Fr. Jim Henderson, first gently suggested that I begin praying the *Liturgy of the Hours* (the Divine Office). When I politely resisted, he firmly insisted. So I relented. It was in the Roman Breviary's Office of Readings that I met the early Church Fathers. From that moment, they, along with Fr. Jim, became my first spiritual guides. Shortly thereafter, Fr. Jim put into my hands a book by a French Jesuit named Henri de Lubac. It was this French scholar who taught me just how critical was the rediscovery of the Fathers for the renewal of Christianity today. His massive study on the Fathers' way of interpreting the Bible became the subject of my doctoral dissertation.

So this book is the fruit of the labors of many great teachers who have brought the Fathers alive for me: Fr. Jim, Henri de Lubac, Jean Daniélou, Louis Bouyer, Godfrey Diekmann, George Berthold, Giles Dimmock, Boniface Ramsey, Robin Darling Young, Francis Martin, and Avery Dulles, to name a few. To them I shall be ever grateful.

But this book has been the fruit of the labors of many more people beyond these. First, I wish to thank the team from Franciscan Media, especially Louise Paré, Claudia Volkman, Barbara Baker, Katie Carroll, and Chris Holmes. Then, of course, comes the staff, benefactors, and volunteers of the Crossroads Initiative, especially Cyndi Lucky and Cyndi Clancy who covered for me in so many respects while I was busy on this project. A multitude of friends and advisors also gave input on everything from the title, to the cover, to the style and content of individual chapters. They include Naomi Lehew and Kurt Klement from St. Ann's parish in Coppell, Texas; Frs. John Schroedel and George Gray of the Orthodox Church of America; Pastor Bob Bonnell; Professors John and Ashley Norohna; Fr. Taylor Albright of the Episcopal Church; Gloria Zapiain of the Archdiocese of San Antonio; Sarah Reinhard from CatholicMom.com; Matt Swaim of the *Sonrise Morning Show*; Alan Napleton of the Catholic Marketing Network; speaker Marc Cardaronella; author David Calvillo; evangelist Kelly Wahlquist; Dan Mansell of Basecamp Creative; and Ascension Press president Matt Pinto.

Finally and most especially, I want to acknowledge the invaluable role played by my family, without whose help this book would have never been completed. My mom, Patricia, and my daughter Cristina Joy covered the whole process in prayer on a daily basis. My son Nick was constantly warning me not to get distracted with unessential things. Marisa, Marcellino, and Anthony read chapter after chapter, making invaluable suggestions for improvement of style and content. But greatest thanks goes to my wife, Susan, who not only proofread every chapter but blocked for me and had to do all the things I couldn't do while barricaded in my study.

This book has been a labor of love undertaken by an amazing team. It is always a privilege to serve the Lord. But it is an even greater pleasure to do so in such good company.

(c. = approximate)

c. A.D. 30:   Death and resurrection of Jesus, followed by Pentecost

50:   Earliest document of the New Testament (*1 Thessalonians*) written; Paul leaves his base in Antioch on his second missionary journey

60:   Paul begins two-year house arrest in Caesarea before being sent to Rome

64–68:   First persecution of Christians in Rome under Nero; Peter and Paul martyred; approx. date first Gospel (Mark or Matthew) written; Polycarp born

70:   Destruction of Jerusalem and its temple by Roman armies under Titus

81:   Domitian becomes emperor, adopting the title *Dominus Deus* (Lord God)

c. 95:   Gospel of John completed; Clement's letter to the Corinthians written, beginning the era of the early Church Fathers

c. 110:   Letters and martyrdom of Ignatius of Antioch

144:   Marcion is excommunicated by the Church of Rome

c. 151:   *First Apology* of Justin written in Rome

155:   Martyrdom of Polycarp in Smyrna; approximate beginning of Montanism

165:   Justin martyred in Rome; approximate date for Hippolytus's birth

c. 185:   Irenaeus writes *Against Heresies*; Clement takes over the catechetical school at Alexandria to be followed twenty years later by Origen; earliest surviving list of New Testament books made, the Muratorian Canon

---

1. See *New Jerome Bible Commentary* (NJBC), p. 1045 for Raymond E. Brown's dating of all New Testament books. Raymond E. Brown, et al., eds. *The New Jerome Biblical Commentary* (Englewood Cliffs, N.J.: Prentice Hall, 1990).

337:	Constantine dies, succeeded in the East by pro-Arian son, Constantius
339:	Athanasius, deposed by Constantius, flees to Rome
356:	Athanasius again deposed by Constantius and flees into the desert; death of Antony
357:	Athanasius writes *Life of Antony*; Basil visits the Egyptian monks in the desert
359:	Most bishops in both East and West forced to sign Semi-Arian Creed of Council of Rimini-Seleucia; "the world groaned to find itself Arian" (Jerome)
367:	First list of all 27 books of our New Testament in Athanasius's 39TH Festal Letter
369:	Valens names Arian bishop of Constantinople; 80 protesting clerics burnt alive
370:	Basil becomes bishop in Cappadocia; next year consecrates Gregory Nazianzen bishop
372:	Basil consecrates his brother Gregory as bishop of Nyssa
373:	Ambrose elected bishop of Milan, replacing the Arian Auxentius; Athanasius dies
c. 375:	Basil writes On the Holy Spirit; Jerome studies Hebrew in the Syrian desert
379:	Theodosius made emperor of the East; death of Basil and Macrina
380:	Theodosius outlaws Arians, makes Gregory Nazianzen Bishop of Constantinople
381:	Council of Constantinople I expands Creed to clarify the divinity of the Holy Spirit
386:	Ambrose refuses to surrender churches to Arians; John Chrysostom ordained priest; Jerome settles in Bethlehem
387:	Baptism of Augustine by Ambrose in Milan; death of his mother, Monica
389:	Gregory Nazianzen dies; Gregory of Nyssa dies a few years later
390:	Ambrose excommunicates Theodosius for the massacre at Thessalonika

395:	Theodosius, last emperor of both East and West, dies; Augustine ordained bishop
c. 397:	Augustine writes his *Confessions*; Ambrose dies
398:	John Chrysostom made bishop of Constantinople
403:	Augustine begins a ten-year battle against the Donatists
405:	Jerome finishes "Vulgate" translation of the Bible, begins commentaries on the Prophets
407:	Death of John Chrysostom after three years of harsh exile
410:	Sack of Rome by Alaric signals the collapse of the Empire in the West
412:	Augustine begins his battle against the Pelagians
419:	Death of Jerome
428:	Nestorius becomes bishop of Constantinople
430:	Death of Augustine during the Vandals' siege of Hippo
431:	Council of Ephesus condemns Nestorius, proclaims Mary as Theotokos (Mother of God)
440:	Leo becomes pope (bishop of Rome)
449:	"Robber Council" of Ephesus
452:	Pope Leo turns back Attila the Hun from the gates of Rome
451:	Ecumenical Council of Chalcedon teaches that Jesus is fully human and divine, one person, two natures, relying heavily on the Tome of Leo
461:	Death of Pope Leo
c. 500:	Benedict begins his life as a monk at Subiaco, in the hills east of Rome
590:	Gregory made pope (bishop of Rome)
595:	Gregory sends 40 monks to evangelize England; they settle at Canterbury
604:	Death of Gregory the Great
636:	Isidore of Seville dies, concluding the Age of the Church Fathers in the West
749:	John of Damascus dies, concluding the Age of the Church Fathers in the East

CHAPTER 1

The Church Fathers: Who Is Included?

When I first heard people refer to "the Fathers of the Church," I had no idea who they were talking about. So I searched for the official list. I was surprised to discover there isn't one. That's because the term "Father of the Church" or "early Church Father" is not a formal title officially bestowed on someone by a pope or Church council. It is a family term, informally coined by somebody in the early Church to refer to some other people in an even earlier era of the Church. Occasionally, when a person comes up with a new term, it just sticks, and others start using it. Before long, everybody is using it. That's apparently what happened in this case.

A New Definition

Still, my question remained. Who is included in this class of people called the "early Church Fathers," and why are they important? One often finds the following standard definition in encyclopedias and textbooks: The Fathers of the Church are those characterized by *orthodoxy, holiness, antiquity,* and *Church approval.*

But actually, this stock definition raises more questions than it answers. *Antiquity*—that's vague. For many today, something is ancient if it was before the Beatles. *Holiness*—some men often called Fathers of the Church, like Origen and Tertullian, never became recognized as saints. *Church approval*—since there is no official list, how do you determine this? And finally there is *orthodoxy.* Many of the Fathers, including great ones like Gregory of Nyssa, had some idea or another that, centuries later, the Church in hindsight officially rejected.

So after lots of years of researching and teaching about the history of Christian thought, I developed an improved definition that describes how the term "Fathers of the Church" is actually used. *The Church Fathers are those great Christian writers who passed on and clarified the teaching of the apostles from approximately the second through the eighth centuries.* Note: This does not include the century when Jesus and the apostles lived; the era of the New Testament stands in a class all its own. The era of the Church Fathers begins where the original eyewitnesses leave off and carries us through the period of the first seven great universal or ecumenical councils that hammered out the two most central issues in the Christian faith: How one God could be conceived of as three distinct persons and how Jesus could be both God and Man. Thus, these teachers helped bring Christianity out of its diapers into adulthood. No one can ever again play the role that they played during those exciting, formative years when the Church was young.

An Era in Four Phases

From A.D. 100 to A.D. 800—that's a long period of time. A lot of things change during so many years. So let's break it down into two main sub-categories. First of all, we have the period of about three hundred years when being a Christian was a capital offense in the Roman Empire. Right after the Edict of Milan (A.D. 313) granted religious freedom in the Roman Empire, a groundbreaking event in Christian history occurred: the first great Universal or Ecumenical Council of the Church—the Council of Nicaea (A.D. 325). The

Church Fathers who wrote during the age of persecution are referred to as "the ante-Nicene Fathers" (*ante* means "before" in Latin). We can distinguish two sub-groups among the ante-Nicene Fathers. First comes the group of writers who were alive when the apostles were alive. They were either immediate disciples of the apostles or had some contact with them and learned from them. They are therefore called the "Apostolic Fathers." They lived from A.D. 50 through about A.D. 150 and their writings come to us beginning around A.D. 95. The importance of these writers is hard to exaggerate. They help us identify both what the apostles actually meant by what they wrote and also what the apostles orally taught but neglected to include in what came to be known as the New Testament writings.

Following the Apostolic Fathers comes a distinctive group of writers, often very bright and gifted. In some cases, they were secular scholars who were won for Christ and then used all their learning to advance the cause of the Gospel. We call these men "apologists" since a major focus of their writings was to defend the faith against Christian heretics, Jewish critics, and pagan persecutors. The apologists lived and wrote from about the year A.D. 150 all the way through the pivotal Council of Nicaea in A.D. 325.

The Edict of Milan ushered in a phenomenal era of ferment and development. The Fathers following this watershed are known as the Nicene and post-Nicene Fathers. For the next two centuries, the central teachings of the faith were hammered out by four successive Ecumenical Councils. The styles of formal worship that we now know—the Roman liturgy of the West, the Byzantine and Maronite liturgies of the East—took shape during this time. The canon, or official list of the various books of the New Testament, also took its final shape during this fertile time.

I like to refer to this period, the fourth and fifth centuries, as the "Golden Era of the Fathers." It includes such personalities as Ambrose and Augustine in the West and Athanasius and Basil in the East.

Following this, we have a period, the sixth through eighth centuries, which is sort of an afterglow, when the remaining Fathers like Gregory the Great and John of Damascus[2] summed up, amplified, and passed on the teaching of previous Fathers and Councils.

Voices That Must Be Heard

This great and diverse group of people provides us with something that we desperately need. They are a mighty cloud of witnesses to what the apostles lived and taught. But many of them were creative contributors to this tradition as well since they provided new vocabulary, key insights, and critical clarifications, enabling the Church to more profoundly understand and more clearly express the apostolic truth that these witnesses passed on to us.

This book is not an exhaustive treatment of seven hundred years of patristic writings. Such a project would have resulted either in a library or a very superficial single volume. Instead, my goal has been to tell the stories of some of the most intriguing fathers of both East and West, from the dawn of the patristic period to its sunset. Since all roads lead to Rome, our story will both start and end in this city of Peter and Paul.

---

2. John of Damascus, also known as John Damascene, is usually regarded as the last of the Church Fathers. He died around A.D. 749.

CHAPTER 2

Clement and the Corinthian Coup

Everybody has heard of Emperor Nero, who reportedly fiddled while Rome burned. The area destroyed by the great fire of A.D. 64 conveniently cleared a section of the city that Nero wanted for the building of his grandiose palace. It was no wonder, then, that some suspected that Nero himself was responsible for the blaze. To deflect the blame, Nero pinned the arson on a sinister new religious sect from the East and, in so doing, launched the first great persecution of Christians in the Roman Empire. Horrible spectacles followed, with Christians serving as human torches to illuminate evening games in the amphitheaters. In the same festivities, other Christians were cast as tragic figures from mythology whose demise was reenacted before the eyes of the bloodthirsty mob.[3] Among the victims of this persecution, which lasted several years, were the apostles Peter and Paul.

After Nero was forced by his own officials to commit suicide in A.D. 68, the Church had a respite. After all, Roman generals were too busy fighting each other to bother with the Christians. But peace did not last long. In A.D. 81 a new tyrant by the name of Domitian came to power. This emperor was, in some ways, an even greater megalomaniac than Nero. He demanded that everyone refer to him as *"Dominus et Deus"*—Lord and God! And the pledge of allegiance that he required was that his subjects burn incense before his divine image.

---

3. See Clement's *First Letter to the Corinthians*, 1 Clement 6.

Obviously, this didn't play very well with Jews and Christians. Fortunately for the Jews, they were exempted because of their ancestral belief in one God. But Christians were no longer regarded as Jews. They were instead considered a new and dangerous sect with no history, no standing, and therefore no privileges. A great persecution ensued, putting the Christian community under intense pressure.[4] In Corinth, this stress apparently led to a breakdown in relationships. Younger elements in the community maneuvered to depose the Church's established leaders and declare themselves the new authorities.

Was such a move legitimate? Is leadership in the Christian community simply a function of popularity, talent, or political power?

Authority in Crisis

The *Letter of Clement* provides a very firm answer to these questions. The leader of the Church in Rome, a man by the name of Clement, had known Peter and Paul before they died. Yet he was very humble, so humble, in fact, that he neglected to mention his own name on this letter addressed to the Church in Corinth from the Church in Rome. Humility, in fact, is one of the central themes of the letter. We know that Clement was the author of this epistle thanks to Church Fathers of the second century who told us about it in their writings.[5]

The main reason for the letter was to let the Corinthian church know in no uncertain terms that the leadership coup that occurred was entirely illegitimate. In the letter, Clement insisted that the apostles had intended an orderly succession of authority in the Church. The apostles themselves, he stated, had commissioned leaders to shepherd

---

4. 1 Clement 1:1.
5. See, for example, Irenaeus, *Against Heresies,* III.3.3.

the Corinthian church and these elders and bishops commissioned others to succeed them in turn. This process of succession from the apostles was to be preserved unbroken. This provides us with the earliest written references to the idea of apostolic succession.[6]

So in each local church, founded by the apostles, there needed to be an orderly succession of leaders that went back to the apostles. But how about in the wider Church? Did one community have the right to meddle in the affairs of another? Did one apostolic church have special responsibility to provide leadership and oversight to other apostolic churches? Clement, who is our earliest witness of the martyrdom of Peter and Paul,[7] answered this question as well. But he did so in his very act of writing this letter and having it carried to Corinth by four prominent envoys whose job it was to help resolve the crisis by following the counsel of the letter.[8]

Clement took it upon himself to speak to the members of a church founded by the apostle Paul and tell them, gently, lovingly, but very firmly, that what they had done was wrong and that they needed to restore the properly authorized leaders of the church. It is fascinating to note that as he describes the offended leaders, he emphasizes their liturgical role as leading Christian worship and sees that worship in sacrificial terms: "For we shall be guilty of no slight sin if we eject from the episcopate men who have offered the sacrifices with innocence and holiness."[9]

His approach is not a heavy-handed bureaucratic one. Rather, as a brother and a father, he exhorts the Corinthian Christians to recover the authentic Christian focus on holiness and charity, which is

6. 1 Clement 40, 42, 44.
7. 1 Clement 5.
8. 1 Clement 63:3.
9. 1 Clement 44.

characterized not by self-exaltation but rather by humility. He brings forth example after example from the Bible, which in his day was still limited to the Jewish Scriptures, to show the danger of rivalry and the power of humble obedience. But he also says that we need to take note of the example of the heroes of "our own generation,"[10] meaning the recent Christian martyrs. Quoting from an unknown source, he is witness to the beginning of a key feature of Christian spirituality: "Follow the saints, for those who follow them will become saints."[11]

In Defense of Unity

Clement is kind and fatherly. But in the ancient world, "father" also meant "authority," and he does not hesitate to engage his authority, insisting that the Corinthians "prove obedient to what we, prompted by the Holy Spirit, have written."[12] Clement wrote before what we know as "the New Testament" was completed and widely available. But he was clearly familiar with Paul's first letter to the Corinthians and reminded his readers of Paul's teaching that the Church is indeed the very body of Christ.[13] To divide the Church is therefore to do violence to Christ.

Devotion to Christ means absolute and passionate commitment to the unity of the Church. Christians today casually accept as a fact of life the existence of thousands of different Christian churches that are separated from and sometimes hostile to each other. Clement and other early Church Fathers, on the other hand, regarded division among Christians with utter horror. Clement condemns the scandalous Corinthian revolt as an "abominable and unholy schism, so

---

10. 1 Clement 5.
11. 1 Clement 46:2.
12. 1 Clement 63:2.
13. See 1 Corinthians 12:12ff.

alien and foreign to those whom God has chosen."[14] On the other hand, Clement invokes "the glorious and holy rule [*kanon*] of our tradition [*paradosis*]," which for him includes not only the truth about who Jesus was and what he did for us, but a commitment to conserve and protect the unity of his body. He calls them to be faithful to "our tradition of noble and righteous harmony."[15]

Clement had the nerve to send this bold letter to Corinth. How was it received? The Corinthians apparently not only heeded his direction, but they continued to read his letter as part of their Sunday worship for the next several hundred years. But better than that, they considered this letter so important that they copied it and sent it all around the empire for other communities to read. Thus the letter survived not only in its original Greek, but in Latin, Coptic, and Ethiopian. And that letter of Clement, which became the first papal encyclical, if you will, was regarded so highly that it was even regarded as part of the New Testament in many parts of the empire, including Alexandria, one of the most important early Christian centers. That is a compelling testimony to the respect for the Church of Rome and its bishop which existed in the earliest days of the Church.

Interesting thing, though—this wonderful letter was lost to Western Christians until the year 1623 when the patriarch of Constantinople gave the king of England a precious gift. It was a copy of the fifth-century bound volume of the Bible called the *Codex Alexandrinus* that contained, along with the Gospels and the epistles, the letter of Clement. That means that, unfortunately, Clement's letter was not available during the prior century when great arguments arose that shattered Christian unity in the West. But it clearly shows that, even

---

14.   1 Clement 1:1.
15.   1 Clement 51.

in the first century, around the same time John's Gospel was likely put into its final form (c. A.D. 95), the successor of Peter and Paul in Rome had a special role. And that role was to defend and preserve the precious unity of the Church.

CHAPTER 3

The *Didache*: Out of the Mist of History

Istanbul had always been a hotbed of intrigue and mystery. But the monk rummaging through the monastery library that fateful day in 1873 was looking for neither. He just wanted something edifying to read. When he happened upon a dusty old volume and opened the cover, he realized that he had found more than he had bargained for. It turns out that this tome had been compiled by a scribe named Leo in 1053 and was actually a collection of even older documents. Leo recognized some of them—copies of letters by Clement and Barnabas dating back to the earliest days of the Church. One of the documents was strange—he had never heard of it. So at first, he ignored it. But this is precisely the one that caused a sensation when he finally published it a decade later.

Entitled "The Teaching of the Lord According to the Twelve Apostles," it quickly became known simply by the Greek word for "teaching," *Didache*. The reason for the furor was that though this work had been mentioned by several of the Church Fathers, it had disappeared and remained hidden away for nearly a thousand years until rediscovered in that monastery library in Istanbul.

As scholars pored over it, they were puzzled. Who wrote it and when? Neither question could be answered with certainty. But here's what the evidence suggests—an anonymous Christian editor in Alexandria, Egypt, sometime in the first half of the second century, got his hands on two Christian documents that were already old in his day. One, called "The Two Ways," was what appears to be the earliest surviving Christian catechism. The second is the very first "Church order," or instructional manual on how to conduct worship. Such practical directions on worship are conspicuously absent in the New Testament. It is this second section that is most fascinating since it apparently reflects the life of rural Christian congregations in Palestine or Syria during the time of the apostles.

A Distinctive Lifestyle

Before we turn to this, though, we have to review a few important things to be gleaned from the catechism. The Ten Commandments had been a classic framework for teaching the moral life among the Jews, and they continued to have this role with Christians. But sometimes what is allowed and not allowed by a given commandment is not exactly clear. Take, for example, "Thou shalt not kill." Since God sent his people to war against the Canaanites, he obviously makes an exception for self-defense. Were there other exceptions? Then there is "Thou shalt not commit adultery." That strictly means a married person can't have sex with anyone other than his or her spouse. But how about an unmarried man and woman (fornication)? How about unmarried men with each other? Or unmarried men with unmarried boys?

A good catechism addresses such situations and questions with which people really grapple. So the first part of the *Didache* provides some interpretation of these two commandments:

> Do not murder; do not commit adultery; do not corrupt boys; do not fornicate; do not steal; do not practice magic; do not go in for sorcery [*farmakeusein*]; do not murder a child by abortion or kill a newborn infant.[16]

---

16. *Didache* 2:2.

Here we find the earliest specification in Christian literature that the murder forbidden by the fifth commandment includes abortion. One thing that may not be clear to the modern reader is that the word that translators often render as "sorcery," *farmakeusein*, really means "pharma," or drugs that could be used in magic potions. Here, the word certainly refers to drugs taken to induce abortion or sterility, namely abortifacients and contraceptives. Obviously, the science of the day was a bit rudimentary, but it did not stop people of the era from trying, sometimes successfully, to prevent birth. Tertullian, writing a century later, would describe in gruesome detail the surgical instruments employed by the abortionists of his time.

Clearly, the sixth commandment's prohibition of adultery included for early Christians any relations outside of marriage between man and woman, whether heterosexual or homosexual. In the Greco-Roman society of the time, religion had very little to do with sexual morality. Adventuresome sexual exploration was the fashion, pedophilia included.

Christians were to be starkly different in their lifestyle. In a culture of gladiator games and infanticide where human flesh was cheap, the Christians were to witness to a culture of life, dignity, and charity. Not only were murder and adultery forbidden, but generosity was expected and commanded:

> Do not hesitate to give and do not give with bad grace; for you will discover who He is that pays you back a reward with a good grace. Do not turn your back on the needy, but share everything with your brother and call nothing your own. For if you have what is eternal in common, how much more should you have what is transient![17]

---

17. *Didache* 4:7–8.

Instructions for Worship

Now we turn to the worship manual. The first directions provided are instructions for baptism:

> Baptize in running water, "in the name of the Father and of the Son and of the Holy Spirit." If you do not have running water, baptize in some other. If you cannot in cold, then in warm. If you have neither, then pour water on the head three times "in the name of the Father, Son, and Holy Spirit."[18]

There were no church buildings yet, and the Church was under persecution, so finding a place to baptize presented a problem. Note the practical, pastoral common sense provided by the *Didache*. Running or "living" water is preferred (after all, Jesus was baptized in a river), but you have to make do. The Romans had hot and cold bath complexes that were a feature of every city or town. Perhaps Christians could discreetly use one of these. But if necessary, pouring over the head is even allowed, which shows that immersion was not considered absolutely necessary to make baptism valid. What is necessary, besides water, is that the name of the Triune God—Father, Son, and Holy Spirit—be invoked.

The author insists that before baptism, the candidates and the ministers must fast for a few days, along with as many others who can join them.[19] Within a century or two, baptisms were customarily done in large groups and reserved for Easter and Epiphany (January 6). The fast of a few days grew to forty days, in honor of Christ's example. Here we see both the origin and the original meaning of the penitential seasons of Lent and Advent.

---

18. *Didache* 7:2.
19. See *Didache* 7:4.

Sometime in the second half of the first century, a rupture occurred between the synagogue and the Church. Neither the Jews nor the Christians nor the pagan Romans any longer considered Christians as a particular group of Jews. Exactly when this took place we are not sure. But we do see reflections of it in the *Didache* where the author is concerned that Christians distinguish themselves from the Jews by their patterns of fasting and prayer. "Your fasts must not be identical with those of the hypocrites. They fast on Mondays and Thursdays; but you should fast on Wednesdays and Fridays."[20] This pattern of Wednesday and Friday fast became virtually universal in the early Church and is preserved by the Eastern churches to this day.[21] While Wednesday has disappeared as a penitential day in the Roman Catholic tradition (except for the start of Lent), each Friday remains a day of penance in honor of the passion of Christ. So the tradition of meatless Fridays has a very ancient origin.

For Jews, the distinctive daily prayer, repeated at least morning and evening (and in the prophet Daniel, at noon also), was the *Shema Yisrael:* "Hear, O Israel, the Lord is our God, the Lord alone. And you shall love the Lord your God with all your heart, and with all your soul, and with all your strength" (Deuteronomy 6:4–5). The *Didache* says that Christians are also to pray three times per day using the Lord's Prayer, in exactly the form it is given in the Gospel of Matthew, substituting for the *Shema.* Jews did not address God as "Father"; to do so is a distinctive mark of the disciples of Jesus who, through him, are sons and daughters of God. Also interesting is that

---

20.   *Didache* 8:1.
21.   We refer here to both Eastern Orthodox and Eastern Catholic (such as Maronite or Byzantine) Churches.

the *Didache* concludes the Our Father with a doxology that is not found in the New Testament text: "For yours is the power and the glory forever."[22]

Christians are to gather weekly, not on the Sabbath or Saturday, but on the first day of the week, Sunday:

> On every Lord's Day—his special day—come together and break bread and give thanks, first confessing your sins so that your sacrifice may be pure. Anyone at variance with his neighbor must not join you, until they are reconciled, lest your sacrifice be defiled. For it was of this sacrifice that the Lord said, "Always and everywhere offer me a pure sacrifice."[23]

Not only does this show us that weekly worship in the Church of this era centered on the Eucharist, but that this Eucharist was understood in terms of a sacrifice, specifically the pure oblation that the prophet Malachi predicted would be offered by the Gentiles.[24] There are echoes too of Jesus's words in Matthew 5:23–24: "So if you are offering your gift at the altar, and there remember that your brother has something against you, leave your gift there before the altar and go; first be reconciled to your brother, and then come and offer your gift." The Eucharistic sacrifice needed to be preserved from both the defilement of personal sin and the strife among brethren that wounded the unity of the Church. So we see the beginning of a penitential rite before the Eucharist and find the reason for the exchange of peace later found in the Roman, Maronite, and other liturgies; this rite is a pledge and a sign that there is no unresolved strife that would prevent anyone from taking part in the sacrifice of unity.

---

22. *Didache* 8:2.
23. *Didache* 14:1–3.
24. See Malachi 1:11.

There is no explanation given by the *Didache* of the relation between the consecrated elements and the Body and Blood of Christ. However, it is clear that the Eucharist is no empty symbolic reminder, but something holy, the purity of which must be safeguarded. "You must not let anyone eat or drink of your Eucharist except those baptized in the Lord's name. For in reference to this the Lord said, 'Do not give what is sacred to dogs.'"[25]

There is a beautiful section of the Eucharistic Prayer to be considered in this connection: "As this piece [of bread] was scattered over the hills and then was brought together and made one, so let your Church be brought together from the ends of the earth into your Kingdom."[26] This hints at something we'll see elaborated in subsequent Church Fathers as time goes on: The Eucharist is not just about the communion of each person with the Lord, but a manifestation and deepening of the unity of his body, the Church.

But Who Wrote It?

The compiler of the *Didache* wished to remain anonymous, and the Church Fathers who refer to it pass over the authorship issue in silence. This is actually most fitting, in light of the name given to the work. This is not offered to us as a creative composition. The compiler's aim was to record not his own teaching but the teaching of the Lord himself that had come down to us from the apostles. He was passing on to the Church of his day the apostolic tradition of faith and worship that he himself had been privileged to receive. And thanks to an eleventh-century scribe named Leo and a monk from Istanbul, it has been passed on to us as well.

---

25. *Didache* 9:5, quoting Matthew 7:6.
26. *Didache* 9:4.

CHAPTER 4

Ignatius: Prophet, Pastor, and Witness

W e now come to one of the most inspiring figures of the early
Church. Not to be confused with the founder of the Jesuits,
this Ignatius lived in Antioch, which had won renown fifty years
earlier as the missionary base of Barnabas and Paul. But these were
not the only apostles to have left their mark on the church in Antioch.
Around the time of the famous council of Jerusalem in A.D. 49 (see
Acts 15), Peter relocated to this city, which at that time was one of
the preeminent cities of the Roman Empire. In the first decade of the
second century, Ignatius was the bishop of this notable place influenced by at least three apostles, the city where Jesus's disciples had
been called Christians for the first time (see Acts 11:26).

We are not sure what year Peter left Antioch to make his way to
Rome. But we do know that Ignatius was Peter's second successor as
leader of the church there.[27] The insight that Ignatius's writing gives
us into the mind of the apostles is therefore incomparable.

But Ignatius gives us something else that is absolutely unique. No
other writer of the early Church so effectively opens a window into
the soul of a Christian on the eve of martyrdom.

---

27. Both Eusebius *Eccl. Hist.* 3.22.36 and Origen, *Hom. 6 In Luc* (P.G. 13, 1814) attest
to this. Eusebius names Euodius as the connecting episcopal link between Peter and
Ignatius.

Martyr as Witness

Before we peer into this window, we need to pause for a historical note. During the almost three centuries that Christianity was a
capital crime in the Roman Empire, persecution was a mostly local
and sporadic affair. Often a civic crisis or natural disaster would lead
a city's populace to look for a reason for the gods' anger. Since it was
known that the Christians insolently refused to worship any god but
their own, these troublemakers would be blamed, rounded up, and
executed to appease offended deities. Something like this apparently
occurred in Antioch around A.D. 110 when a violent but short-lived
persecution broke out and Ignatius, the bishop, was apprehended. As
a top leader of this sect, he was too big a catch to waste on the locals.
Instead, he was sentenced to fight wild beasts in Rome for the amuse-
ment of the mob and the pleasure of the emperor himself.

So Ignatius was chained to a squad of soldiers. He called them "ten
leopards"[28]—men who were brutal and crude. They marched him on
foot across Asia Minor and then up the western coast of what is now
Turkey. He walked in chains all the way to the end of the road, to
Troas, site of ancient Troy, where he finally was put on a ship that
carried him to Rome where the wild beasts awaited him.

Ignatius's captors made rest stops in several towns along the
way. Since no persecution was occurring in the area, delegations of
Christians came to encourage him and to kiss the chains of a holy one
about to die for Christ.[29] Ignatius and his leopards then resumed their
grim march. At subsequent rest stops in Smyrna and Troas, Ignatius
wrote to the churches that had sent representatives to honor him. The
seven brief letters he managed to finish before embarking at Troas

---

28. *Letter of Ignatius to the Ephesians* 5:1.
29. *Letter of Ignatius to Polycarp* 2:3.

serve as his last will and testament. By the providence of God, these letters survived, have been verified as authentic, and have been available to us since the nineteenth century. And in these letters we see what was on the mind and heart of a bishop marching to martyrdom.

The first thing that stands out is that this is a man passionately in love with Jesus Christ. Three hundred years after Ignatius's death, the great preacher John Chrysostom described Ignatius as "a soul seething with divine eros."[30] Yes, he was a prominent bishop, the leader of the one of the most famous of all Christian communities in one of the empire's greatest cities. He was to the end a teacher whose letters addressed various doctrinal and disciplinary issues that were of vital importance.

But before he was a bishop, Ignatius was first and foremost a disciple. And although he did not voluntarily surrender to the authorities, he understood that his arrest only could have happened by the will of God. In his condemnation, he saw the greatest opportunity of his life to give witness to Jesus Christ. That's actually what the word *martyr* means. It comes from the Greek word for "witness." So Ignatius gave witness to Christ with the written words of his letters but even more poignantly with his blood. He saw as his final destiny the laying down of his life as a sacrifice, a sacrifice of love for Christ Jesus.

However, Ignatius also saw his death as a sacrifice of love *with* Jesus, a sacrifice, united to Christ's sacrifice, for the Church. To each of the churches, he wrote again and again, "I am giving my life for you."[31] And this suffering with Christ for the Church was, for him, the perfection of discipleship. The thing that drove him forward was

---

30. John Chrysostom, Homily for the Feast of St. Ignatius (*In S. Martyrem Ignatium I, P.G. 50:588*).

31. *Letter of Ignatius to the Ephesians* 21; *Letter of Ignatius to the Trallians* 13:3; *Letter of Ignatius to the Smyrnaeans* 10:2; *Polycarp* 6:1.

the burning desire "to imitate the passion of my God"[32] and, in so doing, to become at last a "real disciple,"[33] a "genuine Christian." He will not rest until he "gets to God."[34]

All seven of Ignatius's letters are compelling. But the most moving is his letter to the church of Rome. In it, he begs the Roman Christians not to interfere with his martyrdom through some misguided love. He is called to give witness, to be one with his Savior, and so pleads with them not to intervene with the imperial authorities. "Forgive me," he says. "I know what is good for me. Now is the moment I am beginning to be a disciple."[35]

> I am voluntarily dying for God—if, that is, you do not interfere. I plead with you, do not do me an unseasonable kindness. Let me be fodder for wild beasts—that is how I can get to God. I am God's wheat and I am being ground by the teeth of wild beasts to make a pure loaf for Christ.[36]

It is revealing, though, that Ignatius is all too aware of his frailty and so adds this: "If, when I arrive, I make a different plea, pay no attention to me!"[37]

Ignatius's letter to the Romans is the only surviving writing from the ancient Church that tells us, in a martyr's own words, what martyrdom meant and why it was so powerful a stimulus to the growth of the Church. Ignatius and his fellow martyrs died for a person, not an ideology. "To share in his Passion I go through everything."[38]

---

32. *Letter of Ignatius to the Romans* 6:3.
33. *Letter of Ignatius to the Romans* 4:2.
34. *Letter of Ignatius to the Romans* 7:2.
35. *Letter of Ignatius to the Romans* 5:3.
36. *Letter of Ignatius to the Romans* 4:1–2.
37. *Letter of Ignatius to the Romans* 7:2
38. *Smyrnaeans* 4:2.

Prophet and Pastor

The story of Ignatius's march is first and foremost the story of his own quest for perfect union with Jesus Christ in love. But Ignatius, the second successor of the apostles in Antioch, knew that his letters were his parting shot against the heresies and divisions that threatened the legacy of apostolic teaching in this area to which Paul and Barnabas had first brought the Gospel sixty years earlier. Ignatius was proud of the nickname that had been given to him: "God-Inspired."[39] His people considered him a prophet who taught with supernatural insight in the power of the Spirit. Therefore, Ignatius's letters also stand as prophetic and apostolic messages addressing the specific needs of the churches of Asia Minor at this moment in history.

Smyrna, Ephesus, Magnesia, Tralles, Philadelphia—the churches of some of these cities had been founded by Paul. Others number among the seven churches of the Apocalypse (see Revelation 1:11). They were beset with false teaching in the apostles' day, and they evidently were in Ignatius's time as well.

Sunday and the Divinity of Christ

First of all, there existed a group that denied the divinity of Christ. Evidently coming from a Jewish or Judaizing background, they couldn't quite cope with the idea of God becoming man. In the face of this denial, Ignatius strained to make it very clear that Jesus Christ is indeed "God incarnate."[40] In the New Testament, we find only a handful of texts that explicitly call Jesus *theos* or God (John's Gospel contains two: 1:1 and 20:28). In Ignatius's seven short letters, he calls Jesus Christ God (*theos*) sixteen times!

---

39. He's called *Theophorus*, which can also be rendered "God-bearer." See *Trallians* 4:1, "God has granted me many an inspiration."
40. *Letter of Ignatius to the Ephesians* 7:2.

Could he possibly be using the term "God" in some loose or metaphorical sense? Could he mean that some demigod or powerful angel created by God before the visible world was made became incarnate in Jesus? Not at all. He is absolutely unambiguous about what he means.

Jesus is the incarnation of the one who is "above time, the Timeless (*achronos*), the Unseen (*aoratos*), the one who became visible for our sakes, who was beyond touch and passion, yet who for our sakes became subject to suffering, and endured everything for us."[41]

The Jehovah's Witnesses and some other sects claim that the doctrine that Jesus is God, equal in nature and dignity to the Father, was a pagan invention of the emperor Constantine. This general-turned-emperor, so the story goes, introduced this idea into Christianity when he seized power in A.D. 312 and soon formalized it as doctrine through the puppet Council of Nicaea.

Ignatius proves this to be nonsense. Two hundred years before Nicaea, Ignatius bears clear witness to the apostolic teaching that Jesus Christ is, in the later words of the Nicene Creed, "God from God, light from light, true God from true God."

The same group of Judaizers who denied Christ's divinity insisted on worshipping God on the Sabbath, as commanded by Moses. To them, Ignatius responds that it was the apostles, all raised as Jews, who transferred the weekly day of celebration from the Sabbath (Saturday) to Sunday, the first day of the week, because this was the day of the Lord's resurrection.[42] Here we find the earliest explicit testimony to the apostolic origin of Sunday worship and the meaning behind it.

---

41. *Polycarp* 3:2.
42. *Letter of Ignatius to the Magnesians* 9.

....

The Eucharist and the Humanity of Christ

But Ignatius also finds it necessary to inveigh against another very different error. A party had arisen, evidently of pagan Greek rather than Jewish origin, which had no problem seeing Jesus as divine, but which simply could not stand the idea of divinity polluting itself through involvement with material things. And so they claimed that the divine Word did not truly become incarnate in Jesus, but rather just "appeared" in human form. Jesus then couldn't actually have been born, have died, or have risen from the dead. Ignatius has no patience with such people. Christian historians may label them Docetists (from the Greek word for "appearance"), but Ignatius brands them "atheists" and "unbelievers." They dare to call Christ's sufferings a sham? Ignatius retorts, "It is they who are a sham!"[43] Ignatius is adamant that Jesus is fully man, that his body was not a mirage, an appearance, or a phantasm. We believe, he proclaims, in:

> Jesus Christ, of David's lineage, of Mary; who was *really* born, ate, and drank; was *really* persecuted under Pontius Pilate; was *really* crucified and died, in the sight of heaven and earth and the underworld. He was *really* raised from the dead, for his Father raised him, just as his Father will raise us, who believe in him.[44]

In this statement, we can see the kernel of both the Nicene and Apostles' Creeds, which are nothing more than expressions of the ancient, apostolic tradition, sometimes called "the rule of faith" or the "rule of truth," which Ignatius received from Peter, Paul, and Barnabas and valiantly defended with his last breath.

It is notable that the very same people who were squeamish about

---

43. *Letter of Ignatius to the Trallians* 10.
44. *Trallians* 9.

the incarnation were also uneasy about the Eucharist, and for the very same reason. Ignatius says, "They hold aloof from the Eucharist and from services of prayer, because they refuse to admit that the Eucharist is the flesh of our Savior Jesus Christ, who suffered for our sins and who, in his goodness, the Father raised."[45]

Ignatius is not a sophisticated theologian seeking to explain how Jesus could be God and man at the same time. His role is to witness to and defend the true apostolic faith about Jesus Christ, true God and true man, the one who is the object of his love, the one for whom he is about to die. And so he does, with vehemence.

The same is true for the Eucharist. Ignatius does not explain how it could continue to maintain the appearance of bread and wine and still become the Body and Blood of Christ. He simply asserts emphatically that just as the historical body of Jesus is no mere phantasm, neither is the Eucharistic body of Christ some empty symbol. God takes on flesh and blood. And that flesh and blood is truly given to us in the Eucharist, which he calls "the medicine of immortality and the antidote which wards off death but yields continuous life in union with Jesus Christ."[46]

The Unity of the Church Catholic

There is one more topic that Ignatius touches upon repeatedly in his letters, namely the nature of the Church, the community that Christ left behind. The hero whose letters provide us the very earliest surviving use of the term "Christianity"[47] also gives us the earliest written designation of the Church as "catholic."[48] And for him

---

45. *Smyrnaeans* 7.
46. *Letter of Ignatius to the Ephesians* 20.
47. *Letter of Ignatius to the Romans* 3:3.
48. *Smyrnaeans* 8:2.

catholic means that the Church is more than a collection of isolated and disconnected congregations. Rather, it is the united, universal community of believers in Christ that is, in contrast to regional cults common in his day, intended to include *all* people and extend over the *whole* world. We find everywhere in the letters of Ignatius a passionate commitment to express, deepen, and preserve the catholic unity and solidarity of all Christians. Through his letters, we see that his pastoral concern could not limit itself to his congregation in Antioch, but extended to all the churches of Asia Minor. Indeed, he was concerned about the Church everywhere.

And we see that universally, each local church addressed in Ignatius's letters has the very same structure: It is led by one bishop who alone appears to have the fullness of pastoral authority, assisted by a group of elders or presbyters (from which comes the English word "priests") together with a group of deacons. In the various New Testament allusions to the resident leadership set up by the traveling apostles in newly planted churches, we see the terms presbyters (elders) and bishops (overseers or superintendents) applied to these local leaders rather interchangeably. And it is not absolutely clear that there is one principal leader, other than the apostolic founder, for each local church.

Since the sixteenth century, some Christians have alleged that the "monoepiscopate" was invented sometime in the Middle Ages. However, roughly ten to twenty years after the last book of the New Testament was completed, Ignatius was finding it in every church he visited. Moreover, he took this structure completely for granted as if it had existed for a long time. And he went further to say that every church *must* have this structure: one bishop to whom is owed obedience and allegiance, around whom is gathered the priests, the deacons, and the people. "You cannot have a church without these."[49] The one bishop in his mind seems to be both a symbol and instrument of the unity of the Church as well as of the authority and care of our one God and Father. And so, to preserve the unity of the Church, nothing is to be done without the bishop's consent.

With regard to the wider Church beyond Asia, the Church "catholic," Ignatius looked to the Church of the imperial capital with a special reverence. The letter he wrote to Rome has a different tone than his other letters. Obviously, the fact that he was to be martyred in Rome had a lot to do with it. But it was also because the Roman Church, in his view, had a certain precedence. In addressing his letter to the Romans, he told them "you rank first in charity." As he proceeded with his message, he mentioned that the Roman church had the benefit of being taught by both Peter and Paul.[50] This comment provides us with one of our first clear testimonies to Peter's residence in Rome. Later in the same letter, he makes what appears to be a reference to the martyrdom of these apostles and many of their disciples.[51] In begging the Romans not to intervene to stop his martyrdom, he seems to be saying that they, who are renowned for so many martyrs, so many who witnessed with their blood to the love of the Good Shepherd, should not greedily reserve this privilege for themselves. True charity demands that they should allow this poor bishop from Antioch to share in this honor.

> If you quietly let me alone, people will see in me God's Word. But if you are enamored of my mere body, I shall, on the contrary, be a meaningless noise. Grant me no more than to

---

49. *Trallians* 3:1.
50. *Letter of Ignatius to the Romans* 4:3.
51. *Letter of Ignatius to the Romans* 3:1.

be a sacrifice for God while there is an altar at hand. Then you can form yourselves into a choir and sing praises to the Father in Jesus Christ that God gave the bishop of Syria the privilege of reaching the sun's setting when he summoned him from its rising. It is a grand thing for my life to set on the world, and for me to be on my way to God, so that I may rise in his presence.[52]

For Ignatius, in the end it all comes down to discipleship as the imitation of Christ. Even the preeminence of the church of Rome is related to this: It is first at least in part because through its illustrious martyrs, it is first in witness, first in love.

---

52.   *Letter of Ignatius to the Romans* 2:2.

CHAPTER 5

The Martyrdom of Polycarp

Along the route of Ignatius and his ten leopards lay a bustling port town named Smyrna. Upon their arrival there, the bishop and his captors found waiting for them a delegation of Christians led by Polycarp, the bishop of that place. The church in this city, located sixty miles north of Ephesus, was an important apostolic church, one of the seven churches of the Apocalypse (see Revelation 1:11). Peter and Paul had died a few years before Polycarp was born in A.D. 69 or 70. But the apostle John was still alive in nearby Ephesus into the late 90s, and we are told that Polycarp was acquainted with him and was perhaps even appointed bishop by him.[53]

Of Ignatius's seven letters, only one was addressed to an individual instead of a church. That individual happened to be Polycarp. Ignatius says, "While I was impressed with your godly mind, which is fixed, as it were, on an immovable rock, I am more than grateful that I was granted the sight of your holy face. God grant that I may never forget it!"[54]

Ignatius's Friend from Smyrna

Polycarp was a relatively young bishop at the time he met Ignatius, probably about forty years old. In Ignatius's advice to his younger colleague, he reveals the intimate, personal acquaintance a bishop was

---

53. See Iraneus, *Against Heresies*, III.3.4. and Jerome, *Illustrious Men*, 17.
54. *Polycarp* 1:1.

expected to have with his flock in this era, reminiscent of what we see in the letters of Paul: "Take a personal interest in everyone you talk to, just as God does…. Seek out everybody by name."[55] Ignatius, who is called by the nickname "the God-Inspired," also shows us in his letter to Polycarp that the charisms or supernatural gifts of the Spirit mentioned on several occasions by Paul (e.g., 1 Corinthians 12:4ff and Romans 12:6–8) are still a normal part of Christian life. Far from any opposition between the official and the charismatic in the Church, a bishop is expected to be a prophet. "Ask that you may have revelations of what is unseen. In that way you will lack nothing and have an abundance of every gift."[56]

Ignatius's ship departed Troas for Neapolis, modern-day Naples. But on the way it stopped in Philippi. So Polycarp wrote a letter to the church in Philippi after Ignatius's departure, addressing some current problems there, as Ignatius had addressed issues in Polycarp's church, and asking them for news about Ignatius. The style of the letter shows us that Polycarp is not a scholar but rather a simple man who is practical and to the point. He humbly admits that he is not well versed in the Scriptures (meaning at this time the Old Testament), but he shows a wide acquaintance with many writings of the apostles and evangelists that ultimately became part of the New Testament.

Away with the Atheists!

Forty years after the encounter of these two bishops, persecution flared up in Smyrna. It appears that Quintus, a hothead from Phrygia, induced a few others to join him in voluntarily surrendering to the

---

55. *Polycarp* 1:3; 4:2.
56. *Polycarp* 2:2.

authorities. This may well have been the spark that ignited the fire of persecution. Polycarp sought to hide himself in the countryside but was apprehended after a Christian broke under torture and told the authorities of his whereabouts. Fortunately, the entire story of his capture—his interrogation and his martyrdom—was written down and preserved by Pionus, a member of Polycarp's flock. *The Letter of the Church in Smyrna to the Church in Philomelium,* commonly known as *The Martyrdom of Polycarp* is, after the account of Stephen's death in Acts, the oldest account of a Christian martyrdom that has come down to us.

As he tells the story, Pionus emphasizes the meaning of martyrdom as an imitation of Christ and a communion with his passion. He notes how, in every respect, Polycarp's ordeal echoes the ordeal of his Lord Jesus Christ and is "a martyrdom conformable to the gospel."[57] Polycarp waited to be betrayed, just as the Lord did. He was captured on a Friday, the day Christ died. Like Jesus, he too prayed for his captors and his persecutors. In fact, when the authorities arrived at the farmhouse where he was staying, he got their permission to have an hour to pray before departing. While they waited for him to finish his prayer, Polycarp arranged for food and drink to be served to them.

The chief of police happened to be named Herod. As they rode to the arena together, the cynical Herod, who evidently did not take very seriously the divinity of the emperor, said: "What harm is there to say 'Lord Caesar' and to offer incense and all that sort of thing, and to save yourself?" Polycarp politely declined to follow his advice. When they arrived, the arena was filled with a boisterous crowd. Christians, because they refused to worship pagan gods, were known as atheists

---

57. *The Martyrdom of Polycarp* 1:1.

and condemned as such. He was brought up to be interrogated in the presence of the crowd, and the proconsul said: "Have respect for your age, Polycarp. Swear by the fortune of Caesar; change your mind; say, 'Away with the Atheists!'" So Polycarp, pointing to the pagan crowd in the stands, said "Away with the Atheists!" The proconsul was not amused. He continued: "Take the oath and I will release you. Curse Christ!"

Polycarp responded: "Eighty-six years I have served him, and he never did me any wrong. How can I blaspheme my King who saved me?... If you vainly suppose that I shall swear by the fortune of Caesar, as you say, and pretend that you do not know who I am, listen plainly: I am a Christian. But if you desire to learn the teaching of Christianity, appoint a day and give me a hearing."

The proconsul replied, "I have wild beasts. I shall throw you to them, if you do not change your mind."

Polycarp boldly retorted, "Call them."[58]

But the proconsul had a problem. The night had grown late, and all the beasts had been locked securely in their cages. The crowd suggested an impromptu method of execution in which they could participate. People began running to nearby shops to fetch firewood. They demanded Polycarp be burned alive.

Martyrdom as a Charism

We must stop here and take note of an earlier occurrence recounted by Pionus. Three days before his arrest, the bishop "had a vision and saw his pillow blazing with fire, and turning to those who were with him, he said, 'I must be burned alive.'"[59] So Polycarp had followed

---

58. *The Martyrdom of Polycarp* 9–10.
59. *The Martyrdom of Polycarp* 5:2.

Ignatius's advice to pray for revelations, and the Lord had answered his prayer.

But the Lord had also given Polycarp another charism in addition to visions. Pionus tells us that the Phrygian who surrendered himself voluntarily ultimately buckled in fear and offered the required sacrifice. Polycarp, on the other hand, held his ground and was even exuberant after being condemned to death. "He was inspired with courage and joy, and his face was full of grace, so that not only did it not fall with dismay at the things said to him, but on the contrary, the proconsul was astonished."[60] Martyrdom is a charism, a grace (the Greek word being *charis*), a gift of supernatural love powered by the Holy Spirit. It cannot be something one presumptuously volunteers for, since it is impossible to accomplish by the power of natural zeal. The crowds at Roman games saw people die every day before their eyes. But not like this. The death of a martyr was not an ordinary execution or even like the courageous death of a fallen gladiator. It was a visible testimony to something most people had never witnessed before—the flame of divine love. This is why public martyrdoms like Polycarp's, far from stamping out Christianity, stimulated its growth through all sectors of Roman society.

Polycarp was tied to the stake, and Pionus recorded for us the prayer he uttered before the execution began:

> Lord God Almighty, Father of thy beloved and blessed Servant Jesus Christ, through whom we have received full knowledge of thee, "the God of angels and powers and all creation" and of the whole race of the righteous who live in thy presence: I bless thee, because thou hast deemed me worthy of this day and hour, to take my part in the number of the martyrs, in the cup of thy

---

60. *The Martyrdom of Polycarp* 12.

Christ, for "resurrection to eternal life" of soul and body in the immortality of the Holy Spirit; among whom may I be received in thy presence this day as a rich and acceptable sacrifice, just as thou hast prepared and revealed beforehand and fulfilled, thou that art the true God without any falsehood. For this and for everything I praise thee, I bless thee, I glorify thee, through the eternal and heavenly High Priest, Jesus Christ, thy beloved Servant, through whom be glory to thee with him and Holy Spirit both now and unto the ages to come. Amen.[61]

This prayer is remarkable, for it is almost certainly an adaptation of the prayer that Polycarp had prayed over the Eucharist on each Lord's Day. It is valuable because it is one of the earliest examples of such a prayer and because it also makes clear that both martyrdom and the Eucharist have something in common—they both put us in touch with the one sacrifice of Christ and invite us to enter into that sacrifice.

A marvelous thing happened when the fire was lit. The flames, instead of burning Polycarp, fled outward, away from his body, forming a sort of chamber around him "like a ship's sail filled by the wind." Suddenly, the arena was filled with a sweet aroma, "as the breath of incense." Since he could not apparently be killed by fire, someone was dispatched to run him through with a dagger. Such "a great quantity of blood came forth, so that the fire was quenched and the whole crowd marveled that there should be such a difference between the unbelievers and the elect."[62]

---

61. *The Martyrdom of Polycarp* 14.
62. *The Martyrdom of Polycarp* 16.

Relics and the Cult of the Martyrs

After Polycarp's death, the Christians wanted to take possession of his unburned body. But the pagans and Jews in the crowd objected. They were afraid that the Christians would "abandon the crucified and begin worshiping this one."[63] Here the author pauses the story to make a very important point. He says that such a concern could only arise because these people were "ignorant that we could never forsake Christ…nor could we ever worship any other. For we worship this One as Son of God, but we love the martyrs as disciples and imitators of the Lord, deservedly so, because of their unsurpassable devotion to their own King and Teacher."[64]

This shows clearly that the cult of the martyrs and saints goes back to the earliest days of the Church, but that there was a very clear distinction in the minds of the early Christians between the adoration due to God alone and the honor due to his disciples. For them, these were not mutually exclusive, but flowed naturally one from the other.

To prevent the Christians from taking the body, it was burned. But somehow the Christians managed to gather up his ashes:

> So we later took up his bones, more precious than costly stones and more valuable than gold, and laid them away in a suitable place. There the Lord will permit us, so far as it is possible, to gather together in joy and gladness to celebrate the day of his martyrdom as a birthday, in memory of those athletes who have gone before, and to train and make ready those who are to come hereafter.[65]

---

63. *The Martyrdom of Polycarp* 17:2.
64. *The Martyrdom of Polycarp* 17:2–3.
65. *The Martyrdom of Polycarp* 18:2–3.

This helps explain the image that so many of us have today of the early Christians hiding from the Romans in the catacombs. Yes, Christian were often found in the catacombs of Rome and other places such as Smyrna, but not because they were hiding. Rather, they went there to celebrate the Eucharist over the bones of the martyrs on the anniversary of their martyrdom. They spent lots of time in the catacombs because there was an ever-increasing number of birthdays to celebrate as persecution dragged on for nearly three hundred years.

We also find here a witness to the ancient origins of the veneration of relics. When Christianity became legal and churches began to be built, some of the remains of the martyrs were brought into the churches. Sometimes they were interred under the main altar, or churches were built so that the main altar was situated directly above the ancient tomb of a martyr (e.g., St. Peter's Basilica in Rome). In other circumstances, the relics of the martyrs were actually inserted into the main altar. This traditional practice of embedding relics of the martyrs and the saints in the altar of a church survives today in the Orthodox and Catholic churches. It can all be traced back to the days when, in the catacombs, the tombs of the martyrs themselves served as Eucharistic altars.[66]

Finally, this document, which we can date with relative certainty to A.D. 155 or 156, demonstrates where the whole liturgical calendar of saints' days[67] comes from. Pionus identifies February 23 as the date of Polycarp's martyrdom. Ever since the year of his death, Polycarp has been honored each year by Orthodox, Catholic, and Anglican churches throughout the world on this very same day.

Besides Peter and Paul, Polycarp and Ignatius, many others died

---

66. See also *Revelation* 6:9.
67. Known as the sanctoral cycle in the Roman Catholic Church.

as martyrs. After the first three centuries of persecution had passed, exceptionally holy and inspiring Christians continued to be born into eternal glory, but mostly through natural death. The remains of these saints came to be venerated in the same way as the remains of the martyrs. And the commemoration of each of these heroes usually occurred, following the pattern of the martyrs, on the day of their death, their eternal birthday. The various birthday celebrations of the saints, superimposed over the great seasons associated with Christ's birth and resurrection, form the liturgical calendars used by many Christian churches today.

So devotion to saints, saints' days, and relics are not pagan practices imported into Christianity by Constantine. Nor are they an invention of medieval superstition. Rather *The Martyrdom of Polycarp* shows that these practices go back to the earliest ages of the Church, the days of the apostles and martyrs.

CHAPTER 6

Diognetus and the Mystery
of Christian Newness

The moving example of Polycarp captures our imagination. But our next author's personal story cannot possibly inspire us—because we don't know for sure who he was.

This mystery author penned a document that, like many other early Christian writings, took the form of a letter. But equally mysterious is the identity of the person to whom this letter is addressed: a certain Diognetus. Almost certainly a pseudonym or nickname of sorts, the name tells us nothing.

A Mysterious Apology

As scholars put the puzzle together, a plausible theory is that the *Letter to Diognetus* is a lost defense of the faith written in Asia Minor and addressed to the Emperor Hadrian in about A.D. 129, roughly twenty years after the martyrdom of Ignatius and twenty-five years before the martyrdom of Polycarp.

But the important thing is this: The mystery letter is the earliest surviving piece of Christian literature not addressed to fellow Christians, but rather to a pagan, and intended as a defense and explanation of the Christian faith.

A letter of this sort is called an apology. It became a very popular type of Christian literature later in the second century. The *Letter to*

Diognetus is classified among the Apostolic Fathers, however, because it appears to have been written so close to time of the apostles, by someone who perhaps, like Polycarp, had heard John and still had the apostle's teaching ringing in his ears.

There is something that we do know about the author based on his vocabulary and literary style. Unlike Polycarp, this man is highly cultured. His Greek is impeccable, and he puts together words in a masterful way. He evidently understands very well the mentality of the sophisticated ruling class of his day. And one thing he recognizes is that they are cynical. They may not say so publicly, but most no longer believe in the Greek and Roman gods. And they, even Caesar himself, don't actually believe that Caesar is divine. For them, burning incense to the emperor is a civic duty, something akin to the pledge of allegiance to the flag. In fact, many are not sure what they really believe. Many are agnostic. And they're rather tired, bored, and jaded.

Christianity bursts into this scene and gets considerable attention. Some people hate it, but some, even some of the persecutors, are intrigued by it. The *Letter to Diognetus* is an attempt to capitalize on this curiosity.

The first thing this letter teaches us is the proper starting point for the presentation of the Gospel to non-Christians. One should not just start expounding, but should rather first identify the real questions that the audience is asking. That's precisely what our author does. He commences his letter by acknowledging three questions that pagans were asking their Christian neighbors: (1) Who is this God of yours that you worship? (2) What is the source of this extraordinary love that you all seem to have for each other? and (3) Why is it that it took so long for this new way of living to appear on earth?

The second notable thing about his approach is that he does not back his statements up with authorities that his pagan reader does not acknowledge. He doesn't quote the Jewish Scriptures or the apostolic writings because these are not authorities as far as his audience is concerned. Instead, he stands on common ground and appeals to common sense.

Keeping in mind the rather tired cynicism that characterizes the mindset of the day, he sounds a theme at the beginning of the letter that he repeats over and over again. This theme is that Christianity brings something brand new into the world.

A Radical Newness

The author at the outset wants the reader to dispose himself properly and be of the right frame of mind to hear his message:

> Now, then, clear out all the thoughts that take up your attention, and pack away all the old ways of looking at things that keep deceiving you. You must be like a new man from the beginning, since, as you yourself admit, you are going to listen to a really new message."[68]

The Christians themselves are a "new race" with a new "way of life."[69] Though he does not employ the distinctively Christian terms *catholic* or even *church* in his efforts to meet the pagan audience on its own terms, our author goes on to describe the remarkable universality of the Christian community. Religion in the ancient world was typically a local and ethnic affair. Sects like that of Osiris (Egypt) or Mithras (Persia) could spread, but sects they remained. The Christians were, on the other hand, anything but a mere cult or regional sect:

---

68. *Letter to Diognetus* 2.
69. *Diognetus* 1.

For Christians cannot be distinguished from the rest of the human race by country or language or customs. They do not live in cities of their own; they do not use a peculiar form of speech; they do not follow an eccentric manner of life. This doctrine of theirs has not been discovered by the ingenuity or deep thought of inquisitive men, nor do they put forward a merely human teaching, as some people do. Yet, although they live in Greek and barbarian cities alike, as each man's lot has been cast, and follow the customs of the country in clothing and food and other matters of daily living, at the same time they give proof of the remarkable and admittedly extraordinary constitution of their own commonwealth. They live in their own countries, but only as aliens. They have a share in everything as citizens, and endure everything as foreigners. Every foreign land is their fatherland, and yet for them every fatherland is a foreign land. They marry, like everyone else, and they share their board with each other, but not their marriage bed.[70]

The last statement is telling. Adultery, prostitution, and fornication were widespread in the Greco-Roman world of the second century. The Christians' regard for the sanctity of the marriage bond was something altogether new.

When Jesus taught his followers how they should see themselves in relation to the rest of the world, he used the metaphors of light and salt. Our author, realizing that his pagan readers were familiar with the body-soul distinction found in Plato's works, chose to explain the Christians' role in society in these more familiar terms:

To put it simply: What the soul is in the body, that Christians are in the world. The soul is dispersed through all the members of the body, and Christians are scattered through all the cities of

---

70. *Diognetus* 5:1–7.

the world. The soul dwells in the body, but does not belong to the body, and Christians dwell in the world, but do not belong to the world. The soul, which is invisible, is kept under guard in the visible body; in the same way, Christians are recognized when they are in the world, but their religion remains unseen. The flesh hates the soul and treats it as an enemy, even though it has suffered no wrong, because it is prevented from enjoying its pleasures; so too the world hates Christians, even though it suffers no wrong at their hands, because they range themselves against its pleasures. The soul loves the flesh that hates it, and its members; in the same way, Christians love those who hate them. The soul is shut up in the body, and yet itself holds the body together; while Christians are restrained in the world as in a prison, and yet themselves hold the world together. The soul, which is immortal, is housed in a mortal dwelling; while Christians are settled among corruptible things, to wait for the incorruptibility that will be theirs in heaven. The soul, when faring badly as to food and drink, grows better; so too Christians, when punished, day by day increase more and more. It is to no less a post than this that God has ordered them, and they must not try to evade it.[71]

The next thing our author wants his audience to know is that the God of the Christians is fundamentally a God who cares, a benevolent God who is a true friend of the human race. He actually calls the Christian God a "philanthropist," which literally means lover of man.

For those of us who are heirs to two thousand years of Judeo-Christian culture, this may seem self-evident. But for pagans of the second century, this is a new idea. The gods that they'd heard about since childhood were fundamentally selfish. The gods of the Greek and Roman myths were simply human beings writ large. All the

---

71. *Diognetus* 6:1–10.

positive characteristics we find in people, such as beauty, intelligence, and power, were magnified in the gods. But so were all the human foibles. The gods cheated on their spouses. They came down to earth from time to time to use and abuse people. They were often fickle, volatile, even treacherous, taking your side one minute and switching sides the next. The goal of pagan worship was basically to placate and, if possible, manipulate the gods through bribery and gifts. And certainly, by all means, one must avoid arousing their anger through pride (*hubris*).

Cultured pagans believed in or at least were aware of the god of the philosophers. But this god, the unmoved mover, though not hostile or capricious, was nonetheless apathetic. So he was a noble god, unlike the deities of the Greeks and Romans, but he was a god who was self-absorbed, remote, even aloof. He had better things to do than trouble himself with petty human concerns.

So a God who cared about, even passionately loved, the human race, was a novel concept. In emphasizing just how much the God of the Christians was committed to man, our mystery author expounds the incarnation. God reached out to touch us, but he did not do so.

> By sending to men some subordinate—an angel, or principality, or one of those who administer earthly affairs, or perhaps one of those to whom the government of things in heaven is entrusted. Rather, he sent the Designer and Maker of the universe himself.... Now, did he send him, as a human mind might assume, to rule by tyranny, fear, and terror? Far from it! He sent him out of kindness and gentleness, like a king sending his son who is himself a king. He sent him as God; he sent him as man to men.[72]

---

72. *Diognetus* 7:2.

Once again, hundreds of years before the Councils of Nicaea and Chalcedon formally defined the divinity and humanity of Christ, we have a striking affirmation from an Apostolic Father that Jesus Christ is true God and true man.

Now this God who cares is a God who cares enough to respect human freedom. The *Letter to Diognetus* is very clear that God does not force himself upon human beings. Our author follows his ode to the incarnation with a very forceful assertion: "He willed to save man by persuasion, not by compulsion, for compulsion is not God's way of working."[73] This pithy statement was evidently a common Christian saying in the second century since it is echoed nearly verbatim in several other documents from this era. So it must be recognized that the practice which we find much later whereby Christian kings and Church leaders compelled Christian orthodoxy by force was a clear departure from not only Scripture but ancient apostolic tradition. Vatican's II's *Declaration on Religious Freedom* is no more than a recovery of that apostolic tradition. If compulsion is not God's way of working, neither should it be ours.

So what makes it possible for the Christians to love one another and exhibit a way of life that is so utterly new? The *Letter to Diognetus* makes plain that the Christians are driven not just by ideas but by the supernatural power of God. Their martyrdom is itself a testimony to this power of divine love:

> Do you not see how they are thrown to wild animals to make them deny the Lord, and how they are not vanquished? Do you not see that the more of them are punished, the more do others increase? These things do not seem to come from a

---

73. *Diognetus* 7:4.

human power; they are a mighty act of God, they are proofs of his presence.[74]

....

Divine Delay

One question still remained: Why did it take God so long? If God is so loving and God cares so much, why didn't he send Christ earlier in history?

As evil increased over the centuries, it certainly could seem that God was neglecting us, concedes our author. However, God was actually exhibiting his patience and forbearance. And he was teaching us something. We had to learn through experience that we are utterly incapable of entering into the kingdom of God by our own efforts and really deserve eternal punishment. As soon as this was utterly clear, God acted:

> In his mercy, he took up the burden of our sins. He himself gave up his own Son as a ransom for us—the holy one for the unjust, the innocent for the guilty, the righteous one for the unrighteous, the incorruptible for the corruptible, the immortal for the mortal. For what else could cover our sins except his righteousness?[75]

Our mystery author follows this masterful expression of John 3:16 and Paul's teaching on salvation by grace with an appeal to the reader. He is not just interested in winning toleration so Christians can be left alone. He goes further and invites his pagan audience to come to know and accept the Father's love. And he promises, as a fruit of accepting the true God in Christ, something that must characterize his own life and the life of the Christians of this era: "Think with

---

74. *Diognetus* 7:7–9.
75. *Diognetus* 9:2–3.

what joy you will be filled! Think how you will love him, who first loved you so!"[76] He holds out the hope to his readers that in knowing God, they too can become imitators of God and be empowered to love like God loves, taking upon themselves the burdens of others as God does.[77]

From this anonymous letter to the mysterious Diognetus, we learn how to evangelize. We can win the world today in the same way our author and his brethren won the world in their day. Not by making Christianity look just like pagan culture so that it will be more palatable, but by presenting it in all its newness and distinctiveness, attracting our audience with the exhilaration and joy produced by the youthful power of supernatural, sacrificial love. Throughout the ages, people have searched for a fountain of youth. The *Letter to Diognetus* presents the living water of Christ as the fulfillment of this age-old quest: "This is he who was from beginning, who appeared new and was found to be old, and is ever born young in the hearts of the saints."[78]

---

76. *Diognetus* 10:2.
77. See *Diognetus* 10:6.
78. *Diognetus* 11:4.

CHAPTER 7

Justin and the Philosopher's Cloak

A hundred years after the babe of Bethlehem, a boy was born about twenty miles to the north of the City of David in the ancient biblical town of Shechem. Though this was in Samaria, the child was neither Samaritan nor Jewish. By then the Romans had renamed the town Flavia Neapolis (today called Nablus), and the boy was from a pagan family that named him Justin. As he grew, Justin acquired a thirst for truth that led him to philosophy, which literally means the "love of wisdom." In those days, clergy wore no distinctive garb, but philosophers did. They often went from city to city attracting attention through their special attire and gathering around themselves groups of disciples. Justin donned the philosopher's cloak and began his journey. His quest for wisdom led him to Alexandria and Ephesus, home to the most famous libraries, and to numerous systems of thought—the Stoics, then Pythagoras, then finally Plato.

One day, as he strolled along the seashore wearing his philosopher's cloak, Justin was wrestling with one of Plato's more difficult ideas. Suddenly, he noticed a venerable old gentleman walking but a few paces behind him. A conversation ensued, and Justin shared with the man the problem that puzzled him. The old man asked him if he had ever heard about the seers and prophets of the Jewish people. These had all spoken of a mysterious figure to come who would be the key to all knowledge. That figure, said the old man, had indeed already come. In fact, this figure, Jesus of Nazareth, had actually lived, taught, and worked miracles within miles of where Justin had been born.

Justin was fascinated. Though a native of Samaria, he had never read the Hebrew prophets, and he now raced to procure some scrolls. Poring over them, he found their predictions converging on Jesus of Nazareth. He soon witnessed some of Jesus's disciples die in the arena rather than renounce their faith, and that clinched it for him. He took instruction and submitted to baptism. He was about thirty years of age.

The interesting thing is that Justin did not then take off his philosopher's cloak. Rather, he believed that it was only after baptism that he was finally entitled to wear it. In Christ, he had found the answer to every question, the key that unlocked all doors, just as the old man had promised. And now he was to dedicate the rest of his life to loving this true Wisdom and sharing it with anyone who would listen.

However, you can't give what you don't have. So at this point, Justin went to Ephesus, but not for its world-famous library. Rather, Ephesus was now important to him because Paul had founded the community there and John had died there. What better place to drink from the fountain of apostolic wisdom? The only place with a better pedigree was perhaps the church of Rome, heir to the legacy of Peter and Paul. So after a season in Ephesus, he was off to Rome to live, learn, and teach. He rented a home in the city in which he offered public seminars on Christianity. This was indeed living dangerously; being a Christian was a capital crime, and the locations of Christian meetings were usually a closely guarded secret.

In Rome, Justin wrote two defenses of the faith, called apologies, addressed to the emperor and the Senate. The approach of an apology, as we have already seen with the *Letter to Diognetus,* is to identify common objections to the Christian faith and then address them, clearing up misconceptions and laying out arguments for the truth of the Gospel. As Justin goes about this task in his two apologies, he covers an enormous amount of ground. We will limit our discussion here to two important areas. First of all, we'll examine his attitude toward pagan culture and how Christians should engage it. Secondly, we will discuss the fascinating glimpses Justin provides us into the life of Christian worship in the middle of the second century.

Justin develops his idea on both of these important topics against the backdrop of the three charges leveled against the Christians: atheism, incest, and cannibalism.

Pagan Morality

We have already seen why Christians were denounced as atheists. But incest and cannibalism? Rumors had arisen, based on Christians' terminology, that their secret meetings were "love feasts" between "brothers and sisters" who "consumed the flesh and blood of a man called Christus."[79]

So Justin had no choice but to address issues of morality and Christian worship. In doing so, part of his approach was to follow a tried and true strategy, namely, that a good offense is often the best defense. He begins his *First Apology* by blasting the idolatry and sexual immorality of the pagan society of his day. It should be remembered that adultery and promiscuity, including homosexual liaisons and pedophilia, were rife in the empire at this time. Prostitution, both male and female, was widespread and legal. The government even had a vested interest in the practice since the sex business produced

---

79. Justin alludes to these charges in *1 Apol* 26: "the upsetting of the lamp, promiscuous intercourse, and the meals of human flesh."

considerable tax revenue. The goal of the pagans was to enjoy erotic love while escaping the responsibilities of raising and educating children. When the attempts at contraception and abortion through drugs and surgery failed, people typically abandoned unwanted babies in some well-known spot in town. There they either died of exposure or were picked up by pimps and raised for prostitution. Because of this, says Justin, it was the pagans who were often unwittingly guilty of incest since the prostitutes they patronized could actually be close relatives, even their own illegitimate offspring.[80] Justin points out to the emperor the irony of situation: "You charge against us the actions that you commit openly and treat with honor."[81]

Far from holding incestuous orgies, Justin states, Christians rejected all sexual relations except in the context of a marriage ordered toward the begetting of children. These marriages are exclusive and unto death; Justin witnesses to the early Christian prohibition of divorce and remarriage. He also boasts that lifelong chastity was highly prized in the Christian community. "Many men and women now in their sixties and seventies who have been disciples of Christ from childhood have preserved their purity; and I am proud that I could point to such people in every nation."[82]

But Justin wants to impress upon his readers the fact that this new approach to the dignity of human sexuality is just one sign of the utter newness of the Christian lifestyle. Reminiscent of the *Letter to Diognetus*, Justin insists that Christianity is not just a belief system but a whole new way of living:

---

80. *First Apology of Justin Martyr* 27–29.
81. *1 Apology* 27.
82. *1 Apology* 15.

Those who once rejoiced in fornication now delight in continence alone; those who made use of magic arts have dedicated themselves to the good and unbegotten God; we who once took most pleasure in the increasing of our wealth and property now bring what we have into a common fund and share with everyone in need; we who hated and killed one another and would not associate with men of different tribes because of their [different] customs, now, after the manifestation of Christ, live together and pray for our enemies.[83]

The apologist objects to many aspects of the pagan culture of his day. But the thing most outrageous in his mind is what we today call relativism: the notion that there are no moral absolutes, no objective right or wrong. For him, the "greatest impiety and wickedness" is this idea "that there is no real virtue or vice but only by opinion are things considered good or bad."[84]

Greek Philosophy and the Logos

Certainly, Justin's approach to Greco-Roman culture is highly critical. But critical does not mean entirely negative. The word "critic" means judge; and in all sound judgment, evidence is weighed. What is found wanting is rejected and what is sound is accepted. There was not much of value in pagan religion or morality. But as for the Greco-Roman philosophers that Justin had studied, it was a different story. Yes, Plato and the others had made many mistakes. But what amazed Justin was just how much they actually got right. He saw glimmers of the cross in Plato's *Timaeus* and discovered in the oracles of Sibyl, in the Stoics, and even in the Persian sage Hystaspes a prediction that the universe would end in fire.[85]

83. *1 Apology* 14.
84. *1 Apology* 43.
85. See *1 Apology* 20.

One explanation for all this, according to Justin, is that the philosophers, who lived after the prophets, borrowed from them.[86] There is not much historical evidence to support this theory. However, the second reason Justin gives for finding truth in the pagan philosophers, prophets, and poets is much more intriguing.

John 1:9 calls the divine Word the "Logos," who is made flesh in Jesus, "the true light that enlightens every man." The philosophers, notably the Stoics, had spoken about the divine Logos (word or reason) that was responsible for order in the universe. This is the very same Logos who became flesh in Jesus of Nazareth (see John 1:1), said Justin, but from the beginning of time, all things had been made through this Logos.

> Next to God we worship and love the Word, born of the eternal God who is beyond our understanding, because he became man for us to heal us of our ills by sharing them himself. And it is thanks to this same Word who had been placed in them that pagan writers were able to perceive the truth, if in a confused way. Still, it is one thing to possess a seed in proportion to one's capacity and quite another to possess the reality itself.[87]

There are thus "seeds of the Word," glimmers and reflections of his truth, scattered in everyone and in many systems of thought. This means that there are elements of pagan thought and culture that are in accord with the Word and, for that reason, can be incorporated into Christian culture. These elements can serve as a common ground where pagans and Christians can meet to discuss the fullness of truth, as occurred on that day when Justin met the old man on the seashore.

---

86. See *1 Apology* 44.
87. See *Second Apology of Justin Martyr* 13.

But there is much distortion in pagan culture as well. The criterion to separate the wheat from the chaff is Jesus Christ in whom we find the fullness of life and truth. Justin's approach to pagan culture is neither an unqualified rejection nor acceptance with open arms, but a critical assimilation, with the cross as the measuring stick.

This seminal insight of Justin proved to have an enormous impact on the history of Christian thought. Avery Dulles states it well: "From this it followed that there could be no divorce between faith and reason, between religion and philosophy. The wisdom of Socrates was akin in its source to that of the prophets."[88]

Early Christian Worship

Turning to the charge of cannibalism, Justin does something unexpected for which we are ever indebted to him. Christian worship was secret, for obvious security reasons. But it was also secret due to respect for the holy mysteries, as the Christian rites were called. Even converted catechumens were not allowed to be present at or even learn much about some of the ceremonies of Christian worship until they had been baptized and initiated into those mysteries.

Since misconceptions about Christians' liturgy gave rise to charges against them, Justin decided that it was appropriate, under the circumstances, to pull back the veil and tell the emperor, in terms he would understand, exactly what really went on during these Christian gatherings.

Justin lays out how baptisms occurred and, in the course of doing so, he shows us that Roman Christians around A.D. 150 were baptizing in the name of the Father, Son, and Holy Spirit and that what Jesus

---

88. Avery Dulles, S.J., *The Assurance of Things Hoped For: A Theology of Christian Faith* (New York: Oxford University Press, 1994), p. 20.

said to Nicodemus about being born again by water and the Spirit (see John 3:3) was understood as referring to baptism. Echoing the *Didache*, he tells us that before baptism, candidates fasted and the whole community fasted, and prayed along with them.[89] Though Justin does not mention how long this period lasted, we see here, as in the *Didache,* the origin and meaning of Lent, the forty-day fast preceding Easter, the great day of baptism in the early Church.

We also see how serious a commitment baptism was in the minds of the people of the Church of his day. Justin compared it to the sacred military oath taken by a new Roman soldier called a *sacramentum* by which the legionary swore lifelong loyalty unto death to his commander who in turn promised food, wages, protection, and, if the legionary survived, a parcel of land after twenty years' service. Justin points out how much more fitting and necessary it is that Christians be ready to die rather than break their baptismal vows since their promised prize, unlike the soldier's reward, is an eternal one.[90]

In Justin's description of the weekly meeting, we see the outline of the Mass of the Roman rite today—liturgy of the Word, homily, prayer of the faithful, eucharistic prayer, even the collection:

> And on the day called Sunday there is a meeting in one place of those who live in the cities or the country, and the memoirs of the apostles or the writings of the prophets are read as long as time permits. When the reader has finished, the president in a discourse urges and invites [us] to the imitation of these noble things. Then we all stand up together and offer prayers. And, as said before, when we have finished the prayer, bread is brought, and wine and water, and the president similarly sends up prayers

---

89. See *1 Apology* 61.
90. See *1 Apology* 39.

and thanksgivings to the best of his ability, and the congregation assents, saying the Amen; the distribution, and reception
of the consecrated [elements] by each one, takes place and they
are sent to the absent by the deacons. Those who prosper, and
who so wish, contribute, each one of as much as he chooses to.
What is collected is deposited with the president, and he takes
care of orphans and widows.[91]

One of the goals of the Second Vatican Council (1962–1965) was
the reform of the Eucharist of the Roman or Latin rite, commonly
known as the Roman Catholic Mass. Much controversy ensued in
the wake of these liturgical changes. It should be noted that rather
than intending a modernizing departure from tradition, the Council
sought to renew the Mass according to the most ancient pattern of
the Roman liturgy as recorded by Justin.

The final accusation Justin had to rebut was that the Christians
were cannibals because they consumed the body and blood of Jesus
Christ. It is telling how Justin handles this. When it would be most
advantageous for the Christian cause to downplay any realistic interpretation of communion, Justin refrains from an empty symbolism
and attempts to impress upon the emperor just how profound and
true this communion with the flesh of Christ really is:

> For we do not receive these things as common bread or common
> drink; but as Jesus Christ our Saviour being incarnate by God's
> word took flesh and blood for our salvation, so also we have
> been taught that the food consecrated by the word of prayer
> which comes from him, from which our flesh and blood are
> nourished by transformation, is the flesh and blood of that
> incarnate Jesus.[92]

---

91. *1 Apology* 67.
92. *1 Apology* 66.

Notice the phrase "we have been taught." All throughout this letter, Justin repeats this and similar phrases again and again. The words used here are variants of the word "tradition" or the process of handing over or handing on something from person to person. Justin is bright and has the inquisitive, speculative mind of a philosopher. But in explaining Christianity to the emperor, he takes pains to be conservative, not creative. What he is sharing is an apostolic legacy going back from the communities of Ephesus and Rome to Peter, Paul, and John, and ultimately to Christ himself. This teaching, this heritage that has been handed on to him, is exactly what he, in turn, is carefully handing to his students and to the emperor, whether he is dealing with doctrine, morality, or worship.

His Ultimate Act of Witness

The final writing that survives from Justin is his Second Apology. In it, he criticizes the Cynic philosopher Crescens for ignorant prejudice against the Christians. Crescens apparently did not appreciate the criticism. His response was to turn in Justin's name to Rusticus, the prefect of the city of Rome. Fortunately, the account of his interrogation and martyrdom, evidently based on court records, has survived.

> RUSTICUS: Listen, you who are said to be eloquent and who believes that he has the truth—if I have you beaten and beheaded, do you believe that you will then go up to heaven?
>
> JUSTIN: If I suffer as you say, I hope to receive the reward of those who keep Christ's commandments. I know that all who do that will remain in God's grace even to the consummation of all things.
>
> RUSTICUS: So you think that you will go up to Heaven, there to receive a reward?

JUSTIN: I don't think it, I know it. I have no doubt about it whatever.

RUSTICUS: Very well. Come here and sacrifice to the gods.

JUSTIN: Nobody in his senses gives up truth for falsehood.

RUSTICUS: If you don't do as I tell you, you will be tortured without mercy.

JUSTIN: We ask nothing better than to suffer for the name of our Lord Jesus Christ and so to be saved. If we do this we can stand confidently and quietly before the fearful judgment-seat of that same God and Saviour, when in accordance with divine ordering all this world will pass away.

RUSTICUS: (rising to his feet) "Let those who have refused to sacrifice to the gods and to yield to the command of the emperor be scourged, then let them be led away and beheaded, according to the laws."[93]

Ten years after Polycarp gave his witness, Justin gave his final lecture. He at last bore witness in deed to what he had taught by the pen. Baptism is indeed a mystery more powerful than the legionary's *sacramentum*. It celebrated a love that was stronger than death. The philosopher's cloak had become a military cloak. Bleached white in baptism, it was now dyed a brilliant red.

---

93. See *Butler's Lives of the Saints*. vol. II, p. 90.

CHAPTER 8

Irenaeus and the Gnostic Threat

By the middle of the second century, the Roman Empire had played itself out. For over a hundred years the *Pax Romana* had reigned over the Mediterranean world, a peace kept in place by the unrivaled power of the Roman military machine. But it was an empty peace. Roman society suffered from a gnawing sense of futility. Traditional sources of meaning and purpose were coming up short. By this time, no one took the religion of Jupiter, Juno, and the Vestal Virgins very seriously.

In such an environment, people often look to far-off, exotic lands for something new and exciting. So it is no wonder that ideas from Persia, married to a mishmash of notions drawn from Greek philosophy, magic, and other mysterious cults, coalesced into an intoxicating brew known as "Gnosticism." Gnosticism was not a tightly organized religion, but rather a general way of thinking that characterized a wide variety of sects that often disagreed sharply on numerous points of detail.

The important thing here, though, is not the distinctive features of the Valentinians or other Gnostic sects or even precisely where they got their ideas. What we want to understand is the essence of Gnosticism, the basic ideas that people called Gnostics held in common and which presented such a threat to Christianity in the second century.

Alienation and Elitism

Have you ever had the feeling that you don't quite fit with the people and society around you? That you are a fish out of water?

That's probably because you *are* different, the Gnostics would say. This material world, they insisted, was not created by the Supreme Being. He dwells in the realms of light and is purely spiritual. It would never cross his mind to create the slime and muck of this material world. The physical realm is a work of darkness created by a lower spiritual being called the "Demiurge." Some Gnostics taught that the Demiurge was malevolent. Others said he was just incompetent. In any case, this physical world he created is not "good" as it says in Genesis 1, but rather a terrible mistake. And the most tragic mistake is that some sparks of divinity, some truly spiritual realities, managed to get trapped in human bodies. Redemption for them is to discover their true spiritual identity, escape from the body and its disgusting passions, and return to their true heavenly home.

Such liberation required *gnosis*, the Greek word for knowledge. Some spiritual being had to descend from the realms of light and bring us this redeeming gnosis. Most of humanity was "carnal" and truly belonged to this realm of decay. The savior did not come for these pitiful folk who were destined for everlasting destruction.

But to those elite few who were fallen angels imprisoned in flesh, the savior brings the liberating knowledge of their true origins and a complicated set of esoteric passwords so that, after death, these divine souls could navigate past the Demiurge and his minions and make their way back at long last to the realm of light.

So the Gnostic was someone "in the know" who was better than others, discovered meaning in an otherwise meaningless world, and who, sensing a need for redemption, found it through complicated myths and exotic rituals.

Christian Gnostics?

Some Gnostics, hearing the proclamation that "the Word became flesh and dwelt among us" (John 1:14), supposed that Jesus must have been the heavenly messenger destined to bring salvation. Of course, they realized that the stories of Jesus's birth and death could not possibly have been right. No true heavenly being would ever defile himself with matter, for matter and spirit were utterly opposed. So, picking up the idea of the Docetists, the Gnostics said Jesus just *appeared* to be human. Certainly, the bearer of heavenly revelation had no body and therefore couldn't have died. Salvation was not, after all, accomplished through sacrifice, but through knowledge.

So how did these folks deal with the Gospel accounts? Some tossed out the Gospels save one, regarding the others as forgeries. For Marcion, who was not a thorough Gnostic but held many Gnostic ideas, the Gospel of Luke minus the infancy narratives was the only Gospel. Others preferred the view of Jesus as the wandering guru who uttered profound discourses full of riddles, and so John's Gospel seemed a better fit. Others championed gospels that many Christians today may have never heard of, such as the Gospel of Thomas.

But all the so-called Christian Gnostics had one thing in common: theirs was a "Christianity" without the cross. The crucifixion was either explained away or, in the case of the Gospel of Thomas, left out of the story entirely. If salvation was by knowledge, why did they need a story at all? All that was needed was a collection of sayings. And that's exactly what we find in the Gnostic Gospel of Thomas.

So what kind of lifestyle should the true Gnostic lead? Here is where the various sects diverged a bit. They all agreed that the body was of no consequence. Some said that it was a drag on the spirit and, therefore, we must deny it as much as possible. Their ideal was an ascetic lifestyle of severe fasting from food and sex.

Others drew the opposite conclusion. Since the body is just a hunk of meat that has no relationship to the spiritual life, what we do with the body simply does not matter. That means there is no law; anything goes. So some Gnostic sects celebrated this license through ritual orgies. It would appear that the Nicolatians, condemned in the book of Revelation, were an early form of such a sect (see Revelation 2:6, 14). The body, then, could either be indulged or starved. The one thing it couldn't be was saved.

But how could the Gnostics claim that their vision of Jesus was the true one? Simple. Jesus realized that most couldn't handle his true teaching, so he secretly entrusted it to a few elite confidants. (The appealed to Corinthians 2:6: "Among the mature we do impart wisdom.") These confidants passed on this secret tradition to those elite few who were worthy of it, from generation to generation.

The Shepherd Attacks

As strange as this whole religious system may seem to us today, it swept rapidly throughout the Roman world and posed a great threat to the Church. A bishop from what is now France decided that someone had to confront it head on. The name of this theological warrior was Irenaeus, which ironically means "peaceful one." Originally, Irenaeus came from Asia Minor and had, as a boy, heard Polycarp, the disciple of John. As a young man, he went to Rome, where apparently he became a student of Justin. Ultimately, he made his way to the Greek-speaking port city of what is now Lyons,[94] France, and soon discovered that the Gnostic balderdash had reached

---

94. The actual Latin name of this city was Lugdunum, rendered in English today as "Lyons."

even there and posed a danger to the flock entrusted to his care. The shepherd felt that he had no choice but to attack the Gnostic wolf. He must expose this ridiculous and illogical doctrine, this foolishness "craftily decked out in an attractive dress and made to seem truer than the truth itself."[95] So his task was simple. Gnosticism must be stripped naked and shown up for the nonsense that it is. And then, as an antidote to the poison of the heretics, Irenaeus must go on to offer a full exposition of the "rule of the truth,"[96] handed down from the apostles. If he could just lay this preposterous fantasy alongside the compelling truth of the Gospel, the battle would be won. He wanted to deal Gnosticism a knockout blow straightaway, so he held nothing back. A full five volumes later, around A.D. 185, his book *Against the Knowledge Falsely So-Called* (a.k.a. *Against Heresies*) was complete.

Apostolic Succession and Authentic Tradition

First of all, Irenaeus had to confront the issue of legitimacy. How are we supposed to know what Jesus truly taught and who he really was? Who is to say that the Gnostic Jesus is not the original one? The entire case of the Christian Gnostics hinged on their claim to possess a secret tradition going back to Jesus.

It is interesting that Irenaeus did not respond with a *sola scriptura* argument. He did not say, "Forget tradition—only Scripture is infallible."[97] That would not have worked since one of the contested issues was precisely which Christian writings were the authentic. Rather, Irenaeus just used common sense. If Jesus had secret, deeper knowledge to pass down, wouldn't he have entrusted it to the twelve

---

95. *Against the Knowledge Falsely So-Called* (aka, *Against Heresies*) Book I, 1.1.
96. *Against Heresies* III, 11.1.
97. See *Against Heresies* III, 2.1.

confidants, called apostles, whom he personally selected? And toward the end of their lives, would not these have entrusted any secrets to their chosen successors, and so on? Yet, Irenaeus protested around the year A.D. 185, the Catholic bishops of apostolic cities such as Ephesus, Corinth, and Rome could all trace their lineage back in a continual, unbroken line to the apostles. Since they knew nothing of the silly doctrines of the Gnostics, it proves that these doctrines couldn't possibly have come from Jesus and his followers.[98]

To demonstrate how clearly each bishop knew his pedigree, he gives the example of the Roman church and traces the pope of his day all the way back to Peter and Paul, naming every pope in between.[99] "For every church must be in harmony with this church because of its outstanding pre-eminence, that is, the faithful from everywhere, since the apostolic tradition is preserved in it by those from everywhere."[100] So Irenaeus recognizes the Roman church, which had been his home for several years, to have special status not only because of its foundation by the two greatest apostles, but because it was a microcosm of the universal Church, the Church catholic.

This doctrine of apostolic succession of teaching offices solves the problem of which was the authentic tradition. But it also is the key to deciding which were the true and authoritative apostolic writings. Simply put, those gospels and epistles are authentic which have been in continuous use in churches founded by the apostles.

---

98. See *Against Heresies* III, 3.1.
99. The English word *pope* derives from the Greek *pappas,* meaning "papa" or "father." In the third century, this began to be used affectionately for the bishops of Rome, Alexandria, and other places as well. Eventually, the term became a title exclusively reserved for the bishop of Rome, as is commonly used today. However, the Coptic Orthodox still apply the term to their Patriarch.
100. *Against Heresies* III, 3.2. Irenaeus does not use the term *pope* (Greek *pappas*) for the bishop of Rome. It will be another hundred years before written evidence of the use of this term, meaning Pappa or Father, for a Roman bishop.

We ought to...love with the greatest zeal the things of the Church, and so to lay hold of the tradition of the truth. What if there should be a dispute about some matter of moderate importance? Should we not turn to the oldest churches, where the apostles themselves were known, and find out from them the clear and certain answer to the problem now being raised? Even if the apostles had not left their Writings to us, ought we not to follow the rule of the tradition which they handed down to those to whom they committed the churches?[101]

While Irenaeus conceives of the episcopacy in terms of a succession of teaching chairs, he does not view this merely as a sort of bureaucratic transfer of authority from one office-holder to the next. Rather, he sees the bishops as charismatic teachers, each one receiving, through the good pleasure of the Father, "a gift of truth."[102]

The Sacraments: Invisible through the Visible

Having exposed the Gnostic nonsense and established the legitimacy of the true apostolic tradition, Irenaeus goes on to expound the true teaching of a material world that is a blessing, not a curse, and a savior who truly becomes one of us so that he can truly die for us. This Savior continues to nourish us still through sacraments, material realities that become transmitters of holiness. In these tangible vehicles of God's saving power, we see "the incomprehensible [acting] through the comprehensible and the invisible through the visible."[103]

Irenaeus, in the face of Gnostic scorn of the material world, beautifully brings out how the creation, incarnation, Eucharist, and

---

101. *Against Heresies* III, 4.2.
102. *Against Heresies* IV, 26.2.
103. *Against Heresies* III, 11.5.

resurrection of the body are all inextricably intertwined. They stand or fall together:

> They say that the flesh, which is nourished with the body of the Lord and with His blood, goes to corruption, and does not partake of life.... But our opinion is in accordance with the Eucharist, and the Eucharist in turn establishes our opinion. For we offer to Him His own, announcing consistently the fellowship and union of the flesh and Spirit. For as the bread, which is produced from the earth, when it receives the invocation of God, is no longer common bread, but the Eucharist, consisting of two realities, earthly and heavenly; so also our bodies, when they receive the Eucharist, are no longer corruptible, having the hope of the resurrection to eternity.[104]

Recapitulation: The New Adam, the New Eve

The Gnostic Jesus redeemed the world through knowledge, not sacrifice. Irenaeus develops the theme of Jesus as the New Adam. The original head of the human race had radically failed from the very first—he raised his hand to the tree in disobedience and pride. Jesus starts the human race anew and is the new head of a new humanity. He raises his hand to a tree as well, in obedience, love, and humility, undoing the bondage to Satan forged by Adam's disobedience. This "re-heading-up" of the human race is called the doctrine of recapitulation and is a wonderful development of a note first sounded by St. Paul. As Irenaeus goes about this task, he also develops a theme touched upon by his teacher, Justin, but which might very well date back to the apostles. In the first false start for the human race, Adam had an accomplice in his rebellion. In the renewal and recapitulation

---

104. *Against Heresies* IV, 18.5 (*Ante-Nicene Fathers*, vol. 1, p. 486).

of all things, God has not only given the human race a new Adam but a new Eve as well.

Speaking of the Virgin Mary he declares: "And thus, as the human race fell into bondage to death by means of a virgin, so is it rescued by a virgin; virginal disobedience having been balanced in the opposite scale by virginal obedience."[105] This theme of the Virgin Mary as the New Eve is the earliest theme of Marian theology to be developed in Christian tradition.

The Fate of Gnosticism

So what happened to Gnosticism after Irenaeus's blistering attack? Not long after his book was written, Gnosticism faded out of the picture. When darkness is exposed, it vanishes, swallowed up by the light. If this exotic religion initially appealed to a generation thirsty for spiritual life, in the end it failed to satisfy.

So the Gnostic gospels were lost, buried under the sands of time. The only reason that we have the Gospel of Thomas today is because the arid sand of Egypt that entombed it proved too dry for the bacteria that cause decay. In 1945, a peasant from Upper Egypt unearthed a copy of this document. As scholars examined the find, they saw that it confirmed the remarkable accuracy of Irenaeus's description of ancient Gnosticism.

But we must today be on guard. Heresies are a lot like the common cold. They keep coming back, but in a slightly changed form. Usually the change is just enough to help them sneak past the defense of our immune system and pose a new threat to our spiritual health. The New Age movement and the popular novel *The Da Vinci Code*

---

105. *Against Heresies* V, 19.1

both borrow heavily from ancient Gnosticism. They each rely on key Gnostic ideas that have as much appeal now as they did in the second century. For who does not eventually feel the emptiness and ennui of a life without the spiritual dimension, a life devoid of mystery?

To modern society, which has lost its soul, the New Age has appeal because it restores a sense of mystery. It imitates the syncretism of the Gnostics, blending together esoteric ideas from the East with home-grown, Western traditions to produce a hodgepodge that may be incoherent but nevertheless intriguing. *The Da Vinci Code* resurrects the claim of a secret tradition that is earlier and more faithful than the New Testament Scriptures. It offers us a way to feel connected to Jesus even while we scorn the Church said to be founded by him.

Ironically, the appeal of these currents also constitutes their undoing. Both the New Age movement and *The Da Vinci Code* seek spirituality without sacrifice, without authority, without the cross. They follow ancient Gnosticism in preserving a veneer of Christianity while emptying it of its content.

But the fate of Gnosticism ought to serve as a warning here. A Christianity with no cross is a Christianity with no power. And a religion with no power doesn't last very long. *The Da Vinci Code* may have sold a few million copies in the first years of the third millennium. But here is my guess: In the fourth millennium, it will take an archeologist digging in the sands of Egypt to find a copy.

CHAPTER 9

Irenaeus and the Battle for the Bible

Everybody in Christendom today, from Protestant to Catholic to Orthodox, professes that the sacred Scriptures, inspired by the Holy Spirit, are the ultimate norm of our faith and life. That's agreed. But stop and think. In the Bible, there is a very important page that was not inspired by the Holy Spirit. And that is the table of contents.

The Fathers of the Church had to ask questions that never occur to many of us. What books are truly inspired by the Holy Spirit? The thick, bound collection that we know today as the Bible did not yet exist in the second century. Instead, Christians had access to various parchments and scrolls written by different authors. First, there were books by Hebrew authors before Jesus, going back to Moses. These are what Christians generally meant by the "Scriptures" up until the time of Irenaeus. There were also collections of Jesus's words and deeds, called Gospels, and various letters, histories, and collections of prophecies and visions. Should some of these be put on a par with the Law and the Prophets? And if so, which ones? Another thing that is not included in the text of the books called Gospels: The names of their authors. Who wrote them? How do we know?

This problem is what we call the problem of the canon.

But there is a further problem. The writings and laws of the old dispensation are different in notable ways from the new dispensation brought by Jesus Christ. Are the two opposed so that we should reject one and embrace the other? Or do we just add the laws of the Sermon on the Mount to the 613 commandments in the Jewish Scriptures and do our best to keep them all? Or should we expect new prophets to bring us further laws and revelations to substitute for the outmoded ones of Moses and Jesus?

This is the problem of the covenants or testaments.

Neither of these big questions was answered either conclusively or officially in Irenaeus's great five-volume work. But it is doubtful that anyone in Christian history did more to help Christianity resolve them than the peaceful warrior of Lyons.

The Ebionites, Marcion, and Montanus

Unfortunately, the Gnostics were not the only heretics that Irenaeus had to worry about. He was forced to do battle on three additional fronts at the same time.

His foes, other than the Gnostics, had this in common: They all came from same part of the world that Irenaeus originally hailed from, Asia Minor. The first were a particular group of Jewish Christians whom Irenaeus calls the Ebionites. In the early Church, many Jewish Christians, including Peter and Paul, took pride in their special Hebrew heritage. But Paul noted in his letters repeatedly that some Jewish believers really weren't willing to go all the way in recognizing the newness of the Gospel. This "Judaizing" party viewed Christianity just as God's final touch upon the masterpiece of Judaism. Thus, they insisted that everybody, including Gentile Christians, must observe circumcision, the Jewish holidays, and the dietary prescriptions of the law. Moreover, it was necessary to do so, not just for preservation of culture and tradition, but in order to be saved. Ignatius showed us that these Judaizers rejected the idea of Jesus's divinity. Irenaeus goes on to tell us that the only apostolic writing they accepted was the

Gospel of Matthew minus the infancy narrative (since they denied the virgin birth). They utterly rejected Paul as an apostate to the Law. For them, Jesus was just the last and greatest of the prophets. These Ebionites did not have a two-covenant problem at all since, for them, there is only one. Jesus does not represent, as he does for Paul, an entirely new covenant, but only a minor embellishment.

The Ebionites, their name deriving from the word *poor*, appear to have been a small sect with little influence, mainly confined to Asia Minor, Syria, and Arabia. But the next movement coming from Asia Minor made it all the way to the imperial capital where Polycarp, Justin, and Irenaeus all encountered it. It was led by the son of a bishop who himself may have been ordained a bishop before he developed his heretical ideas. His name was Marcion, and he tackled the problems of the canon and the covenants in his own distinctive way.

To prepare to understand Marcion's point of view, it is best to ask yourself a few questions. Have you ever read the Old Testament and run across a passage, let's say in Judges or in Joshua, where the brutal warfare carried out by the Israelites, seemingly at God's command, was a bit disturbing? Have you ever had problems reconciling such passages with the Sermon on the Mount? Did you ever wonder how the Old Testament image of God's wrath squares with the merciful Father revealed by our Lord Jesus Christ? Well, Marcion wondered about the very same things. And the answer he came up with resolves all the problems entirely. He taught that the reason for the two very different pictures is simply because there are two very different Gods. For Marcion, the God of Moses and the prophets was the evil Demiurge who created the matter that entrapped all of our noble souls. Therefore, the Jewish Scriptures are evil—they are to be thrown out entirely.

What should Christians read then? It appears that Marcion was the very first to come up with a canon: a list of inspired writings to be considered "Scripture." He accepted only one Gospel, Luke. For, he asked, how could there be more than one authentic gospel account? The others had to be either spurious or superfluous. And obviously, since the created world is evil, Jesus couldn't really have been born. So Marcion took a pair of scissors and snipped the infancy narratives right out of the Gospel. He assumed these had to have been inserted later, by some heretic employed by the Demiurge. He added to this truncated Gospel a collection of ten Pauline letters, "purified" of any nonsense about the created world coming from God the Father. Problem solved—a clear canon and only one Testament.

As if Marcion and the Ebionites weren't tough enough adversaries, there was yet another movement from Asia Minor led by a man named Montanus. He and two women in his company were self-proclaimed prophets. Some believed that their oracles were verbatim from the Holy Spirit and superseded Jesus just as Jesus had superseded Moses. The "New Prophecy," as it was called, raised a very important question. Maybe God is not finished yet. Perhaps there is totally new revelation to come from these three prophets and future prophets as well.

Harmony and Pedagogy

In response to all this, Irenaeus realized that he needed to lay out for his readers a reasoned and comprehensive account of just how the history of salvation fit together. True wisdom does not involve inventing new doctrines like Gnosticism and Montanism or cutting out what we don't like as did the Ebionites and Marcion. Rather, "It consists in working out the things that have been said in parables, and building them into the foundation of the faith."[106]

Irenaeus developed an image that St. Paul first introduced in Galatians, that of the pedagogue. He said God is the wisest of all educators. As the Most High looked down upon the first Israelites whom he had chosen, he knew he couldn't oblige them to embrace the whole truth at once. They simply couldn't come that far that fast. So he accepted them where they were and gradually, over nearly two thousand years, brought them to the point where they were finally ready for Christ.

> He took his people in hand, teaching them, unteachable as they were, to follow him. He gave them prophets, accustoming man to bear his Spirit and to have communion with God on earth. He who stands in need of no one gave communion with himself to those who need him. Like an architect he outlined the plan of salvation to those who sought to please him. By his own hand he gave food in Egypt to those who did not see him. To those who were restless in the desert he gave a law perfectly suited to them. To those who entered the land of prosperity he gave a worthy inheritance. He killed the fatted calf for those who turned to him as Father, and clothed them with the finest garment. In so many ways he was training the human race to take part in the harmonious song of salvation.... Through many acts of indulgence he tried to prepare them for perseverance in his service. He kept calling them to what was primary by means of what was secondary, that is, through foreshadowings to the reality, through things of time to the things of eternity, through things of the flesh to the things of the spirit, through earthly things to the heavenly things.... Through foreshadowings of

---

106. *Against Heresies* I, 10.3.

the future they were learning reverence for God and persever-ance in his service. The law was therefore a school of instruction for them, and a prophecy of what was to come.[107]

So the Old Testament Scriptures prepare for and prefigure Christ. But when Christ finally arrived, he brought the fullness of truth with him. God held nothing back from us—in Christ, says Irenaeus, he gives us everything. There is no further revelation to expect. So here's the magnificent balance presented by Irenaeus. Between old and new covenants, the Law and the Gospel, there is perfect continuity. Nonetheless, the cross of Christ introduces a dramatic shift. The harmonious song of the history of salvation is one continuous melody. But in Christ, there is a sudden transposition, a unique change of key. This decisive shift, this new key, is the final key. The fullness has been given, and there is nothing further to be added.

The harmony image introduced by Irenaeus is a rich one that describes the difference between the heretics' approach and Irenaeus's approach not only to the relationship between the covenants, but to the very idea of the canon of Scripture as well. The word *heresy* comes from the Greek word for choice. It usually involves a selective picking and choosing leading ultimately to impoverishment. Irenaeus points out that it is a hallmark of most of the heretics that they choose only one Gospel, rejecting the rest. The same goes for the apostles: Marcion chooses only one apostle, Paul, rejecting all others.

For Irenaeus, as the two Testaments are different but harmonious, making a rich and beautiful melody, so the differences of style, vocab-ulary, and perspective of each evangelist and New Testament author blend together to give us a symphony of praise of Jesus Christ. In

---

107. *Against Heresies* IV, 14.2–3.

writers prior to Irenaeus, we see references to this gospel or that, to a letter of Paul here and the first letter of Peter there. In Irenaeus for the first time, we find a Christian teacher working with a New Testament much the same as the one we have. He is also the first Christian author who provides an explanation of why to accept this book and not that one. Irenaeus is also the first of the Fathers who, when referring to "Scripture," at least half of the time means New as well as Old Testament books.

The name of the authors of each of the Gospels is not included in the original text. It is Irenaeus who identifies the four legitimate Gospels and tells us who wrote them:

> So Matthew among the Hebrews issues a Writing of the gospel in their own tongue, while Peter and Paul were preaching the gospel at Rome and founding the Church. After their decease Mark, the disciple and interpreter of Peter, also handed down to us in writing what Peter had preached. Then Luke, the follower of Paul, recorded in a book the gospel as it was preached by him. Finally John, the disciple of the Lord, who had also lain on his breast, himself published the Gospel, while he was residing at Ephesus.[108]

For Irenaeus, the fact that there are four Gospels is highly symbolic. In the ancient world in general and in the book of Revelation in particular, the number four, reflecting the four points of the compass, stood for the whole world. It was a symbol of universality or catholicity, which is of course an essential characteristic of the Church. For Paul, the Church is the pillar and foundation of the truth (see 1 Timothy 3:15). Here Irenaeus says that the catholic Church requires a catholic foundation and finds it in the fourfold Gospel:

---

108. *Against Heresies* III, 1.1.

The Gospels could not possibly be either more or less in number than they are. Since there are four zones of the world in which we live, and four principal winds, while the Church is spread over all the earth, and the pillar and foundation of the Church is the gospel, and the Spirit of life, it fittingly has four pillars…a gospel fourfold in form but held together by one Spirit.[109]

There is something else Irenaeus contributes to Christian culture in the course of his discussion of the fourfold Gospel. He sees these four documents mysteriously prefigured in the four faces of the cherubim in Ezekiel 1: the lion, the ox, the man, and the eagle, which ultimately come to be the symbols of Mark, Luke, Matthew, and John, respectively. So they have remained in Christian art throughout the Christian centuries down to this day.

Legacy and Synthesis

There is probably nothing that Christians so much take for granted as the Bible. They can argue with each other about its interpretation, but seldom does it occur to them to question the table of contents. Never, that is, until a book comes along, such as the *Gospel of Thomas*, *The Da Vinci Code*, or Reza Aslan's *Zealot*, that challenges our assumptions and rattles our complacency. Often, these radical attacks on the truth of the Bible leave Christians reeling and stammering.

A man of peace once fought fiercely to preserve and explain to us the foundation on which we stand. Today Muslims, neo-Gnostics, and supposed critical historians all question the picture the New Testament provides us of Jesus and claim to have some better access to him. The commonsense arguments of Irenaeus against the naysayers of his age are exactly what we need to face the challengers of our own.

---

109. *Against Heresies* III, 11.8.

If we are to believe anyone when it comes to the truth about Jesus, who more than those who lived with him and later died for him? And if anyone should be trusted to know these shepherds' true teaching, who more than those to whom they entrusted their sheep, many of whom also died for Christ?

All Christians, whether they are aware of it or not, depend on apostolic tradition, preserved by the early Church Fathers, every time they pick up their Bibles. It is time that they learn to appreciate and articulate the sound reasons for the confidence they place in the book they hold in their hands.

CHAPTER 10

Clement and the School of Alexandria

We really don't know much about the details of his life. But around A.D. 150, a boy named Clement was born to a pagan family, probably in Athens. We are not sure where and when he accepted the Christian faith, but we do know that once converted, he wanted to learn that faith from the very best of teachers. So he did what high school graduates today still do. He moved away from home in search of the best education. His quest led him far and wide until he came to the place where he should have started. This was the city the Greek conqueror of Egypt so humbly named after himself—Alexandria.

This conqueror, by the way, though he lived three hundred years before Christ, is the reason that the New Testament was written in Greek. Alexander had a goal of uniting the world through the spread of Greek culture, and he was wildly successful. From his time forward, the common language and culture of the whole Mediterranean world was Greek. The Roman conquest did not change this. In fact, the Romans simply co-opted the Greek gods, the Greek classics, and Greek philosophy. The sign on the cross over Jesus's head was written in Aramaic, Latin, and Greek because, outside of Italy and North Africa, Latin was only used in the government and the army. In the marketplace and in the schools, people communicated mainly in Greek.

When Clement arrived in Alexandria, it was one of the largest and most vibrant cities in the world, second only to Rome. Located on the sea at the mouth of the Nile, it was unrivaled as a center of trade; its lighthouse was one of the seven wonders of the ancient world. It was also the intellectual capital of the empire with a legendary library. A large Jewish community lived in this city where the Hebrew Bible had been translated into Greek for the first time. Christians had been there since New Testament times, and among them, Clement found the teacher he'd been long looking for. Pantaenus was a convert to Christianity from the Stoic school of philosophy. We don't know much more about him, except that, though he was a layman, he had a very important role in the Christian community. Evidently, the local bishop had put him in charge of the very first Christian school in history, a catechetical institute where new Christians were prepared for baptism. Clement soon became his assistant, and around A.D. 200 he became Pantaenus's successor.

Clement's Problem

The church in Alexandria had evidently enjoyed a respite from persecution for some time. Nonetheless, it was now menaced by heretical sects of every stripe. The main Gnostic groups that prompted Irenaeus's book had headquarters here. Gnostic ideas were in the air. So were the ideas of Plato and the Stoics. Many Christians evidently reacted by shunning any sort of pagan learning and withdrawing into a sort of intellectual ghetto. Clement himself notes this: "The multitude are scared of Greek philosophy, as children are of masks, fearing that it will lead them astray."[110] He goes on to say that, like the companions of Odysseus passing the Sirens, "they stop up their

---

110. *Stromateis* VI, 80.

ears because they know that if they once allow themselves to listen to Greek learning they will not be able afterwards to find their way home again."[111]

In another place, he describes the negative and defensive posture he observes on the part of many of his brethren:

> I am well aware of what is said by some who stupidly take fright at any noise. They assert that one must concern oneself only with what is necessary and is bound up with faith, that we ought to pass by anything outside this as superfluous because it distracts us to no purpose and absorbs our energies in studies which are of no help towards our ultimate end. There are others who even think that philosophy was introduced into human life by some evil inventor for the ruin of men.[112]

As a faithful disciple of Christ and son of the Church, Clement is of course critical of the Gnostics and aware of the limitations of philosophy. But as someone entrusted with evangelizing and training new enquirers, many of whom were cultured members of the upper classes, he saw this unqualified rejection of learning as nothing short of disastrous. It played right into the hands of those who ridiculed Christianity as having no rational basis whatsoever. Just a few years before he took over as head of the school, a pagan critic of Christianity by the name of Celsus had written that while there may be a few cultured Christians, the majority say, "Do not ask questions, only believe. Faith will save you. Wisdom is an evil thing and foolishness good." Galen, a famous physician and philosopher of the day, made much the same observation.[113]

---

111. *Stromateis* VI, 89.
112. *Stromateis* I, 18.
113. See Richard Walzer, *Galen on Jews and Christians* (Oxford: Oxford University Press, 1949) pp. 15, 48–56.

Clement saw knowledge of philosophy and literature not only as important for outreach to cultured enquirers, but as tools for defense of the faith. "The Hellenic philosophy does not, by its approach, make the truth more powerful; but by rendering powerless the assault of sophistry against it, and frustrating the treacherous plots laid against the truth, is said to be the proper fence and wall of the vineyard."[114] Part of philosophy is logic, and in the face of often irrational and baseless attacks, Christians need to know how to use it.

Above all, Clement is a man of Scripture and Tradition. But evidently, secular learning had prepared him to accept the Gospel, as it had for Pantaenus and Justin. So he advances significantly beyond Justin, who had seen "seeds of the Word" present throughout the pagan intellectual world. Clement goes so far to say that Greek philosophy is actually of divine origin. Though philosophy is not on a par with the Old Testament, God, in his Providence, sent it to the Greeks as a preparation for the Gospel in a similar way that God sent the Law and prophets to the Jews to prepare them for his Son.

Granted, Greek philosophy neither comprehends the truth in its entirety nor conveys the strength to fulfill the Lord's command. Yet, it at least prepares the way for Christianity by making a man self-controlled, by molding his character, and by making him ready to receive the truth.[115]

Clement had to fight the same foes as Irenaeus, but he employed a different strategy. He refused to ridicule his Gnostic and pagan critics. Instead, he aimed to steal their fire. The word *gnostic* means the person "in the know" who possesses saving knowledge. Baptism in the early Church was called the "illumination." Clement maintains that the real "gnostic," the true enlightened one, is the person who

---

114. *Stromateis* I, 20.100.
115. *Stromateis* I, 80.

receives the light of faith in baptism and is determined to penetrate the profound meaning of that faith by making use of every available aid. Living out this faith, growing daily in virtue as well as understanding, the Christian gnostic attains love and, ultimately, heaven.

....

A Dynamic Journey

Around the year Clement arrived in Alexandria, Irenaeus had written, "The glory of God is man fully alive."[116] In his book called the *Stromateis*, Clement sought to sketch what man fully alive looks like, and he called him the true gnostic.

Clement wants both his catechumens and his pagan critics to understand something. The true Christian life does not consist in simply accepting the deposit of the faith, getting baptized, and then attending the required services. On the contrary, this just begins a process of ever-deepening insight and sanctification. For the "knowledge" that Clement is talking about consists not only of intellectual understanding but of an intimate experience of God and his truth that leads to a transforming union. It is a knowledge that assimilates us to God and to the truth that we contemplate. "This, therefore, is the life-work of the perfected gnostic, viz., to hold communion with God through the great High Priest, being made like the Lord, as far as may be…and in being thus assimilated to God, the gnostic is making and fashioning himself and also forming those who hear him."[117]

As he goes about describing the journey of the "true gnostic," we learn much of the features of Christian life of the day. Clement does not want his people to go mindlessly through the motions of prayer

------

116. *Against Heresies* IV, 20.5–7.
117. *Stromateis* VII, 3.13.

or to fast out of mere custom. Rather, he wants them to do everything intentionally, aware of the deeper meaning of their external actions.

For example, it was already a part of Christian tradition to pray facing east. Clement directs the Christian gnostic to do this, but to have understanding of its meaning:

> And since the east symbolizes the day of birth, and it is from thence that the light spreads, after it has first "shone forth out of darkness," aye, and from thence that the day of the knowledge of the truth dawned like the sun upon those who were lying in ignorance, therefore our prayers are directed towards the rise of dawn.[118]

The *Didache* told us that Christians are to fast on Wednesdays and Fridays. But Clement wants the Christian gnostic to understand the reason for this. The gnostic "understands too the hidden meanings of the fasting of these days, I mean of Wednesday and Friday: for the one is dedicated to Hermes, the other to Aphrodite. At any rate he makes his life a fast both from love of money and love of pleasure, which are the springs of all the vices."[119]

We see also, as we did in the *Didache,* that Christians have set times of prayer including the Sunday Eucharist and the prayer three times per day specified by the *Didache.* The Christian gnostic observes these fixed times but would never just leave it at that. Following St. Paul's counsel in Philippians 4, his goal is to pray always, maintaining a continual conversation with God:

> Accordingly all our life is a festival: being persuaded that God is everywhere present on all sides, we praise him as we till the

---

118. *Stromateis* VII, 7.43.
119. *Stromateis* VII, 11.75. Aphrodite (Venus) was the goddess of love; Hermes, the god of fortune, chance, thieves, and gain in general.

ground, we sing hymns as we sail the sea, we feel his inspiration in all that we do. And the gnostic enjoys a still closer intimacy with God, being at once serious and cheerful in everything, serious owing to his thoughts being turned towards heaven, and cheerful, as he reckons up the blessings with which God has enriched our human life.[120]

Clement likens the life of the Christian gnostic to a life of spiritual training. "So in every difficulty the soul of the gnostic proves its strength, being in first-rate condition and vigour, like the body of the athlete."[121]

Plato had said that good is diffusive of itself. Clement sees that the crowning act of charity in the life of the gnostic is to share his knowledge with others. Certainly, sharing perishable goods with those in need is part of the lifestyle of the gnostic. But if the duty to share earthly things is a solemn one, even more so is the duty to share heavenly truth. It is a duty, but it is the greatest joy of the gnostic as well. Clement may be director of the catechetical school, but all authentic gnostics, all Christians who desire perfection, must be evangelists and catechists. Heretical Gnostics were elitists and kept their knowledge a secret. The true gnostic shares that truth with anyone and everyone.

> But the dignity of the Christian gnostic is carried to an even further pitch by him who has undertaken the direction of the teaching of others, assuming the management in word and deed of that which is the greatest blessing on earth, by virtue of which he becomes a mediator to bring about a close union and fellowship with God.[122]

---

120. *Stromateis* VII, 7.35.
121. *Stromateis* VII, 11.64.
122. *Stromateis* VII, 9.52.

Teaching others, for Clement, is a matter of both word and deed. Both Ignatius and Justin poured their energies into teaching by the spoken and written word. Yet their ultimate witness was the laying down of their lives. For Clement, living in a period of relative peace, teaching must be accompanied by the "white martyrdom" of a life of virtue dedicated to Christian perfection.

Marriage

Despite the sensuality of pagan society at this time, the more philosophically minded held sexual abstinence in high esteem and wondered whether a true philosophic life could be carried out amidst the cares that accompany a spouse and children. Marcion, whose heretical church had branches in Alexandria and all over the empire, totally rejected marriage as cooperation in evil. The evil Demiurge had commanded, "Be fruitful and multiply," and the last thing Marcion wanted to do was encourage anyone to help this fiend carry out this wicked plan of entrapping even more souls in the muck of matter.

Clement found it necessary to counter these errors with a defense of marriage. In doing so, he made an early and invaluable contribution to the Christian theology of marriage and family.

For Clement, marriage and procreation are not only permitted or even, as the Stoics taught, a duty to society. Rather, we are in the presence of something more than natural and good. Marriage is truly something sacred. In becoming parents, man and woman have communion with God in his creative work. "Thus man becomes an image of God in so far as man cooperates in the creation of man."[123]

Clement appreciated both celibacy and marriage, seeing each

---

123. See *Paedagogus* II and *Stromateis* III.

person as receiving their particular calling and gift from God. But he did not mind sharing his opinion on which is a higher calling. Unlike the other Fathers who weigh in on the subject, he voted for marriage, due to the opportunities it provides for self-denial and the testing of virtue:

> True manhood is shown not in the choice of a celibate life; on the contrary the prize in the contest of men is won by him who has trained himself by the discharge of the duties of husband and father and by the supervision of a household, regardless of pleasure and pain—by him, I say, who in the midst of his solicitude for his family shows himself inseparable from the love of God and rises superior to every temptation which assails him through children and wife and servants and possessions. On the other hand he who has no family is in most respects untried.[124]

Clement did not hold that procreation is the only reason for matrimony. The intimate sharing of all things and the mutual support between spouses is something that is most precious in Christian marriage:

> The virtue of man and woman is the same. For if the God of both is one, the master of both is also one; one Church, one temperance, one modesty; their food is common, marriage an equal yoke; respiration, sight, hearing, knowledge, hope, obedience, love all alike. And those whose life is common, have common graces and a common salvation; common to them are love and training.[125]

In the Christian family, the Lord himself is present. Subsequent Church Fathers would further develop the theme that the family is

---

124. *Stromateis* VII, 11.70.
125. *Paedagogus* 1.4.

the domestic Church, but we find the idea suggested in the beautiful way that Clement interprets a familiar saying of Jesus: "But who are the two or three gathered in the name of Christ in whose midst the Lord is? Does he not by the 'three' mean husband, wife, and child? For a wife is bound to her husband by God." [126]

The First Christian Scholar

This, of course, is not the only Gospel text Clement cites. Although Clement wrote only a few years after the appearance of Irenaeus's book, we know that Clement, like Irenaeus, recognizes "the four gospels that have been handed down to us."[127] Following Irenaeus, Clement cites from nearly every book of what came to be known as the New Testament. In total, in the course of the four works of his that have come down to us, he cites passages from the New Testament 2,000 times, texts from the Old Testament over 1,500 times, and Greek classics over 360 times. Writing two centuries later, St. Jerome calls Clement the most learned of all the early Fathers.

Of course, Justin had been the explorer who made the initial contact between the divine wisdom of the Gospel and the philosophy of the Greeks. But Clement was the pioneer who settled down, cleared the stumps, and planted a garden in the field of Christian philosophy, a garden that yielded much fruit. The famous patristic scholar Joannes Quasten says of Clement, "We owe it above all to him if scholarly thinking and research are recognized in the Church. He proved that the faith and philosophy, Gospel and secular learning, are not enemies but belong together."[128]

---

126. *Stromateis* III, 10.68.
127. *Stromateis* III, 13.93.
128. Johannes Quasten, *Patrology, Vol. II: The Ante-Nicene Literature After Irenaeus* (Allen, Tx.: Christian Classics, 1983), p. 7.

One could only imagine what more Clement could have accomplished had he had more time to cultivate his garden. But his tenure at the catechetical school was cut unexpectedly short. Seemingly out of nowhere in A.D. 202, a fierce persecution erupted in Alexandria under the Emperor Septimius Severus. The catechetical school shut its doors, and Clement fled the country. He was never again to return to his beloved Alexandria before departing in A.D. 215 for his heavenly homeland.

CHAPTER 11

Origen: Zeal and Genius

As he stood over the sleeping youth, Leonidas beamed with pride. He lifted up his hands and glorified God for giving him such an extraordinary son. He had provided him the best education that Alexandria had to offer. Though he was only seventeen, Origen was clearly Clement's brightest student. It was sad that the recent trouble had caused the school to shut down. No matter. The most important thing was that the boy continue to make progress in prayer and the study of God's Word, and he could do that at home for now. Leonidas was especially grateful that his son's zeal for God was even greater than his zeal for his studies.

A knock at the door interrupted his thoughts. The trouble that had driven Clement from town had now come to his doorstep. The soldiers took Leonidas into custody and dragged him away. As Origen awoke and realized what was happening, he abruptly bade his mother farewell. He was determined to run after the soldiers and die with his father. His mother pleaded with him to no avail but then had an idea. The boy had leapt up from bed wearing no more than undergarments. She knew him well. He was too modest to run naked into the street. So while he was saying good-bye to his five younger siblings, she stealthily hid every single garment he had.

As the heat of the moment passed, she reasoned with him. Those who surrender themselves, she reminded him, are not martyrs, but suicides. Martyrdom is an honor that you cannot seize for yourself.

Your duty now is to care for me and your five younger brothers and to continue your studies. Who knows? Your opportunity to suffer for Christ may yet come.

Indeed, she understood him. For one who was so passionate, bright, and impetuous, he was remarkably humble. As she expected, he submitted to what was manifestly the will of God. Still, no one could prevent him from writing a note to Leonidas who was in prison awaiting execution. His final communication to his father was a plea not to buckle, not to shrink back but to hold firm and be faithful to Christ unto death. Leonidas went to his death grateful—his legacy would be his witness and the amazing boy he left behind.

This episode, recounted to us by Eusebius,[129] historian of the early Church, tells us everything we need to know about the remarkable prodigy from Alexandria named Origen.

If Origen could not witness to Christ through martyrdom, he knew he was free to die with Christ through a life of self-sacrifice. So from that day, he took literally the counsel of Jesus to the apostles—he wore no shoes and permitted himself no more than one set of clothing. Till his dying day, he slept not in a bed, but on the floor. And he consecrated his sexuality to Christ, embracing celibacy for the sake of the kingdom (see Matthew 19:12).

The Student Becomes the Headmaster

All the family's property was confiscated by the government in punishment for Leonidas's great crime of sharing Christ with others—for the government crackdown was not so much for being a Christian,

---

129. Eusebius was born in Caesarea around the year of Origen's death (253). He wrote his *Ecclesiastical History* shortly before A.D. 300. The history of Origen is recounted extensively in Book VI of this history.

but for making others Christians. Origen did what he knew to earn money for the family—he taught the Greek classics. But soon the persecution died down, and the bishop, Demetrius, wanted to reopen the catechetical school. With Clement somewhere in Asia Minor, who would lead it? Demetrius selected the child wonder, not yet eighteen, to succeed a mature, published scholar in his fifties.

When we think of a catechetical school, we naturally assume that it provided Bible and catechism classes since the main goal was to get new converts ready for baptism. And of course, it did. But remember Clement's vision of the Christian life—the true "gnostic" must understand what he believes and share it with others. That meant he must pray and study like an athlete. And so we find out from Origen that the catechetical institute of Alexandria included study of astronomy, mathematics, physics, and philosophy, everything to help the student not only understand Christian doctrine, but to explain it to their neighbors.

Over all this activity, Origen presided uninterrupted for over ten years. But as his reputation for brilliance and holiness spread throughout the Christian world, he was invited abroad to speak and serve as a consultant. He traveled to Rome in A.D. 212 and heard the preaching of the brilliant, though troublesome, Hippolytus. A few years later, some bishops invited him to Palestine to speak. But when Bishop Demetrius found out that Origen, a layman, had preached during the divine liturgy, he was incensed. Such a thing was not permitted in Alexandria. Origen was promptly summoned to return home.

It is then that Origen began to write or, more precisely, to dictate. He had opened the eyes of a Valentinian Gnostic who then renounced heresy and accepted the true, orthodox faith. This man, Ambrose, was forever indebted to Origen and wanted more people to benefit from his teaching. And so, being a man of means, he offered to employ a secretary for Origen, who was too busy to write for himself. The first assistant was worn out in a few days, so another was hired, and then another. It ultimately took a staff of more than fifteen to keep up with the tireless teacher—seven stenographers worked in shifts, taking dictation by shorthand with as many others converting the shorthand into normal script and others finally into finished texts. Origen was one of the certifiable geniuses of Church history; for the next forty years, he typically dictated four different books at any one time.

Out of Egypt to the Promised Land

About fifteen years after the incident in Palestine, Origen was invited to come to Athens to help resolve an issue there, and Demetrius let him go. On the way, he made a brief stop in Palestine. Once again, the bishops begged him to preach during the liturgy. Origen declined, reminding them of his bishop's objections to a layman preaching. His hosts fully understood his dilemma and came up with a simple solution to the problem—they ordained him to the priesthood on the spot. Instead of appeasing Demetrius, this enraged him. Eusebius identifies jealousy as the motive for what happened next. Demetrius evidently began to circulate the story that, in a moment of rash, youthful zeal following his father's martyrdom, Origen had not only embraced celibacy, but had taken Matthew 19:12 too far by castrating himself. Since tradition forbade the ordination of eunuchs, the ordination, he insisted, was invalid.[130]

---

130. Eusebius simply accepts this as a fact. But he wrote seventy years after the events he was recording and could very well have uncritically accepted as true a bit of slander spread by Origen's enemies. There is no record of Origen either affirming or denying this allegation. However, when he interprets Matthew 19 in his writings, he encourages people *not* to take Jesus's words literally and do what he was accused of doing.

Once again, Demetrius recalled Origen. This presented Origen with the most difficult cross of his life, and his greatest fear was that he would be tempted to lash out in bitter resentment against the injustice. The Lord helped him to hold his tongue and forgive from his heart; he humbly submitted and said not a word in his own defense.[131] Shortly thereafter, Demetrius died, and the bishops of Palestine invited Origen to start a new school for them in the coastal town of Caesarea.[132] Thus begins Origen's greatest period of productivity, which continued for some twenty years.

How many books did he ultimately write? No one knows for sure, since all but a few have been lost. Two hundred years later, St. Jerome reported that he saw a list of Origen's works in the library of Caesarea, and they numbered over two thousand. In one of his letters,[133] Jerome lists over eight hundred of them.

The First Theologian

Christian theology, classically understood as "faith seeking understanding,"[134] began with Matthew, Mark, Luke, and John. Theology as the scientific and systematic exposition of all Christian doctrine, explained logically as a coherent whole—that began with Origen. His book *De Principiis* (On First Principles) is the first serious attempt to put it all together in a work of systematic theology.

For all his originality, however, it must be made clear from the beginning that Origen's humility ruled. Like other Fathers before him, he submitted entirely to the apostolic tradition. He was no

---

131. Origen alludes to this in his *Commentary on John* VI, 2.
132. Paul had been held in Caesarea under house arrest for about two years. See Acts 23:33—25:32.
133. Jerome, *Letter 30 to Paula*.
134. A phrase made famous by St. Augustine c. A.D. 400.

arrogant maverick, but was a loyal disciple and son of the Church first, theologian second:

> I want to be a man of the church. I do not want to be called by the name of some founder of a heresy but by the name of Christ, and to bear that name which is blessed on earth. It is my desire, in deed as in Spirit, both to be and be called a Christian.[135]

Far from wanting to avoid oversight and accountability, he invited it: "If I who seem to be your right hand and am called presbyter and seem to preach the Word of God, if I do something against the discipline of the Church, then may the whole church in unanimous resolve, cut me, its right hand, off, and throw me away."[136]

Everywhere in the writings of the early Fathers we see evidence of the Church's belief in the divinity of Christ. Origen is certainly a witness to the apostolic tradition on this point. Before creation and time, God the Father begot the Son, but this generation of the Word is an eternal happening. Origen says clearly, "There is no time that He was not."[137] This is nothing new. But Origen contributed something of great importance to the Tradition. In his effort to explain the truth of the Trinity and the mystery of how the divine and human are related in the person of Jesus (Christology), he coined Greek terms and phrases that became classic: being (*ousia*), nature (*physis*), Jesus as the "God-man" (*theanthropos*). One term he apparently borrowed from the Valentinian Gnostics and introduced into Christian theology is even enshrined in the creed many Christians recite every Sunday—the Son is one in being or "consubstantial" (*homoousios*) with the Father.

---

135. Origen, *Homily 16 on Luke*.
136. Origen, *Homily on Joshua* 7.6.
137. *De Principiis* 1, 2.9ff.

With regard to the Virgin Mary, he appears to be the earliest theologian in whose writings we find the term "Mother of God" or "God-bearer" (*theotokos*).[138] In his groundbreaking *Commentary on the Gospel of John,* he witnesses to the importance of devotion to Mary in the earliest days of the Church: "No one may understand the meaning of the Gospel, if he has not rested on the breast of Jesus and received Mary from Jesus, to be his mother also."[139]

As a man of the Church, Origen's life took place against the backdrop of the Church's liturgical and sacramental life. His primary responsibility was preparing adult converts for baptism. It is telling, therefore, that he is so insistent that baptizing babies dates back to the apostles. He writes, "The Church has received from the apostles the custom of administering baptism even to infants. For those who have been entrusted with the secrets of the divine mysteries, knew very well that all are tainted with the stain of original sin, which must be washed off by water and the spirit."[140]

Origen also witnesses to a very realistic understanding of the Eucharist as the body of Christ that prevailed in the Church of his day:

You who are wont to assist at the Divine Mysteries, know how, when you receive the body of the Lord, you take reverent care, lest any particle of it should fall to the ground and a portion of the consecrated gift (*consecrati muneris*) escape you. You consider it a crime—and rightly so—if any particle thereof fall down though negligence.[141]

138. Sozomen, *Ecclesiastical History* 7.32 citing Origen's *Commentary on Romans.* (Sozomen wrote in the year 443.) This is not to say he invented the term; it was in use in at least the Syriac liturgy before it made its way into theology and Scripture commentary.
139. Origen, *Commentary on John* 1.6.
140. Origen, *Commentary on Romans* 5.9. See also *Homilies on Leviticus* 8.3.
141. Origen, *Homilies on Exodus* 13.3.

The First Scripture Scholar

The sum total of Origen's contributions to the development of Christianity are too many to enumerate. The most important thing about Origen is that he was first and foremost a man of the Bible and a pioneer in every aspect of biblical scholarship.

The classic translation of the Law and the Prophets from Hebrew into Greek had been carried out four hundred years before his time. Jewish legend had it that the King of Egypt wanted a Greek translation of the Bible for his library in Alexandria. So he locked seventy rabbis each in separate chambers and told them to translate Moses and the Prophets. Miraculously, so the story went, all emerged from their cells with the very same translation which came to be known as the Septuagint, in honor of the seventy (LXX) translators.

In spite of the legend, Origen felt it was his responsibility to check this translation against the original Hebrew and other Greek translations. So he took it upon himself to do something that few other Christian teachers did after the age of the apostles; he set himself to the difficult task of mastering Hebrew. Once he had that under his belt, he embarked on an unprecedented project called the *Hexapla*: He put the Hebrew original, the Septuagint, and four other Greek translations of the entire contents of the Old Testament in parallel columns so that he could compare them all. He wanted to do everything he could to establish the very best understanding of the letter of the sacred text.

The letter of the text, however, was not the ultimate goal for Origen, and he, following St. Paul, did not think it should be the ultimate goal of any Christian: "The letter kills but the Spirit gives life" (2 Corinthians 3:6). For him, Scripture was like another body of the Lord. The body dies and decomposes without the soul and the spirit. To penetrate to the spirit of the text must be our aim.

True, the Logos, or divine Word, was not incarnated in the letter of Scripture in the same way as it was in the human body of Jesus or, for that matter, in the Eucharist. Yet in a very real but analogous way, the divine Word truly is incorporated in the words of Scripture and dwells there as in a tabernacle. The Church, the Eucharist, and the Scriptures are three bodies of Christ, which all reveal the Word and make him present. The Divine Logos shines through the letter of the Bible just as he shines through the flesh of Jesus.

Following the tradition that had been handed down to him, Origen believed that Scripture is God-breathed, or inspired by the Holy Spirit. For him, biblical inspiration did not mean only that the human authors *were* inspired, but rather that the text *is* inspired. The Bible is full of the Spirit; the Spirit continues to dwell in the texts as in a temple. Origen was well aware that there were many human authors of the books and that they wrote in many different styles. But since they were all inspired by the same Spirit, all the books are held together and made alive just as the soul holds the body together and animates it. For him, one must always approach the text as a unitary body that is pulsating with divine Life.[142] Origen could do very painstaking work of preparatory study and textual criticism, but once the text was before him, he came to it to meet God and adore.

Origen took his cue from St. Paul when it came to the interpretation of the Bible. "Spiritual things must be understood spiritually" (see 1 Corinthians 2:10–16). If a person wants to penetrate beyond the letter to the Spirit, he needs the help of the same Holy Spirit who inspired the text. So the student of Scripture must be eager not only to study but to pray. Origen puts to work "all the resources of his mind" while simultaneously begging for the assistance of the Spirit.[143]

---

142. Origen, *Commentary on John* 10.13.
143. Origen, *Homilies on Exodus* 1.4.

It is therefore not enough to be zealous for the study of the sacred Scriptures, but we must beseech the Lord and implore him day and night that the Lamb of the tribe of Judah might come who, taking the sealed scroll, will deign to open it.[144]

We have seen Irenaeus and others use the image of harmony to describe the relationship between the two Testaments. Origen makes plain that this harmony blends the diverse notes of all the individual texts into a magnificent symphony. As a result, he is fond of a phrase introduced by St. Paul in Romans 12:6, the analogy (or proportion) of faith (*analogia fidei*). Understanding this phrase in light of Paul's exhortation to judge spiritual things by the spiritual, Origen takes the analogy of faith to mean that the interpreter should compare spiritual things in Scripture to other spiritual things in Scripture, thus clarifying one part of Scripture by another. This becomes a classic interpretive principle from Origen onward.[145] The same proportion or connection exists between the truth of Scripture and the truth passed down through apostolic tradition, reflected in the Church's liturgy and creed. There is a harmonious resonance of all the parts of the book with each other, but also between the book and the tradition of the Church, so all of these realities mutually illumine each other.

Many have criticized the allegorical or spiritual method of Origen and other Fathers of the Church for being subjective. But Origen's perspective is quite different. The object of all of Scripture, its ultimate content even in the Old Testament, is Jesus Christ. Everything prepares, prefigures, or predicts Christ, so to see Christ everywhere in the Bible is supremely objective. We can see an example of his

---

144. Origen commenting on Emmaus in his *Homilies on Exodus* 12.4.
145. It is classic in the Catholic and Orthodox traditions but also a key principle of John Calvin and the Protestant reformers who believe Scripture interprets itself (*Scriptura scripturae interpres*).

approach in the beautiful way he interprets the story of Abraham on Mt. Moriah:

> Isaac said to Abraham his father: "Father!" This plea from the son was at that instant the voice of temptation. For do you not think the voice of the son who was about to be sacrificed struck a responsive chord in the heart of the father? Although Abraham did not waver because of his faith, he responded with a voice full of affection and asked: "What is it, my son?" Isaac answered him: "Here are the fire and the wood, but where is the sheep for the holocaust?" And Abraham replied: "God will provide for himself a sheep for the holocaust, my son."
>
> The careful yet loving response of Abraham moves me greatly. I do not know what he saw in spirit, because he did not speak of the present but of the future: God will provide for himself a sheep. His reply concerns the future, yet his son inquires about the present. Indeed the Lord himself provided a sheep for himself in Christ.
>
> Abraham extended his hand to take the sword and slay his son, and the angel of the Lord called to him from heaven and said: "Abraham, Abraham." And he responded: "Here I am." And the angel said: "Do not put your hand upon the boy or do anything to him, for now I know that you fear God." Compare these words to those of the Apostle when he speaks of God: "He did not spare his own Son but gave him up for us all." God emulates man with magnificent generosity. Abraham offered to God his mortal son who did not die, and God gave up his immortal Son who died for all of us.[146]

Origen was moved in preaching about this episode, and he was bringing out its deeper significance. That is the final point about the spiritual meaning of Scripture in the mind of Origen and other

---

146. Origen, *Homilies on Genesis* 8.6–9.

Fathers. The reason Christ comes to meet us in Scripture is not merely to inform us, but to transform us. Therefore, the spiritual understanding of Scripture, or the allegorical meaning, is never just something detached, historical, or catechetical. God speaks to us through Scripture and awaits a personal response. Spiritual understanding of Scripture and the process of conversion are one and the same for Origen. If personal application of Scripture fails to take place, then biblical interpretation is incomplete.

There is yet another thing to understand about the "application" of Scripture. We don't reach out to take the meaning of the text and try to apply it to our lives. Rather, when we put ourselves before God in the Bible, the Spirit that dwells in the words reaches out and assimilates us to himself. God's word is alive and efficacious. Origen, in his response to the ridicule of Celsus, tried to get this across to his pagan opponent. The Christian Scriptures are not like the writings of the Gentiles—beautiful discourses that change nothing. Rather, they are like God himself—they have an efficacious power to change hearts and bring about what they say. This power, declares Origen, is a testimony of their divine origin.[147]

The Confessor

Looming always in the background of his prodigious work was the specter of persecution. After two decades of peace following his father's martyrdom, crisis struck again. This time his patron Ambrose and another friend were endangered. As Origen had written a letter to his father in prison, once again he wrote a much longer letter to his friends, the *Exhortation to Martyrdom*, which has become a classic of Christian spirituality:

---

147. Origen, *Contra Celsum* I, 2.

God says through the prophet: "At an acceptable time I heard you; on the day of salvation I helped you." What time could be more acceptable than when, for our fidelity to God in Christ, we are made a public spectacle and led away under guard, not defeated but triumphant?

...In Christ and with Christ the martyrs disarm the principalities and powers and share in his triumph over them, for their share in Christ's sufferings makes them sharers also in the mighty deeds those sufferings accomplished. What could more appropriately be called the day of salvation than the day of such a glorious departure from this world?[148]

This crisis again subsided, like the previous one. A decade passed, and a new emperor decided to take a new approach—instead of these sporadic, wrist-slapping, local persecutions, he planned a systematic and empire-wide move to crush the Christian non-conformists once and for all. Decius decreed that all inhabitants of the empire were hereby required to carry documents attesting that they had burned incense to the gods and to the emperor. This took a heavy toll on the Church everywhere. In Rome, the pope was executed. In Caesarea, Origen was imprisoned and mercilessly tortured over an extended period of time. But before Origen could fulfill his childhood wish to die for Christ, the emperor who had unsheathed the sword against the Christians himself fell by the sword. Origen was released. But the torture, added to years of penance and exhausting labor, had taken its toll. Within a year or two, the tireless teacher and courageous confessor[149] went home to his Lord.

---

148. Origen, *Exhortation to Martyrdom* 41–42.
149. When someone is called a confessor in Christian history, this means not that he "heard confessions" but that he confessed his faith despite imprisonment and torture. The word *martyr* is reserved for those who are killed rather than deny their faith.

Origen's Legacy

It must be admitted that there was chaff mixed into the wheat of Origen's genius. He was a daring pioneer and so veered off the road into the bush from time to time. But this is only because the road had not yet been marked out by the Church. Some of his ideas, like the pre-existence of the soul and the final salvation of everyone, even the demons, came from Platonism. This philosophy was part of the air that he breathed in Alexandria and one of the tools he attempted to use in theology. Hundreds of years after his death, some of his fans turned these speculative suggestions of Origen into doctrinaire positions that were then condemned by the Church. This cast a cloud of suspicion over Origen's reputation and the entire body of his valuable work. Emperor Justinian secured condemnations against ten doctrines attributed to Origen. This tragically resulted in the destruction of Origen's writings, many of which are most likely lost forever.

But Origen had done what God had called him to do. His approach to theology, Scripture, and prayer had profoundly influenced the best and the brightest all around the Christian world, in both East and West, for two hundred years before the condemnations were pronounced. His legacy was woven into the fabric of the Church's faith and life—no emperor could rip it out. Because of the condemnations and because of the tale of his self-mutilation, Origen was never canonized. But there are few teachers in the history of the Church to whom more is owed. It seems to me we also owe a debt of gratitude to his father, for the example of heroic faith he provided his son. And to his mother as well—for hiding his clothes.

CHAPTER 12

The Tragedy of Tertullian

T unisia today conjures up the image of desert sands and the
sound of the Muslim call to prayer. But in the days of the early
Church, the Mediterranean was a Roman lake, and its North African
shore was dotted with towns as Roman as you could find in nearby
Sicily. Before being conquered by Roman legions some centuries
earlier, North Africa's principal city, Carthage, had been a center of
child sacrifice.[150] In the second century after Christ, blood was still
being spilled here. Only now it was the blood of the martyrs.

A centurion and his wife brought a son into this severe, provincial world of Roman Africa. Quintus Septimius Florens Tertullianus,
Tertullian for short, received an extensive education, mastering both
Greek classics and Roman jurisprudence. After practicing law for a
few years in Rome, he returned to his hometown. Like many young
men of his day, Tertullian amused himself with frequent sexual
adventures, which continued even after he was married. As he was
struggling with a general sense of disgust for the meaninglessness of
his own lust-driven life, he happened to attend public games where
he witnessed the martyrdom of some Christians. He heard the way
they answered the magistrate. He noticed the way they supported one
another. As a lawyer, he knew criminals, and these were not criminals. Rather, they were virtuous people who had both the courage to
die and something worth dying for. Tertullian was so moved that he

---

150. The Phoenicians brought child sacrifice to Carthage when they founded the town in
814 B.C.

102

found himself seeking to know more. Soon thereafter, he presented himself for baptism. He was about thirty-four years of age.

It did not take long for the leaders of the Church to notice his passionate zeal and remarkable eloquence. A later writer says be became a presbyter, but this cannot be confirmed. What we do know is that a few years after his conversion, like the laymen Clement and Origen, he was entrusted with the task of preparing candidates for baptism.

And then he began to write. The original language of the Christian community in Carthage was the same as it was everywhere else in the Christian world up to this point—Greek. But culture was slowly changing all across the Western part of the empire—the knowledge of Greek was slowly fading, and it was becoming more necessary every day to write in Latin. Tertullian was the first Christian theologian to do so. And he proved to be a master both in his Latin prose and in his theology. His eloquence, his turns of phrase, his terse, ironic manner of expression all make him the most quotable of the Fathers—except for another African theologian named Augustine.

A Lawyer Attacks an Empire

Tertullian was a lawyer from first to last. He always wrote with an adversary in mind and always fought as if to win a case. The first adversary he chose to go after was the State. The Roman apologist Justin had approached apologetics as would a philosopher. Tertullian took a more legal approach befitting his background. His *Apology* is considered one of his great masterpieces; it is a mine for famous quotes.

The first thing to point out is that Tertullian turned the State's charge of irreligion back upon its own head. By trying to force religious devotion, he wrote, the State was committing a crime against religion by violating its deepest character. True devotion must be a free-will offering, not a compulsory sacrifice:

> "For see that you do not give a further ground for the charge of irreligion, by taking away religious liberty, and forbidding free choice of deity, so that I may no longer worship according to my inclination, but am compelled to worship against it. Not even a human being would care to have unwilling homage rendered him."[151]

In a subsequent letter to the proconsul of North Africa, he proclaims what could be considered a manifesto for religious liberty: "It is a fundamental human right, a privilege of nature, that every man should worship according to his own convictions: one man's religion neither harms or helps another man. It…is certainly no part of religion to compel religion."[152]

This affirmation is important because it underlines the apostolic tradition mentioned by other early Fathers: Faith is essentially a free act that government can neither compel nor interfere with. In the twenty-first century, religious freedom is once again a hot topic not only in the Middle East where many wish to impose Islamic law, but in Western liberal democracies where secular liberalism has been putting increasing restrictions on the expression of faith.

Tertullian goes on to make the case that if the State wants to contain Christianity's growth, its program of persecution is ironically counterproductive. "Nothing whatever is accomplished by your cruelties, each more exquisite than the last. It is the bait which wins men for our school. We multiply whenever we are mowed down by you;

---

151. *Apology* 24, 6–10.
152. Tertullian's *Letter to Scapula*, proconsul of Africa (written in 212).

the blood of Christians is seed."[153] This last statement, slightly refor-mulated, is one of the most famous quotes from the early Fathers: "the blood of the martyrs is the seed of the church."

Writing some years later to the local governor, Tertullian expresses concern that the emperor will have to answer before the judgment seat of God for the innocent blood he has spilled. This warning both expresses what happened in his own conversion and predicts the Church's triumph over paganism a hundred years later:

> But they whom you regard as masters are only men, and one day they themselves must die. Yet this community will be undying, for be assured that just in the time of its seeming overthrow, it is built up into greater power. For all who witness the noble patience of its martyrs, as struck with misgivings, are inflamed with desire to examine into the matter in question; and as soon as they come to know the truth, they straightway enroll them-selves its disciples.[154]

Tertullian points out to his pagan opponents that it was not only the courage shown through martyrdom but the daily love of Christians for each other that was causing their pagan neighbors to sit up and take notice:

> Every man once a month brings some coin, or whatever he likes, and only if he does wish, and if he can; for nobody is compelled; it is a voluntary offering. You might call them the trust funds of piety. For they are not spent upon banquets nor drinking parties nor thankless eating houses; but to feed the poor and to bury them, for boys and girls who lack property and parents, and then for slaves grown old, and shipwrecked mariners; and

---

153. *Apology* 50.13.
154. *Letter to Scapula* 5.

any who may be in mines, islands or prisons, provided that it is for the sake of God's love.... Such works of love (for so it is) put a mark upon us in the eyes of some. "Look," they say, "how they love one another," for themselves hate one another. "And how they are ready to die for each other," for themselves will be readier to kill each other.[155]

Initiation in the Early Church

As Tertullian went about his work with his catechumens, his class was raided by a sectarian Jezebel who attacked the importance of baptism. So Tertullian, the defense attorney, leapt into action. His drive to repulse the heretical assailant led to the very first treatise on baptism, or any of the sacraments for that matter. And what he tells us is extremely important for identifying the apostolic tradition with regard to the meaning and practice of both baptism and confirmation. He shows that, in second-century Africa, fasting and prayer preceded the event, as every ante-Nicene witness to baptism also mentions. But Tertullian tells us what happens immediately after the baptismal bath, which is not clearly laid out either by the New Testament or previous Church Fathers. The newly baptized was anointed with the special oil that priests, prophets, and kings were anointed with in the Old Testament. Called chrism, it is related to the word *Christ*, meaning "anointed one," and it gave baptized believers their name, "Christian." Then came the laying on of hands by the bishop, the successor of the apostles, for the giving of the Holy Spirit. This is the sacrament of confirmation or chrismation that we see today in the Orthodox, Catholic, and Anglican churches.[156]

---

155. *Apology* 39, 1–7.

156. A few other churches, such as the Lutheran and Methodist, have confirmation, though most Protestants, following Luther, do not see it as a sacrament instituted by Christ.

Baptism, according to the Lord's words in John 3, is needed to enter the kingdom of God. But those catechumens who are martyred before they can be baptized are still considered to have been baptized—but in their own blood. And because baptism is so necessary for salvation, anyone, in a case of dire necessity, can and should baptize. Of course, in normal circumstances this would be the prerogative of the bishop, whom he calls the "chief priest." In conclusion, he instructs the catechumens:

> When you ascend from that most sacred font of your new birth, and spread your hands for the first time in the house of your mother, together with your brethren, ask from the Father, ask from the Lord, that His own specialties of grace and distributions of gifts [charisms] may be supplied you.[157]

This shows that gifts of the Holy Spirit mentioned in 1 Corinthians 12 were expected and requested as a normal fruit of the sacraments of initiation.

The "house of your mother" here, of course, indicates the Church. This is the earliest surviving written witness to the designation of the Church as "mother," though both Church and the Virgin Mary can be seen imaged in the pregnant woman clothed with the sun of Revelation 12. Tertullian also calls the Church "mother" elsewhere in his writings.[158] Incidentally, Tertullian's favorite way to speak of Mary, the Virgin Mother, is in terms of the New Eve,[159] just as we find in Irenaeus and Origen.

---

157. Tertullian, *On Baptism* 20.
158. For example, *To the Martyrs* 1, *On Prayer* 2, and *On Modesty* 5, 14.
159. Tertullian, *On the Flesh of Christ* 17.

Eucharist: Reception and Reservation

Tertullian does not provide us a treatise on the Eucharist, but his references to this sacrament throughout his many works are notable. Like all the Fathers before him, he understood the Eucharist realistically, as the Body of Christ: "the flesh feeds on the body and blood of Christ, that the soul likewise may fatten on God."[160] He says that the bread represents the Lord's Body, but by "represents," he means *re*-presents, that is, makes present again.[161] Communion was clearly taken in the hand at this time, but this does not mean that communion was a casual affair. Tertullian shows a great reverence for the taking of communion and a horror of desecrating the sacrament through receiving it with hands made unworthy through idolatry.[162]

It must be kept in mind that, as of yet, there were no church buildings; meetings for worship generally took place in the spacious homes of the wealthy. Even so, we see a witness in Tertullian to the practice of the reservation of the sacrament between Eucharistic celebrations. We see in his writings that the faithful commonly brought the consecrated species home after the liturgy to reserve it so that they might receive communion daily.[163] In fact, Tertullian, in his treatise on the Lord's Prayer, states that Jesus is referring to the Eucharist when he instructs us to pray "give us this day our daily bread."[164]

Confession and Penance

Baptism is the original sacrament for the remission of sin—all is graciously forgiven, and the white garment received symbolized the purity of the newborn Christian in the sight of God. As we have

---

160. Tertullian, *On the Resurrection of the Flesh* 8.
161. Tertullian, *Against Marcion* 3:19; cf. *Against Marcion* 4.22 and *On the Resurrection of the Flesh* 17.
162. Tertullian, *On Idolatry* 6.
163. *On Prayer* 19 and *Letter to His Wife* 2.5.
164. *On Prayer* 19 and *Letter to his Wife* 2.5.

seen in previous Fathers, baptism was seen as an extremely serious commitment, likened to the *sacramentum* or sacred initiation oath of a Roman legionary. Among the early Christians there was a horror of betraying the baptismal promises and soiling the white baptismal garment through serious sin.[165] But inevitably, such things happened. How did the early Church respond? A document from about A.D. 100, the *Shepherd of Hermas*,[166] makes an obscure reference to a second chance for forgiveness of grave sins after baptism.

But Tertullian is the first Father to provide a general description of what this entailed. In his treatise *On Penance*, he describes a process of repentance with a specific Greek name, a technical term he feels obliged to continue to use even in his Latin text—the *exomologesis (confession)*. This shows that he is not referring to a new practice but something that was well-established and already traditional in the Church, a process of public penance. He tells us that the penitents would dress in sackcloth and ashes, beg the prayers of the faithful of the community, and confess their sins to the presbyters. After a prolonged but unspecified period of prayer and fasting, they would be given "absolution" by the bishop.[167] We find out from later Fathers that a person could be enrolled in the order of penitents for a very lengthy period of time, even years, depending on the gravity of the offense, before being given absolution and being restored to communion. Tertullian says that this process could only be undertaken once; in later authors we see that those who fell again after absolution were absolved and given communion again only on their deathbeds. This was the way the sacrament of penance generally was administered for the entire patristic period (until about A.D. 800).

---

165. See 1 John 5:16 for the distinction between sin in general and sin that is deadly or mortal. See 2 Peter 2:20–22.
166. *Shepherd of Hermas*, Mandate 4, 3:1–6.
167. Tertullian, *On Penance* 9.

Christ and the Trinity

The apostles, like their master, were Jews who grew up declaring every day, several times a day, "The Lord is our God, the Lord alone" (Deuteronomy 6:4–5). It was a hallmark of Judaism that the God of Israel is the only God. Yet, the New Testament and all the early Fathers affirm that Jesus is God. And then there is the Holy Spirit who also appears as divine.

The New Testament itself does not provide a clear explanation on how God can be one and three at the same time, so various teachers of the early Church tried to answer this question. We've seen that Origen, the first systematic theologian, made some important contributions along this line.

Later in Tertullian's life, a teacher from Asia Minor thought he'd made an original contribution. Praxeas, emphasizing the unity of God, taught that the Father descended into the womb of Mary as the Word. He ascended back to heaven only to return as the Holy Spirit. So Father, Son, and Spirit were simply three roles played by the one God, three masks worn by him at different times in salvation history. This doctrine came to be known as Modalism by some, since Father, Son, and Spirit are but three different "modes" of God's presence to us. Some ridiculed it as "Patripassianism" because it dares to infer that it was the Father who suffered on the cross.

Tertullian once again sprang into action. This heretic, for whom he of course had no patience, spurred him to make one of his greatest contributions to Christian theology. In explaining the proper way to reconcile the three-ness and the oneness of God, Tertullian coined the Latin term *trinitas* or trinity. He also introduced the key term *persona* or person. Father, Son, and Holy Spirit are three persons but only one divine substance, nature, and power. The three persons are distinct without being divided, so there is only one God, not three.[168] It is true that Tertullian himself made some serious errors regarding the Trinity which the Church later rejected—but this new terminology became classic and was later incorporated, as were some of the terms introduced by Origen, into the subsequent official expressions of the Church's faith.

When it comes to the explanation of how the human and divine are related in Jesus Christ, Tertullian made another brilliant and decisive contribution. He taught that in Christ, there is one person with two natures (*substantiae*), human and divine. There is no confusion or blending of natures in Jesus; humanity and divinity are distinct but never separated in him, so that it can be said that God died and a man raised the dead. Tertullian was so clear here that he anticipated the dogmatic definitions of the Council of Chalcedon, some 250 years later. Indeed, the great Christological controversies over how Jesus is both human and divine rocked the Eastern churches for several generations, causing two serious schisms. The Western Church was spared such tension largely because it accepted the assistance provided by Tertullian.

Rigorism: A Tragic End

John Henry Newman, a nineteenth-century expert in the history of doctrine, said that the original sin of all heretics is impatience. Sadly, Tertullian, for all his zeal, was afflicted with this sin in the extreme. He was not unaware of his weakness—he confessed in the beginning of his treatise *On Patience* that Tertullian writing about patience is like an invalid writing about health.

---

168. *Against Praxeas* 12.

He always wrote as an angry man. And he never was satisfied with just defeating his opponents; he always set out to annihilate them. First the pagans and then heretics served as the target of his biting and sarcastic invective. But finally, he turned his fire upon the bishops of the Church.

In reaction to his own pre-baptismal lifestyle, he had always been prone to severity and rigidity. So it was no wonder that he would find congenial the "New Prophecy" of the Montanists. Irenaeus had to battle their theology of revelation, their idea that new prophecy could in fact supersede prior revelation. But part of this heresy was rigorism, the idea that serious sexual post-baptismal sins like fornication[169] and adultery, along with murder and apostasy,[170] could not and should not be forgiven by the Church. The bishops, according to Montanist prophecies, had no authority to do so. If anyone could forgive sins in the name of Christ, these prophets proclaimed, it would be the holy and inspired ones such as themselves, not the corrupt bishops of a lax church.[171]

Tertullian gradually fell under the spell of this rigorist sect and remained in it for about twenty years. He apparently died bitter and resentful, in self-imposed exile from the peace and communion of the catholic Church. But Tertullian, in spite of himself, had been used mightily by God. His writings are an important witness to the apostolic tradition, even though he broke with that tradition near the end of his life. Ironically, his most original contributions to clarifying and developing that tradition with regard to Christ and the Trinity were made even as he himself was drifting away.

---

169. Premarital sex, including homosexual acts.
170. Denying or renouncing Christ, usually under the threat of persecution.
171. See Tertullian *On Modesty* 2 and 21.

CHAPTER 13

Cyprian and the Unity of the Church

Alot of things had changed since Tertullian's time. Scarcely a generation had passed, but Gnostics and Marcionites had virtually disappeared from the North African scene. Yes, being a Christian was still technically a crime, but by A.D. 240, you had to talk to the elderly to hear the stories of the martyrs. There had been peace for nearly forty years.

A lot more people were joining the Church in those days. One of the new members even came from one of the richest and most cultured families in Carthage.[172] His name was Cyprian, a prominent professor of rhetoric, or public speaking. He knew how to put words together in a way that could convince people. And he knew how to make money; it was early in his career, and he was already a wealthy man.

Yet, dissatisfaction with his own dissolute life had led Cyprian to the baptismal font, probably in A.D. 246. Shortly after his enlightenment, he put pen to parchment and shared his experience:

> I was entangled in the thousand errors of my previous life; I did
> not think I could get free of them, for I was so much the slave of
> my vices...and I had such complaisance in the evils which had
> become my constant companions. But the regenerating water
> washed me from the stains of my previous life, and a light from

---

172. The actual Latin name of this city was Carthago, rendered in English today as "Carthage."

on high shone into my heart thus purified from its corruptions, and the Spirit coming from heaven changed me into a new man by a second birth. And immediately, in a wonderful way, I saw certitude take the place of doubt.[173]

Though he was of the same profession as Tertullian, Cyprian was totally different in personality. It must be admitted that Cyprian lacked Tertullian's originality and penetrating genius; however, he had what Tertullian lacked—gentleness, self-control, a warm and generous spirit. These attributes, along with his great eloquence, help to explain why he was ordained a priest within a year. They also help to explain why, when the see of Carthage became vacant a year later, the people elected him bishop over the strident protests of the senior clergy.[174]

A New Level of Persecution

Cyprian had scarcely begun his episcopal ministry when a new emperor came to power. Decius wrote a new law that finally put teeth in the ancient statute against Christianity.[175] All citizens were now required to obtain an official document certifying that they had sacrificed to Caesar and the gods. The goal was to swiftly decapitate the Church by first going after her leadership. The new law went into effect on January 1, 250, and within three weeks Pope Fabian was martyred. The crisis fell like a meteor upon the Church. After so many years of peace and so many new converts, the complacent

---

173. Cyprian, *Letter to Donatus* 3–4.
174. It was common in the early Church for the people to elect the bishop. Neighboring bishops would then come to consecrate the one elected.
175. No copy of the original imperial rescript survives today, but based on countless pagan as well as Christian sources, Nero (d. A.D. 68) apparently was the one who officially made Christianity a capital crime and so it remained on the books, whether it was enforced or not, until A.D. 313.

Christian community was unprepared for such a ferocious attack.

The authorities came looking for Cyprian, too, of course. But they did not find him; in a dream, God had warned him to go into hiding, and so he had taken refuge in a friend's villa in the countryside. He directed his flock through letters sent by select deacons who were the only ones who knew his whereabouts.

Though it lasted only fourteen months, the persecution left in its wake many broken relationships. Cyprian returned, joyful to see his flock and proud of the many who had died for Christ. But he was crestfallen to find out that a multitude had compromised, some performing the sacrifices, some purchasing fraudulent certificates saying that they did.

And now they were clamoring to be forgiven and received back? Received back by people who had remained faithful and, as a result, had lost all their property and even their loved ones?

Evidently, it had not been the practice in North Africa to accept the lapsed back into communion, but the intense, systematic persecution of Decius had created an unprecedented number of them. Some of the faithful thought they should never be readmitted. Others said only on their deathbeds. But some wanted to depart from local tradition and welcome them back instantly, without any serious time of penance at all. The presbyters who resented Cyprian's election championed this lax approach and even got some of the confessors to put pressure on Cyprian to see things their way. Everyone respected the confessors. They certainly possessed the Holy Spirit; their faithfulness under torture proved it. Some of the people had such a great regard for them, however, that they insisted that they could command even the bishop. A few even claimed that they had the power to remit sins, since they were full of the Spirit.

Cyprian, the shepherd, had to guide his flock through this crisis. He said all needed to wait until he could meet with his fellow bishops in a synod, where they would decide on a common approach.

The Seamless Garment

But in the meanwhile, Cyprian heard disturbing news from Rome. Now that peace had returned to the Church, an election had been held to replace Fabian, the martyred pope. The most famous and distinguished presbyter, Novatian, was passed over for Cornelius, a less educated man. It was a shock to many, not least to Novatian. When Pope Cornelius granted absolution to some of the lapsed, Novatian found the excuse he needed. Arguing that the new pope had polluted the holiness of the Church by welcoming apostates, Novatian declared that Cornelius's community was no longer the holy, Catholic Church. Then, he found some country bishops, brought them to town, and had himself consecrated and proclaimed the lawful bishop of the truly holy Catholic Church of Rome.

Upon notification of this dispute, Cyprian carefully inquired into the two elections and determined that Cornelius, not Novatian, was Pope Fabian's legitimate successor. And Cyprian saw that the growing resentment, recrimination, and schism created by Novatian and others presented much more grave a threat to the Church than any persecution ever did.

So, he decided to write a treatise, which he read at the African bishops' synod later that year and also sent to those Roman confessors who were supporting Novatian. In it, Cyprian helped develop the teaching on the Church found in the Scriptures and the Fathers.

The Church, he says, is essentially one and indivisible. It is symbolized by the seamless tunic of the Lord, which cannot be rent. "By the type and symbol of his garment he has manifested the unity of the Church."[176] Those who seemingly split the Church do not *actually* do so. Rather they *leave* the Church entirely and set up an assembly that is in no sense part of the one Church of Christ.

Irenaeus and Tertullian had championed apostolic succession as the safeguard of the Church against the claims of heresy because it identified where the true apostolic teaching was to be found. Now Cyprian, fighting schism instead of heresy, enlisted apostolic succession as a guard to unity, since it identified where the true Church was to be found. Which is the true bishop? It is he who is legitimately in the line of succession from the apostles. Which is the true Church? The group that is in communion with the authentic bishop. When Jesus changed Simon's name to Peter and said, "On this rock I will build my church" (see Matthew 16:18), he established a very important principle for the constitution of the Church. "He builds the Church upon one man." Cyprian admitted the other eleven each had their own share in the apostolic ministry. But the Lord wanted this apostolic ministry to be one, so, "in order to make unity manifest, he arranged by his own authority that this unity should, from the start, take its beginning from one man."[177]

While today our first instinct may be to consider the implications of this for the universal Church, Cyprian's problem was primarily one of the local church, in both Rome and Carthage. So he emphasized something we have seen already in Ignatius: the local bishop as the visible sign and instrument of unity in the Church. As Peter was the spokesman and head of the Eleven and of all the disciples (see Acts 2:14), so the bishop is the spokesman and head of the presbyters and

---

176. Cyprian, "On the Unity of the Church," Treatise 1.7, referring to John 19:23–4.
177. "On the Unity of the Church," 4.

the whole local church. He is the rock upon which each local church is built. The unity of the Church coalesces around a structure, the bishop in apostolic succession in each local church. The confessors who have endured prison and torture for Christ are certainly venerable, but the bishop, and the bishop alone, is the one who authoritatively speaks in the name of the Church, the only one entrusted by Christ with the power of the keys. Moreover, there is no sin that is excluded from this power Christ gave Peter and the apostles to bind and loose.[178]

There is another important feature to Cyprian's teaching on the episcopate. Though each bishop is entrusted with a portion of the Lord's flock, the bishops do not function independently. Rather, they make up a sort of college or senate. Just as the peace and communion of each person with the local bishop is a sign and instrument of the Church's unity on the local level, the personal communion of each bishop with the others is the sign and instrument of the unity of the Church catholic. Cyprian declares, "The Church, which is catholic and one, is not split asunder nor divided but is truly bound and joined together by the cement of its priests, who hold fast one to another."[179] The Second Vatican Council's teaching on the collegiality of bishops owes much to the ancient bishop of Carthage.

If the bishops of the world have common responsibility for the unity and orthodoxy of the Catholic Church, what role has the pope? The bishop of Rome is seen by Cyprian as successor of Peter in a special way and serves as a touchstone of unity for the entire episcopate:

> And after the resurrection he also says to him [Peter], "Feed my sheep." On him he builds the Church, and to him he entrusts

---

178. In the New Testament, the power to bind and loose refers to the authority to forgive and remit sin (see Matthew 16:19 and 18:18, John 20:22–23).
179. Cyprian, *Letter 66*, 8.

the sheep to be fed. And although he gives equal power to all the apostles, yet he established one chair (*cathedram*) and arranged by his own authority the origin and principle (*rationem*) of unity. Certainly the rest of the apostles were exactly what Peter was, but primacy is given to Peter (*primatus Petro datur*) and one Church and one chair is demonstrated. And they are all shepherds but the flock is shown to be one, which is to be fed by all the apostles in unanimous agreement. He who does not hold this unity of Peter, does he believe he holds the faith? He who deserts the chair of Peter on whom the Church was founded, does he trust that he is in the Church?[180]

However, it is important to note that Cyprian saw all this in terms of personal communion, not primarily in terms of jurisdiction. The Church is a single body with members of the episcopate attached to one another by the laws of charity and concord.[181] Letters have been preserved that testify to constant communication between Cyprian and the Church of Rome, even during the fourteen months that there was no bishop in the imperial capital. Yet, Cyprian did not see the Roman primacy to mean that the pope could simply decree how, for example, the North African bishops should approach local problems. Each bishop is a successor of the apostles in his own locale; he is not a branch manager appointed by a CEO in Rome. Cyprian witnesses to all the elements of the apostolic and episcopal structure of the Church—the prerogatives of each bishop, episcopal collegiality, and Roman primacy—but does not quite put all the pieces together in a systematic way that would answer all our questions.

---

180. "On the Unity of the Church," 4, primacy texts that do not appear in all recensions of this document, though they are most certainly the words of Cyprian.
181. *Letter 54*, 1; *Letter 68*, 5.

....

Eucharist and Prayer

The Church is one and so the Eucharist is one. In his long letter to his friend Fidus, Cyprian provided us with the very earliest writing completely dedicated to the subject of the Eucharist. Following Tertullian and all the Fathers we have examined so far, Cyprian emphasizes that the Eucharist is a sacrifice. But each Eucharist is not some new sacrifice added to past sacrifices. There is only one sacrifice, Christ's sacrifice on the cross. The Last Supper presented this sacrifice in advance of its historical offering on Good Friday; all subsequent Eucharists simply re-present it, or make this unique sacrifice present and efficacious here and now. "We make mention of His passion in all sacrifices because the Lord's passion is the sacrifice which we offer. Therefore we ought to do nothing else than what he did."[182] As Christ's death on the cross was a sacrament of love that brought about the unity of all believers in one body, so the Eucharist is a sacrament of unity. In its Eucharistic communion, the Church proclaims and deepens its unity as the Body of Christ: "In this very sacrament our people are shown to be made one, so that in like manner as many grains, collected, and ground, and mixed together into one mass, make one bread, so in Christ, who is the heavenly bread, we may know, that there is one body, with which our number is joined and united."[183]

Despite his insistence on a proper understanding of the episcopate as a safeguard of unity, Cyprian saw schism as essentially a spiritual sickness, as did Clement. It ultimately arises from ambition, resentment, and a pharisaical scorn for sinners and anyone who is "soft"

---

182. Cyprian, *Letter 63*, 17. He calls the Eucharist *"dominicae passionis et nostrae redemptionis sacramentum"* (the sacrament of the Lord's passion and our redemption).
183. Cyprian, *Letter 63*, 13. See also *Letter 66*, 4. Compare this with the *Didache 9*.

on sinners. But Cyprian, who wrote a treatise on the Lord's Prayer that became a classic, identified the "law of prayer" (*lex orandi*) as the absolute requirement for forgiveness and reconciliation. Without this, there can be no prayer, no sacrifice that is remotely pleasing to God.

> So when he gave the rule of prayer [*lex orandi*] he added: "And when ye stand praying, forgive, if ye have aught against any one: that your Father also which is in heaven may forgive you your trespasses." He calls back from the altar the one going to the sacrifice with angry feelings and tells him first to be reconciled to his brother and then to come back and offer his gift to God. For God had no respect [for] Cain's gifts, nor could he have God at peace with him when by his envious hate he had no peace with his brother. What peace can the enemies of their own brothers promise themselves? What sacrifices do the rivals of the priests think they celebrate? Do those who gather themselves outside the Church fancy that Christ is with them when they are gathered together?[184]

Without brotherly love, dying for the faith is no true martyrdom, since martyrdom is a witness to charity. St. Paul said as much in his famous ode to love in 1 Corinthians 13: "If I deliver my body to be burned, but have not love, I gain nothing." Cyprian commented on this in light of the schism:

> But the discordant and the dissident and he who has not peace with his brethren, according as the blessed Apostle and the Holy Scripture testify, not even if he be slain for His name, shall be able to escape the crime of fraternal dissension, because, as it is written: "Whoever hates his brother is a murderer," and a murderer does not arrive at the kingdom of heaven nor does

---

184. "On the Unity of the Church," 13.

he live with God. He cannot be with Christ, who preferred to be an imitator of Judas rather than of Christ. What a sin that is which cannot be washed away by the baptism of blood; what a crime that is which cannot be expiated by martyrdom![185]

Outside the Church, No Salvation

When Cyprian's letter was read to his brother bishops, they were deeply moved. Regarding the controversy over the lapsed, they decided together to follow Cyprian's advice and avoid both extremes. The lax approach of reconciliation without a period of penance was rejected. Those who had compromised their faith now needed to strengthen it through penance, which the bishops saw as spiritual therapy more than punishment. But the rigorists were rejected as well. Those who did penance, the bishops declared, could not be denied the fruit of penance, which is forgiveness and an eventual return to communion.

Predictably, this decision did not please everyone. The lax party ordained its own bishop of Carthage. Next, the rigorist Novatianists spread to Carthage and consecrated their own bishop. Cyprian now had to contend with two schismatic groups in Carthage, both claiming to be the true, holy, catholic Church.

Some converts from paganism were baptized by these groups and, soon after, realized they had joined the wrong group. They wound up at Cyprian's doorstep, seeking communion with the Catholic Church. Cyprian, and the other bishops in communion with him, required them to be rebaptized. When Pope Stephen got wind of this, he shot off a letter to the Africans stating that such a position was untraditional. As long as baptism was performed in the name of

---

185. "On the Lord's Prayer," Treatise 4.24.

the Triune God, with water, said the pope, the sacrament was valid, even if conferred by a schismatic.

Cyprian and the Africans said no, that by cutting themselves off from the lawful bishop, the schismatics had left the Church. The sacraments are means of salvation empowered by the Spirit that exist only within the Church. In the context of this controversy, Cyprian uttered some of his most famous statements. "Outside the Church there is no salvation."[186] And "He who does not have the Church for his mother cannot have God as his Father."[187]

Cyprian's opinion was logically consistent. But pushed to its limit, it meant everyone was damned who was not an official member of a church having a bishop with legitimate apostolic succession. And it also meant that the sacramental anointing given in ordination did not convey a permanent power or authority. If it could be suspended by schism, could it also be suspended by other things, such as personal sin on the part of the minister? Pope Stephen's position seemed more moderate, but what was the theological reason for it? What was it that actually made a sacrament valid or invalid? If grace, salvation, and the Holy Spirit were to be found outside the visible boundaries of the true Church, how can this be explained? Such questions remained unresolved.

End of the Story

Decius's persecution had been the most devastating to date. But it was not the last. Cyprian had been back at the helm in Carthage but six years when the next wave broke, under Emperor Valerian.

---

186. The classic phrase used to describe his position is *extra ecclesiam, nulla salus*. But Cyprian's precise words were *"salus extra ecclesiam non est."* (*Letter 73*, 21).

187. "On the Unity of the Church," 6. *"Habere non potest deum patrem qui ecclesiam non habet matrem."*

The first thing was a decree of exile for all bishops, forcing Cyprian once again to leave his flock and take up residence in the countryside, this time under imperial scrutiny. But shortly thereafter, unrepentant bishops were condemned to death. Cyprian gave his witness and was beheaded in A.D. 258 shortly after Pope Stephen, like Fabian, gave his life for his sheep.

The laxist schismatics in Carthage didn't last long. But even after Novatian's death under Valerian, his rigorist schism lived on for several centuries in Carthage and many cities. The crisis of the lapsed did not go away, and the questions raised by the crisis would have to wait nearly two centuries for an answer. Ironically, some of those answers would be provided by a later North African bishop named Augustine who both revered and gently disagreed with Cyprian.

CHAPTER 14

Hippolytus and the *Lex Orandi*

One of the highlights of Origen's life had been the visit he paid to the ancient city of Peter and Paul. While in Rome, he had heard an awe-inspiring homily, "On the Praise of the Lord Our Savior," preached by one of the most prominent clerics of the city.[188] We don't know much about the background of that preacher, a priest named Hippolytus, who was probably born around the time Justin was martyred.

What we do know is that Hippolytus was brilliant and energetic, much like the young man from Alexandria who heard his sermon that day in A.D. 212. Hippolytus was already famous, since he'd already been writing for ten years. Perhaps his example gave Origen the nudge he needed to begin writing. Just a few years earlier, Hippolytus had written the very first biblical commentary in Christian history, on the book of Daniel. He'd also written a book against many heresies, which was followed years later with an even more detailed book on the subject that owed much to Irenaeus.

One of the things we find out from this second book on heresies is that, in Rome, there was such a stress on the fact that there is only one God that the Modalist heresy had gotten some serious traction. Modalism was the theory that God is one, not three; he only appears to be three because at different times we find him playing three different roles—first Father, then Son, then Holy Spirit. Tertullian had written against this.

---

188. Jerome, *On Illustrious Men*, 61.

Hippolytus wrote against this as well. The problem is that in so doing he unfairly accused the pope, Zephyrinus, of being soft on both this heresy and the Roman priest named Sabellius who championed it. Zephyrinus was soft on other things besides, at least so far as Hippolytus was concerned. Sexual sin was one example. Hippolytus did not deny the power of the bishop to forgive repentant sinners, but he thought this pope was far too quick to take people back.

A statue of Hippolytus that dates back to sometime shortly after Hippolytus's death was dug up in Rome in the sixteenth century. This was a sensational find for a few reasons. First, it shows us how much he was admired in Rome during his lifetime and for years afterward; we find no statues of other Christian leaders from this period. The other thing about the statue is that an extensive list of all of Hippolytus's writings had been engraved on its base. Like Origen's works, many of them have been lost. This is due in large measure to the fact that Hippolytus happened to be the very last Christian author in Rome to write in Greek. Within a few generations, the knowledge of the Greek language was just about completely lost in Rome. With no one to read them, there was no one to copy Hippolytus's Greek writings. Thus, those that had not been rather immediately translated into Latin were in most cases simply buried in the sands of time.

The Apostolic Tradition

One of the missing works listed on the statue had an intriguing name: *The Apostolic Tradition*. Scholars scoured ancient archives for this one since they expected it would have preserved a lot of valuable information about early Christianity. But nothing by that name was ever found with the name Hippolytus attached to it.

However, in the early twentieth century, a scholar came forth with what initially sounded like a far-fetched theory. He claimed that a document called *Egyptian Church Order*, surviving in an ancient Egyptian dialect, was actually the lost *Apostolic Tradition* of Hippolytus. Other scholars looked over the text and compared it with an obscure Latin document found in Verona and some similar ancient documents in a few other exotic languages. When all the pieces were finally assembled a few years later, the puzzle was solved. *The Apostolic Tradition* of Hippolytus had been successfully recovered! Evidently, like the letter of Clement of Rome, it was so highly regarded that it had been copied, sent all over the empire by the author's admirers, and translated into a variety of languages. Over time, the name of the author and the original title had been lost, but the document nonetheless had survived, waiting to be discovered.

This reconstructed text, finally published between the two world wars, represents a milestone for the history of early Christianity. Hippolytus, writing about A.D. 215, let us know in the first paragraph of the work that some ignorant men (read "the pope and his advisors") were courting apostasy and that the Roman church was in danger of moving beyond the apostolic tradition. Hippolytus apparently was an extreme "traditionalist" in liturgy as well as in doctrine and morals. Lest the traditional forms of worship and lifestyle passed down from the apostles be forgotten, he decided to set them down in writing. Since he pined for the bygone days of traditional liturgy, he most probably described the liturgy and prayer life of the church of Rome in the days of his youth. That means the second half of the second century. The picture Justin provided us of Roman liturgy dates from about A.D. 155; Hippolytus described the liturgy as he experienced it a mere generation later. When we combine Hippolytus's information with the data we get from Justin, we arrive at a rather full and fascinating picture of how the Christians of Rome worshipped in the second century.

Ordination and Eucharist

The first thing Hippolytus lays out is how a new bishop is to be ordained. Clearly, the bishop was not simply an officer who succeeds to an institutional position. His ordination was a great and sacred celebration. The people gathered with the priests and bishops who were presumably from neighboring regions. Everyone joined in praying, but the only one to lay hands on the new bishop-elect was one of the bishops present. What was conveyed to the new bishop through the laying on of hands was not just authority, but the power of the Spirit. Here is a portion of the ordination prayer:

> Pour out now the power that comes from you, the Spirit of headship, which you gave to your beloved Child Jesus Christ, and whom he handed on to the apostles who built the Church, your sanctuary for the glory and ceaseless praise of your name…. May he always make you merciful to us and offer you the gifts of your holy Church. In virtue of the Spirit of high priesthood, may he have the power to forgive sins as you have commanded."[189]

The bishop, most certainly, was a teacher who preached the word of God. But the emphasis in this prayer of consecration falls on the concepts of priesthood, offering of sacrificial gifts, and power to forgive sin.

Immediately after ordination, the new bishops offered the Eucharist. Hippolytus provides us with the earliest complete "anaphora," or

---

189. Hippolytus, *The Apostolic Tradition*, 2–3.

Eucharistic prayer. The preface dialogue is virtually identical to the one still in use in many churches today:

BISHOP: The Lord be with you!
PEOPLE: And with your spirit!
BISHOP: Let us lift up our hearts.
PEOPLE: They are turned to the Lord.
BISHOP: Let us give thanks to the Lord!
PEOPLE: It is right and just![190]

The exchange "the Lord be with you!—And with your spirit!" must go back to the Eucharist of the apostles in the first century, for not only do we find it here in Rome, but in all the ancient liturgies in the early apostolic centers of Christianity: Jerusalem, Antioch, and Alexandria. An early form of this greeting and dialogue can be seen in various Old and New Testament texts, so it is safe to assume that this dialogue came into the Church from the synagogue service in the time of Jesus.[191]

The invitation, "lift up your hearts," is also found in all liturgical traditions from the ancient apostolic centers, so it goes back at least to the earliest Christian worship, if not the synagogue.

The Eucharistic prayer that follows includes Jesus's words at the Last Supper joined to an *epiclesis*, or invocation of the Holy Spirit. It ends with a doxology, "through your Son Jesus Christ, our Lord," concluded by the final amen. It is interesting that Justin

---

190. *Apostolic Tradition* 4.
191. See Ruth 2:4, "Boaz came from Bethlehem; and he said to the reapers, 'The Lord be with you!' And they answered, 'The Lord bless you.'" Compare David's final blessing to Solomon in 1 Chronicles 22:11,16: "Now, my son, the Lord be with you, so that you may succeed in building the house of the Lord your God." And Paul "The Lord be with your spirit" (2 Timothy 4:22); "The grace of the Lord Jesus Christ be with your spirit" (Philippians 4:23).

said the "president of the assembly" gives thanks extemporaneously. Hippolytus makes clear that the prayer he provides here is just a pattern:

> It is not necessary, however, that he repeat the same words we provided, as though he had to try to say them from memory in his thanksgiving to God. Let each one pray according to his ability. If he is capable of praying at length and offering a solemn prayer, well and good. But if he prays differently and pronounces a shorter and simpler prayer, he is not to be prevented, provided his prayer be sound and orthodox.[192]

Interestingly enough, by the time this work is translated in Egypt into Coptic, this last paragraph was omitted, probably indicating that by then there was no longer an option for the bishop or priest to do his own extemporaneous prayer.

Hippolytus then goes through instructions for the ordination of priests, deacons, subdeacons, lectors, etc. Finally comes a mention of the ministry of healing: "If anyone makes the claim: 'I have received the gift of healing through a revelation,' do not impose hands on him. The facts themselves will show whether or not he is speaking the truth."[193] Thus, charisms of the Spirit, which Tertullian had instructed the newly baptized to pray for with expectant faith, were still alive and part of the normal life of the Church in Rome in this period.

Christian Initiation

The second part of the *Apostolic Tradition* provides us with a marvelous glimpse into how Christian initiation took place in second

---

192. *Apostolic Tradition* 9.
193. *Apostolic Tradition* 14.

century Rome. First, we see here what we have seen elsewhere in the early Church—candidates for baptism were often taught by lay catechists.[194] Those who had introduced the Gospel to them and brought them to enroll in the catechumenate would have to vouch for their willingness to break with a sinful, pagan lifestyle to embrace the Christian way of life. Sexual liaisons outside of marriage had to be renounced. Those cohabitating must marry, separate, or would be turned away. Many would not be accepted without first agreeing to abandon their professions, since so many involved idolatry, lewdness, or violence: actors, artists involved in the creation of idolatrous statues, gladiators and wrestlers, government officials with the power to put people to death, etc.

The time of instruction before baptism was three years, though Hippolytus mentions exceptions could be made to shorten this in the case of those who made particularly rapid progress. Curriculum is not clearly laid out, but prayer over the catechumens by the catechist is mentioned as a feature of every session. And we see that the most important consideration was transformation of behavior, not so much intellectual grasp of doctrine. "When those to be baptized have been selected, their life is to be examined: Have they lived uprightly during their catechumenate? Have they respected widows, visited the sick, practiced all the good works?" He goes on: "If any one of them is not a good man or is not pure, he is to be rejected, for he has not heard the word with faith."[195]

Then came the description of the Easter Vigil. Those to be baptized must fast all day Friday and Saturday. After receiving a final exorcism from the bishop, they must spend all night Saturday in vigil,

---

194. *Apostolic Tradition* 15.
195. *Apostolic Tradition* 20.

praying and reading Scripture. At cockcrow, the water was blessed, and the baptismal ritual began. Echoing the *Didache*, running water was preferred, but if that was impossible to find, any water would do. The candidates removed all clothing. They were told to face west and renounce Satan, his undertakings, and his works. After an anointing to seal this exorcism, the actual baptism began.

"The children are to be baptized first. All of them who can, are to give answer for themselves. If they cannot, let their parents or someone in the family answer for them."[196] Thus, infant baptism was practiced in Rome and believed to be of apostolic origin, as Origen believed it to be as well.

A deacon then descends into the water with the one to be baptized. The one baptizing lays his hand on him and asks:

> Do you believe in God, The Father almighty?
> The one being baptized is to answer: "I believe."
> Let him baptize him then a first time, keeping his hand on the person's head. He then asks him:
> Do you believe in Christ Jesus, Son of God,
> born by the Holy Spirit of the Virgin Mary, who was crucified under Pontius Pilate,
> who died, was raised on the third day, living from among the dead,
> who ascended to the heavens, who sits at the right had of the Father,
> who will come to judge the living and the dead?
> When he has answered: "I believe," he is to baptize him a second time. He is to ask him again:
> Do you believe in the Holy Spirit, in the holy Church, in the resurrection of the flesh?

---

196. *Apostolic Tradition* 21.

The one being baptized is to answer: "I believe." Then he baptizes him a third time.[197]

In earlier Church Fathers, we hear echoes of this baptismal creed in passages reproducing the "Rule of Faith." However, this text from Hippolytus shows us that the creed originated as an interrogation in the actual ceremony of baptism. What became a "Creed" or Rule of Faith initially served as an expression of solemn, personal commitment to the three divine persons. The articles of this baptismal creed do no more than specify the character of the divine persons to whom the new Christian is entrusting himself. As heresies arose that denied various things about the three divine persons, the articles had to be further elaborated to rule out certain heretical denials (for example, that the Father was not the same as the Creator, or that Jesus was never truly born or never died).

Immediately after baptism, the new Christians were led into the assembly. There, they were greeted by the bishop, who laid hands on them, poured the consecrated oil of thanksgiving over their heads, and marked them with the sign of the cross on the forehead.[198] This "sealing with the Spirit" is the sacrament of chrismation, or confirmation. Here we have the earliest clear illustration of this sacrament as a separate rite, distinct from baptism but following immediately after it.[199] Eastern churches still administer the two sacraments together; it wasn't until the ninth century that they were often separated in the Western Church.

---

197. *Apostolic Tradition* 21.
198. *Apostolic Tradition* 21.
199. Tertullian, writing a few years before Hippolytus, also attests to this post-baptismal anointing, which he says "is of ancient discipline." See his *On Baptism,* 7.

It was only after receiving "all this"[200] that the new Christians are allowed to pray with the faithful and participate in the kiss of peace.

Next came the first communion of the newly baptized. The bishop gave thanks over the bread and the cup, as in a normal Eucharist. But in the Roman Church at this time, a cup of water and a cup of milk mixed with honey were also placed on the altar and given to the newly baptized along with the Eucharist. The two other cups symbolized the fact that they were now pure as clean water and had passed not only through the Red Sea but also the Jordan; they had come out of slavery all the way to the Promised Land of milk and honey.[201]

In distributing communion, the bishop would say to each person, "The bread of heaven in Christ Jesus!" And the person would say, "Amen!"[202]

We are not told how often the Eucharist was offered besides Sundays, but we are told that communion was distributed "on other days…in accordance with the bishop's instructions."[203]

Daily Life of Prayer

In the third and final part of *The Apostolic Tradition,* Hippolytus describes the daily life of prayer of ordinary Christian laypeople. How closely the faithful followed the instructions of Hippolytus in these matters is something we can't be sure about. After all, he was harkening back to the days when things were done properly, complaining about laxness in his own day. The earlier Fathers bear

---

200. *Apostolic Tradition* 21.
201. The custom of offering milk and honey to the newly baptized was still observed in Rome in the sixth century. John the Deacon, *Letter to Senarius,* 12 (PL 59:405–406).
202. *Apostolic Tradition* 21.
203. *Apostolic Tradition* 22.

Hippolytus out on this point—that the Christian was expected, as St. Paul counseled, to pray not just once a week, or once a day, or even a few times per day, but to pray continually (see 1 Thessalonians 5:17).

Hippolytus describes an evening prayer service, later called the Lucernary in Christian tradition, where the lighting of the evening lamp announcing sunset was accompanied by prayer led by the bishop. A communal meal followed, which was concluded with the singing of psalms by children and "the virgins."[204] This entire rite appears to derive from the Sabbath meal of the Jews that became the basic pattern for the agape meal of the Christians in the apostolic era (see Acts 20:7).

Hippolytus was writing before there were church buildings per se, but he indicated that there were regular sessions of prayer and Bible study early in the morning before work, presumably in a large home, which everyone is encouraged to attend if able. He called this "going to the church" and repeatedly noted that the Christian assembly is the place "where the Spirit flourishes." Whether people can attend this or not, they are to pray in their homes immediately upon rising, before doing any sort of work.[205]

At this time in history, the Eucharist was kept in the homes of the faithful, and they were to take communion before their meal. The reason he advises consuming the Eucharist before the meal demonstrates Hippolytus's belief in the supernatural nature of this "bread of heaven": "If he receives it with faith, and then some deadly poison is given to him afterwards, it will not have power to harm him."[206] He went on to express the care to be taken with the sacrament:

---

204. *Apostolic Tradition* 25.
205. *Apostolic Tradition* 35.
206. *Apostolic Tradition* 36.

Each person must see to it that an unbeliever, or a mouse, or other animal, does not eat the Eucharist, and that no part of it falls to the ground and is lost. For it is the body of the Lord that the faithful eat, and they must not treat it with contempt.[207]

Besides prayer upon rising, which would be at the first hour of the Roman day (6:00 to 7:00 A.M.), Hippolytus wrote that Christians who were at home should pause what they are doing to praise God aloud at the third, sixth, and ninth hours, which roughly would be mid-morning, noon, and mid-afternoon. When out and about, Christians were to lift up their hearts to God silently at these times since each of these hours serves as a memorial of a different moment in the passion of Christ—the third hour is when Christ was nailed to the cross, the sixth hour darkness fell, and the ninth hour is when blood and water flowed from his side.[208] Christians were to pray before bed, but also to rise in the middle of the night to pray, especially at midnight, when Matthew 25:6 tells us the bridegroom is coming, and again at cockcrow, remembering Peter's denial. The section on prayer concludes with an exhortation frequently to make use of the sign the bishop inscribes on the forehead of every newly baptized Christian, the mark or seal of the cross:

If you are tempted, hasten to sign yourselves on the forehead in a worthy manner. For this sign manifests the Passion which stands against the devil, provided you make it with faith, not for men to see but knowing how to use it like a breastplate. Then the adversary, seeing the power that comes from the heart, will flee. This is what Moses imaged forth through the Passover lamb that was sacrificed, when he sprinkled the thresholds and

207. *Apostolic Tradition* 37. The same practice and attitude is found at this time in North Africa, as attested by Tertullian in his *Letter to His Wife*.
208. *Apostolic Tradition* 41.

sealed the doorposts with its blood. He was pointing to the faith that we now have in the perfect Lamb. By signing our forehead and eyes with our hand, we repulse him who seeks to destroy us.[209]

Note that this is far from some mechanical, superstitious use of the sign of the cross, as if it were a good luck charm. Rather, Hippolytus was encouraging the sign to be made as an act of conscious faith, a proclamation of the power of Christ's death, and a renewal of baptism. The comparison of this original mark on the forehead to the protection provided by a breastplate explains why it was so natural for the sign of the cross to be eventually expanded to cover the breast and shoulders as well as the forehead. The use of the sign of the cross in daily devotional life at this period is also attested by Tertullian.

Hippolytus concluded by expressing the idea of *lex orandi, lex credendi*, literally, "the law of prayer is the law of faith." In other words, if you pray right, you will believe right, since doctrine is implicit in prayer and liturgy. This man who was so worried about heresy saw the tradition of prayer passed down from the apostles as the best safeguard of the faith they passed down:

> I counsel all prudent men to observe these traditions. For if everyone follows and observes the tradition of the apostles, no heretic, and indeed no human being at all, will be able to lead you astray. The reason why heresies have increased is that leaders have been unwilling to make their own the teachings of the apostles and have acted as they pleased and not as they should have.[210]

---

209. *Apostolic Tradition* 42.
210. *Apostolic Tradition* 42.

Final Reconciliation

If there was any leader whom Hippolytus trusted less than Pope Zephyrinus, it was the pope's chief deacon, Callistus. So when the pope passed away and Callistus was elected as his successor, Hippolytus was horrified. He gathered his fans around him, managed to get himself consecrated bishop, and became the first anti-pope in history.[211] Callistus died, and another pope came and went, and Hippolytus still persisted in schism.

Nothing, however, brings people together more than a common enemy. A new emperor took over, Maximinus Thrax, who initiated measures against the leaders of the Church. He couldn't care less about schisms and who was the true bishop of Rome. He simply sent both Hippolytus and Pope Pontianus to Sardinia, known as the "island of death," to die in the mines. Thus, the pope and anti-pope found reconciliation in suffering. They both decided to resign to open up the way for a new pope and a reunification of the Church of Rome. The abject conditions at the mines had their intended effect. The new pope, Fabian, had the bodies of Hippolytus and Pontianus brought back to Rome and, on the very same day, gave these former adversaries a martyr's funeral. The Church of Rome preserved no memory of Hippolytus's schism or his mean-spirited criticism of Fabian's predecessors. The Church instead chose to remember only what was noble and good of Hippolytus's legacy and forget about the rest. Chief among those things was the beautiful anaphora that he provided as a model. If you go to a Latin-rite church for Mass and the priest selects Eucharistic Prayer II, you will still hear the ancient words of St. Hippolytus.

---

211. This schism was a generation before the Novatian schism described in the previous chapter.

CHAPTER 15

The Great Persecution

As time went on, the onslaughts just seemed to get worse. The first, under Nero, was brutal, but at least it was limited to the city of Rome. Beginning with the persecution that made Origen fatherless, however, they began to become more systematic, affecting the entire empire. Decius' persecution, which sent Cyprian into hiding and Origen into prison, was a shock. But Valerian's attack on the Church, just a few years later, reached new heights of ruthlessness.

Just a year after he martyred Cyprian, Valerian got a shock of his own. He won the distinction of being the only Roman emperor ever to be captured in battle. Once the Persians got their hands on him, he was never heard from again. So thankfully, his persecution, like his reign, was short-lived.

The Calm before the Storm

Perhaps Galienus believed his father's disgrace to be a result of God's judgment. That would explain what happened as soon as he became emperor in A.D. 260. This offspring of the most brutal persecutor in history not only eased up on the Christians, he formally decreed by force of law that they could henceforth worship freely, own property, and even hold political office.

It seemed like a dream come true. Church buildings, even large basilicas, went up across the empire. Christians began to work their way up through the ranks of the military and the government.

Granted, it was a bad time for the empire as a whole. Twenty-five different emperors ruled and died within the space of only fifty years, most killed by their own soldiers. The once prosperous Roman economy, based on extensive trade between provinces, was contracting at breakneck speed. Provinces were lopped off left and right as the Persians hammered the empire from the East and the barbarians from the north.

Despite all this, the church grew by leaps and bounds. One prominent historian estimated that in A.D. 260, about one million Christians lived in the empire, but by A.D. 300, there were six million, or about 10 to 15 percent of the empire's inhabitants. Some of the growth even came from prominent families entering the Church. By the end of the third century, Christians could be found in the imperial court and among every profession in the empire. By that time, the myths about incest and cannibalism among Christians had been largely debunked.

Of course, there were many who still hated Christians. The pagan intelligentsia found them ignorant, ridiculous, and appalling. Anybody with a financial interest in pagan worship—priests, priestesses, augurs, diviners, fortune-tellers, and statue-makers—loathed the Christians for destroying their businesses. Many in the army and government still suspected them of disloyalty to the empire. Imagine the gall of Christians refusing to participate in patriotic festivals like the one-thousand-year anniversary of the founding of the city of Rome! Just because they objected to obligatory sacrifices to the gods that had brought such glory and wealth to the city? Fanatical, ungrateful, and treasonous!

Gathering Clouds

This era of instability and turmoil came to an end in A.D. 284 when a man named Diocletian was raised to the imperial purple. Here was somebody with the courage to make bold changes in response to the chaos and decline that had plagued the empire for the previous fifty years. He just faced facts—the empire was simply too large to be ruled by one man alone. In the days of the republic, there had been many to share decision-making power. So Diocletian came up with a far-reaching plan of reorganization: The empire would be divided in half—East and West. These regions also would in turn be divided in half. There would be four emperors: a senior emperor or "Augustus" in the East and another the West. Their junior emperor assistants would be called "Caesars." Every emperor would directly rule a fourth of the empire, with each Caesar reporting to his Augustus and the two *Augusti* keeping in close touch with each other in order to craft common policy and preserve unity. Four new capitals near the frontiers were selected so that the emperors could more quickly respond to any incursion by barbarians or Persians. This was a rather magnanimous and humble thing for Diocletian to do—voluntarily share power with three others.

One of the far-reaching effects of this reorganization was not foreseen by Diocletian but is now apparent in hindsight. The line he drew separating the eastern half of the empire from the western half accelerated something that had already quietly begun—a growing cultural divergence between the Latin-speaking West and the Greek-speaking East. Before Diocletian, in A.D. 200, the North African author Tertullian had written with equal ease in both Greek and Latin. Twenty years later in Rome, Hippolytus was still writing his theology not in Latin but in Greek. By the end of Diocletian's reign, however, few in Rome or Carthage could read a Greek text with any fluency. And no one in the East, besides government employees, bothered to learn Latin, considered by the easterners to be a barbarous tongue.

Nevertheless, Diocletian enjoyed a great deal of success in his program to reverse the disintegration of the Roman government. He reformed the tax code, reorganized the army, and pushed back the enemy. He wanted to restore the glory days of the empire. This, of course, required paying renewed homage to the gods that had made Rome great.

At first, there was no hint that he would put any pressure on the Christians. Indeed, right across the street from his imperial residence in Nicomedia, the new capital of the Eastern Empire, loomed a huge Christian basilica. He even had some Christians in his imperial court. Diocletian was generally a man who wanted to bring different sorts of people together in the great society that was Rome. By temperament, he was not the sort of ruthless, intolerant ruler that many of his predecessors had been.

Diocletian was "Augustus" of the East. His "Caesar," Galerius, was of a different cast of mind altogether. The junior emperor agreed with the cadre of pagan intellectuals and military advisors who disdained the Christians as an unpredictable and heterogeneous element in society. Egged on by Galerius, these imperial advisors tried to convince Diocletian that Christianity presented an obstacle to the very restoration of Roman tradition that was his life's program. Diocletian was reticent to concur. But when Galerius made the case that the loyalty of the army was in question, Diocletian reluctantly agreed to grant Galerius free reign to shore up military discipline by whatever means he saw fit.

At first, it didn't seem too bad. Christian soldiers were not imprisoned or killed; they just had to sacrifice or resign. Resignation, however, entailed the surrender of their pension, which included a parcel of land and a lifetime income. Despite the financial consequences, most

Christian officers chose to resign rather than deny their faith. A few compromised, of course. There are always a few.

A great campaign against the Persians concluded successfully in A.D. 299, and so a formal celebration was planned in Antioch to be attended by Diocletian, Galerius, and their courtiers. Naturally, sacrifices and divination were part of such occasions. But as the festivities got underway, an unusual problem arose. The augurs, responsible to read omens from the gods, could not decipher the entrails of the sacrificed animals, even after repeated attempts. This was an embarrassing disruption of what should have been a triumphant celebration. When Diocletian demanded an explanation for this outrage, the augurs said that they noticed Christians from the emperor's own court making the sign of the cross, and this had blocked their divinations. Diocletian was furious and demanded punishment for the Christians in the palace. The first blood was spilled, and the clouds began to gather.

The Storm Breaks in Fury

Galerius now saw his chance. He capitalized on this incident to lobby for a systematic crackdown on the Christians, but still Diocletian hesitated. They came up with a solution: They would ask the advice of the oracle of Apollo at Miletus. The pagan priestess put their question to the god and got this reply: The "just on earth" had silenced the oracles. Diocletian's advisors told him that this most certainly referred to the Christians. Diocletian finally was convinced that something must be done.

Thus, after forty years of peace, the storm finally broke. On February 23, 303, the Christian basilica across from the imperial palace was razed to the ground. The next day an empire-wide edict was issued: effective immediately, all Christian buildings were to be destroyed, sacred Scriptures and liturgical vessels seized, and meetings forbidden. All Christians holding office in the military or government would immediately lose their positions. This applied even to senators and members of the Equestrian Order. Christian freedmen, the decree stated, would now revert back to their former status as slaves.

Many officials carried out their orders halfheartedly. They knocked on doors and asked Christians for their sacred books. Some gave them nothing and were hauled in for prosecution. Some handed over the Scriptures. Others gave the police heretical volumes or even medical textbooks written in Greek, passing these off as sacred books to the police, who read only Latin. The police often could care less what they got as long as it looked like they were doing their job.

In the following year, a second and even harsher edict was issued: All Christian clergy, of whatever rank, were to be imprisoned. Historians from the era said that the number of bishops, priests, deacons, subdeacons, lectors, and exorcists who flooded the prisons was so great that there was no room for common criminals. Diocletian decided to soften his second edict: Clergy could be released as long as they were willing to offer sacrifice.

Diocletian's second decree was ignored by the Caesar of the Western Empire, a man named Constantius. But Constantius's domain was limited mainly to Gaul and Britain. His Augustus, who was in charge of Italy and North Africa, took both edicts more seriously. In the East, the decrees were implemented everywhere with vehemence. Some clergy caved in and sacrificed. Many of the jailers either sympathized with the Christian clergy or just wanted to get them out of their overcrowded jails. Frequently those who refused to sacrifice were given certificates anyway, just to get rid of them.

However other local officials relished the opportunity to take action against the Christians. No general death sentence was part of the imperial decrees—yet. But governors always had the right to mete out capital punishment at their discretion. When it came to dealing with Christians, some governors were pleased to exercise this option as often as possible.

Diocletian's health declined in the second year of the persecution. So he did something no other emperor had ever done. He voluntarily abdicated, retired to his magnificent seaside palace, and spent the rest of his life tending his vegetable garden. Galerius advanced to become Augustus of the East. Now, unrestrained by the scruples of his former boss, he used his new authority to compel everyone in the empire to offer sacrifice or face death. Thus began the most gruesome phase of a persecution that had already lasted longer than any other. In one case, all the citizens of a Christian town in Phrygia unanimously refused to offer the required pagan sacrifices. The town was promptly surrounded by soldiers and set ablaze, with no one—man, woman, or child—allowed to escape.[212]

"In This Sign, Conquer"

But hope came from the West. In A.D. 306, Constantius died and his army acclaimed his son, Constantine, as the new emperor. Constantine and his father had been worshippers of *Sol Invictas*, the unconquered Sun. This divinity had been the military's deity of choice for more than a generation. However, there was Christian influence somewhere in the family, for Constantine had a half-sister named

---

212. Eusebius, *History of the Church*, 8.11.1.

Anastasia, meaning "resurrection." Immediately upon succeeding his father, Constantine decreed religious freedom in the provinces controlled by him, including Britain and Gaul. His not-too-friendly co-emperor, Maxentius, was not going to allow his colleague to out-do him in winning the allegiance of the sizable Christian minority. So he reluctantly followed suit and took the pressure off the Christians in Rome and Africa where he was in control. Meanwhile, in the East, the persecution continued unabated.

What happened next proved to be decisive for the history of Christianity and Western Civilization as a whole. Maxentius, who had seized Italy, wanted to consolidate and extend his power. He had defeated several of his rivals and built an army in Italy of over one hundred thousand troops. He saw that Constantine stood in the way of his ambitions, and so he declared war on him. Rather than wait for Maxentius to come to him, Constantine decided to make his move. He would boldly march his army from Gaul over the Alps and attack Maxentius on his own turf. This was against all earthly prudence, said his advisors. Constantine had fewer than forty thousand troops to his rival's one hundred thousand. In addition, Constantine would be fighting on enemy territory, where Maxentius controlled both the roads and the food supply.

Constantine nevertheless followed his instincts and launched his daring campaign. He encountered armies and fortified cities every step of his way down the Italian peninsula. After a chain of stunning victories, he found himself directly across the Tiber from the gates of Rome. Maxentius had shrewdly destroyed all the bridges and so was protected behind both the Tiber and the massive Aurelian walls surrounding the city.

Two surprising things happened next. First, Constantine had a dream wherein God showed him a symbol and told him to make it his standard. It was what looks to us today like an *X* with a *P* superimposed on it. In Christian symbolism, it is known as the Chi-Rho, the first two letters of the word *Christ* in Greek, and thus Jesus's monogram. Obedient to the divine command, Constantine had this Christian emblem emblazoned on the shields and banners of his army. He was confident that under this sign, he would be victorious, with the help of God.

The second remarkable thing was a strategic decision made by Maxentius after consulting his gods. He abandoned the safety of both the walls of the city and the Tiber, which served as its moat. Contrary to all common sense, he and his army crossed the Tiber on a bridge made of boats to meet Constantine on the open field of battle, their backs to the river. Despite his superior numbers, Maxentius was pushed back to the Tiber, where the Milvian Bridge lay in ruins. In the confusion of retreat and the absence of a solid bridge, Maxentius fell into the water and drowned along with many of his troops. Constantine entered the city hailed as a liberator. To honor Constantine, the Senate even commissioned a large triumphal arch to be erected adjacent to the Colosseum, elaborately sculptured with scenes from the momentous battle of the Milvian Bridge.

The story of the Chi-Rho, told to us by Lactantius, advisor of Constantine, is borne out by the fact that coins minted under Constantine contained the Chi-Rho symbol. Whatever had been his previous devotion to *Sol Invictas,* he attributed his victory to Christ and considered himself from then on a Christian believer.

So what became of Galerius, the instigator of the Great Persecution? He had taken ill the year previous to the battle of the Milvian Bridge. Knowing he was on his deathbed, be issued a decree of religious toleration for Christians which, believe it or not, included a request that they pray for him!

Before he died, Galerius appointed Licinius to succeed him as Augustus. The year after the battle of the Milvian Bridge, Constantine met Licinius in Milan. Together they promulgated a formal, empire-wide decree of toleration not just for Christians, but for everyone of whatever creed. All would be allowed to follow their religious convictions in peace. But for the Christians, whose property had been unjustly destroyed by the state, there would be monetary compensation. Scriptures, sacred vessels, and churches would all be replaced at government expense. This momentous legislation, enacted in A.D. 313, came to be known as the Edict of Milan.

Constantine had already made good on this pledge of restitution even before the decree was issued. Within two months of his victory, he made the decision to part with a historic palace situated on the Caelian Hill that had come to him as part of the dowry of his wife, Fausta. This patrimony, which had once belonged to the noble Lateran family, was donated to the Church to serve as the site of the city's cathedral and episcopal residence. What came to be known as St. John Lateran was to remain the papal residence for another thousand years. Its basilica still stands today as the official cathedral of Rome and mother church of Western Christendom. The current residence of the pope was originally another gift of Constantine to the Church. A few years after the Edict of Milan, Constantine erected a basilica over the tomb of St. Peter on the hill across the Tiber known as the Vatican, where Peter was martyred.

When the pagan Licinius began to renege on his word and harass Christians in the East, Constantine took military action. After handily defeating Licinius in A.D. 324 both by sea and by land, Constantine became the sole ruler of the empire.

The Great Persecution had lasted eleven long years in the East. The peace that followed put an end to three hundred years of spasmodic persecution of the fledgling Church by the Roman state. Constantine had not forced Christianity upon the empire. But while he lived, he was determined that the empire would never again force paganism on Christianity.

Aftermath

The peace of Constantine left the Christian community jubilant yet, at the same time, divided. New rigorist groups arose in Egypt and Carthage that refused fellowship to anyone who had cooperated with the police in any fashion whatsoever during the Great Persecution. Whether they actually sacrificed to the gods, handed over the Scriptures (or medical textbooks or heretical writings in lieu of the Scriptures) didn't matter. They were all *traditores*—"traitors" who had compromised their faith and could never again be trusted. Their pollution would defile anyone who would accept them into communion. This new rigorist schism made the one in Cyprian's day look like child's play. It would go on to haunt the North African Church for the next three centuries.

But a far greater threat to the unity of the Church began to brew in Alexandria even before the final victory of Constantine over Licinius. This menace represented an attack on the very identity of Jesus Christ and his relationship to God the Father, and so threatened to poison the heart of the Christian faith. This doctrine took only a couple of years to split the Church in Alexandria. Left unchecked, it was apparent that it could divide the Church across the empire. Constantine, not yet baptized, understood little about theology. But even he realized that this challenge had to be dealt with decisively, and done so quickly.

CHAPTER 16

Nicaea, the First Ecumenical Council

Contemporaries described Arius as sophisticated, austere, and serious, even grim. The description fit with his past; he had been part of a rigorist Egyptian sect that refused to associate with sinners or any Christians who associated with them. The bishop of Alexandria had bent over backward to heal the schism. Perhaps the kind old bishop was a bit too gracious. He had not only accepted the somber cleric back into communion, but even gave him care of one of the most prestigious churches in the bustling port district of the city. There, beginning in A.D. 313, Arius built quite a following for himself. It was said that over seven hundred consecrated virgins and many wealthy widows hung on his every word.

To many others, however, his words were disturbing. "God is one," he said. So far, so good. But then he went on to argue that if God is one and unique, then Jesus can't also be God. Certainly, Jesus is the incarnation of the Word[213]; that is plainly taught in Scripture (see John 1:1–4). However, the Word is distinct from God. He is the only-begotten one, the firstborn Son. That means that he is the only one that God created directly. In other words, God made the Word first, out of nothing, so that he could use him to make everything else. This was necessary because the finite creatures God intended to create could not possibly endure the awesome power they would encounter should God create them directly. Almighty God, then,

---

213. The Word (in Greek *logos*, see John 1:1) is the same as the "Son." The preexistent Word or Son becomes incarnate in Jesus of Nazareth.

needed an instrument, an intermediary. So God created the Word, the first of his creatures. This Word was to be the brush in the hand of the Divine Artist.

Of course, taught Arius, since the Son was created out of nothing like everything else, there obviously was a time when he was not. The Son is wonderful, most assuredly. But if a line were to be drawn separating the infinite, uncreated God from finite, created nature, God the Father alone would be on the divine, "supernatural" side of the line, and the Word would be on the other side with us and the rest of the created universe.

An additional corollary to this teaching was also alarming: God the Father is so utterly transcendent that the Word really can't know him as he truly is. Therefore, he can't fully reveal the Father to us. But perhaps that is just as well. For if even the Word himself can't know God, neither can we. Moreover, the Word, being a creature, can change. That means he could have possibly sinned, as Lucifer did. But God, foreseeing his merits, granted him the grace needed to protect him from falling. So yes, he is called "Son." But only by virtue of adoption, thanks to the grace of God, which he needs as much as we do. For Arius and his disciples, this adopted Son is utterly unlike and inferior to God the Father.

Arius's Heresy of Choice

Jesus, Son of God the Father, is himself called "God" at least three times in the New Testament and sixteen times in the *Letters* of Ignatius of Antioch. [214] From the earliest days, it had been part of

---

214. Virtually all agree that Jesus is called "God" in John 1:1, John 20:28, and Hebrews 1:8–9; most commentators agree that he is probably called "God" also in John 1:18, Romans 9:5, and Titus 2:13, but some would translate these texts so as to make the Word "God" refer to the Father. For Ignatius on the divinity of Christ, see chapter four.

the fabric of Christian life both to call Jesus "God" and to worship him as such. The oldest surviving account of a Christian martyrdom, that of Polycarp, clearly testifies to this: "It will be impossible for us to forsake Christ...or to *worship* any other. For him, being the Son of God, we *adore*, but the martyrs...we cherish."[215] Yet, it was also traditional from the time of Moses and the prophets to proclaim that the Lord, our God, is Lord *alone*. Frankly, there is more than a little tension between these two seemingly contradictory affirmations: How can we worship *both* the Father *and* His Son as God and still maintain that there is only one God? No text of the New Testament neatly reconciles these two truths intellectually. For the most part, Christians of the first two centuries did not try to offer an explanation. They were content to profess this double-truth, live it, and reverently bow before it.

As far as Arius was concerned, such a pious approach simply evaded the hard-nosed thinking required to explain this conundrum. He was not the first to offer a rational explanation—several had tried in the third century. In Rome, for example, the Modalists[216] had begun from the vantage point of God's essential unity. Their solution was to say that the Father broke into our history as Jesus and then, after ascending back to heaven, returned once more as the Holy Spirit. God is forever one; the "Trinity" simply consists of three successive roles played by the same supreme God over the course of salvation history. Modalism reduces the Trinity to a divine show.

Arius, starting from the typical Eastern vantage point of three

---

215. *The Martyrdom of Polycarp*, 27:2–3. (Emphasis added) Worship and adoration are due to God alone. Note the contrast between "cherishing" the holy martyrs and "worship" and adoration of Jesus; worship of an angel or saint would be idolatry.

216. The Modalists were also known as "Sabellians," after Sabellius, a Roman priest who championed this opinion. See chapter twelve.

distinct entities, resolved the problem in the reverse. God is one because the Father alone is true God; the Son, and the Holy Spirit as well, are his creatures, like the angels.

But actually, Arius and the Modalists are really not opposites—their views are two examples of the very same kind of one-sided choice. "Choice," by the way, is the meaning of the Greek word *hairesis*, or heresy.

If he is truly infinite and transcendent, the truth about God cannot be fully grasped by the finite human mind. As Augustine would say a century later, "what you understand can't possibly be God."[217] God cannot be solved as if he were a math problem or mastered, once and for all, like a crossword puzzle. The work, and even more so, the very nature of God, cannot appear to the human mind as anything short of mystery. This mystery typically presents itself to us as a series of paradoxes. God is one, yet God is three. Jesus is human, yet Jesus is divine. These paradoxes are truths-in-tension; they strain the brain and summon the human mind to bow in awe and worship.

Heresy arises when thinkers, annoyed by this tension, seek to relax it by eliminating one of the seemingly contradictory truths. Impatient with mystery, heresy seeks to domesticate it. Making a choice of one or the other side of the paradox, heresy attempts to rationalize what is beyond human reason. The Modalists preserved the divinity of the Son at the expense of his individuality—the Son is no more than a role to be played, a temporary mask worn by God. Arius, on the other hand, turned the distinction between the Son and the Father into a rigid separation and preserved the unity of God by sacrificing the divinity of the Son.

---

217. Augustine of Hippo, *Sermon 117*, 3, 5. For more on Augustine, see chapter twenty-one.

For Arius, the Father and the Son are two entirely different beings. The Father is God and the Son is not. His explanation appealed to many because it seemed clear, simple, and logical. If he is the Son, he was begotten, and if he is begotten, he had a beginning, and if he had a beginning, he is not infinite, and if he is not infinite, he is not God. The choice to reduce the mystery of God to such neat little syllogisms as this is one of the hallmarks of heresy.

The Arrogance of Heresy

Bishop Alexander of Alexandria sensed that Arius's teaching did violence to the Church's rule of faith. He assumed this must be a sincere but misguided error on the part of the venerable old priest. Surely, thought the bishop, if we call him aside and point out his error, he will see it and mend his ways. But Arius ignored his bishop and fellow Alexandrian clergy except for the few who agreed with him.

Next, in A.D. 320, Alexander called a meeting of the bishops of Egypt and surrounding areas. Out of the approximately one hundred who gathered, eighty of them agreed to excommunicate Arius if he did not retract his erroneous teaching, which of course he refused to do.

This illustrates another classic hallmark of heresy: It obstinately clings to a private opinion despite correction from the Church and its established authority.[218] The heretic considers himself wiser than his colleagues, wiser than his superiors, more Catholic than the Church. Forced to choose between the Church's teaching and his own, he prefers his own. Thus, heresy is characterized by a double arrogance:

---

218. Later on, this deliberate, obstinate persistence in doctrinal error in defiance of Church authority will be called "formal" heresy in distinction from the unintentional doctrinal error called "material" heresy.

Since it refuses to bow before the mystery, it naturally refuses to bow before the Church.

The pride of Arius becomes even more apparent when it is contrasted with the attitude of Origen, the great Alexandrian theologian who lived and taught a century earlier:

> I want to be a man of the church. I do not want to be called by the name of some founder of a heresy but by the name of Christ, and to bear that name which is blessed on earth. It is my desire, in deed as in Spirit, both to be and be called a Christian…. If I who seem to be your right hand and am called presbyter and seem to preach the Word of God, if I do something against the discipline of the Church, then may the whole church in unanimous resolve, cut me, its right hand, off, and throw me away.[219]

Rather than assume the posture of Origen and humbly submit, Arius fled Egypt and took refuge with an old school chum, Eusebius, bishop of Nicomedia. Evidently, these theological bedfellows had picked up the teaching of the Son's inferiority from their teacher, Lucian of Antioch, who had been martyred in A.D. 312 during the Great Persecution. They began drumming up support from other bishops in various cities—most were former students of Lucian—and so formed a tight-knit cadre of influential leaders. In addition to this political maneuvering, Arius took his ideas directly to the masses by expressing them in poetic lyrics set to catchy tunes. Alexandrian sailors stopping in the port of Nicomedia learned these theological sea shanties and proceeded to carry them back to Alexandria and, indeed, to ports all over the Mediterranean.

---

219. Origen, *Homily 16 on Luke* and *Homily 7.6 on Joshua*. Origen was a pioneer who wrote in an age prior to officially defined dogmas. Later in Church history, it became clear that several of Origen's ideas were incorrect. His errors would then be "material," not "formal," heresies.

....

The First Ecumenical Council

This was the volatile situation faced by Constantine when he arrived to occupy the imperial palace in Nicomedia. He immediately deputized his ecclesiastical advisor, Ossius, a Spanish bishop, to investigate the controversy and summoned an assembly of bishops to resolve the matter in the nearby city of Nicaea.[220]

Gatherings of bishops, called synods or councils, had met since the late second century to address disciplinary and doctrinal issues.[221] They were largely local in their scope and had never presumed to speak definitively for the entire Catholic Church. Never before had a council been convened by a Christian emperor and never, since the council of the apostles in Jerusalem (see Acts 15), had a council been faced with an issue so vital to the very heart of the Christian faith. Soon after it took place, this council came to be described as an "ecumenical" or universal council, in distinction from the regional synods that were part of everyday Church life. The word *ecumenical* comes from the Greek word *oikia,* or "household," and it means "pertaining to the whole world," which the Romans generally identified with the boundaries of their empire. From an ecclesiastical point of view, an ecumenical council can be understood as a representative gathering of bishops from the entire "household" of the faith, the catholic or universal Church, which addresses matters vital to all and therefore makes decisions that are binding upon all.

Neither the term nor the eventual definition of "ecumenical council" had been worked out by the time the council met in A.D.

---

220. Nicaea, now Iznik, Turkey, was only thirty miles south of the imperial capital of Nicomedia. Ossius was bishop of Cordoba. His name is also rendered as Hosius or Osius.

221. The earliest appears to have met around A.D. 177 in Asia Minor in order to deal with the Montanist heresy.

325 at Nicaea. Nonetheless, all who attended this solemn gathering were clearly aware that they were involved in an unprecedented and historic event.

Naturally, Arius, Eusebius, and their supporters were there. So were the bishop of Alexandria, who had excommunicated Arius, and the bishops of Antioch and Jerusalem who supported him. The emperor himself was there accompanied by his advisor, Bishop Ossius. Several of the bishops who came had endured imprisonment and torture fifteen years earlier during the Great Persecution. Paul of Neocaesarea had lost the use of his hands because of torture. Paphnutius of Egypt, having had one eye put out and one leg hamstrung, was personally embraced and kissed by Constantine after the old warrior hobbled into the council.

Prior synods had customarily followed Roman senatorial procedures. Traditionally, the emperor attended the deliberations of the Roman Senate but did not vote. So it was at Nicaea. Roman procedure also dictated that the senior senator always spoke first, voted first, and signed any decrees first. The bishop of Rome, due to the stature of his see, occupied this role of honor. Though he could not personally attend, he was represented by two legates who signed in his stead. The bishop in attendance whose name is most familiar, another confessor for the faith during the persecution, is none other than Bishop Nicholas of Myra, the beloved Santa Claus.[222]

No one knows exactly how many bishops attended the council; one participant said 250, and another said 300. The number came to be symbolically fixed at 318 since this was the number of the armed

---

222. Tradition has it that jolly old St. Nick, upon encountering Arius at the council, slapped him in the face. Although this may well be legendary, it illustrates what a curial cardinal said as Rome prepared for Vatican II: "a council is not a boy scout meeting."

servants of Abraham who came to the rescue of Abraham's kin (see Genesis 14:14). It would be wonderful to have a copy of the official minutes of the council, complete with a list of all participants and the text of all their speeches. But if such written records ever existed, they have been lost.

What we do know is that at Nicaea, the bishops did something that had never been done by Church councils prior to A.D. 325: They expressed their teaching by drafting a creed that all were bound to accept and promote as a universal standard of authentic Christian faith. Prior to this, creeds were used almost exclusively for the instruction and baptism of new Christians. Their exact wording varied somewhat from city to city. The bishops or "fathers" of the council of Nicaea, as they came to be called, evidently took a local baptismal creed and carefully edited it so that the precise wording clearly defined the divinity of Christ and ruled out the teachings of Arius. After stating positively what the Church believes, the creedal statement goes on to condemn Arian opinions that were incompatible with true Christian faith. Those who continued stubbornly to hold such opinions were automatically excommunicated, or, echoing the words of St. Paul, anathematized:[223]

> We believe in one God the Father Almighty, Maker of all things visible and invisible; and in one Lord Jesus Christ, the Son of God, begotten of the Father, only-begotten, that is, from the substance [*ousia*] of the Father,
>
> God from God, Light from Light, True God from True God, Begotten, not made, of one substance [*homoousios* or consubstantial] with the Father, through Whom all things were made.

---

223. "But even if we, or an angel from heaven, should preach to you a gospel contrary to that which we preached to you, let him be accursed" [*anathema* in the original Greek] (Galatians 1:8).

Who for us men and for our salvation came down and became incarnate, and was made man, suffered and rose on the third day, and ascended into heaven, and is coming with glory to judge living and dead, And in the Holy Spirit.

But those who say, There was when the Son of God was not, and before he was begotten he was not, and that he came into being from things that are not, or that he is of a different hypostasis or substance [*ousia*], or that he is mutable or alterable—the Catholic and Apostolic Church anathematizes.[224]

Attempts had been made to write this creed using scriptural language alone, but the results were neither clear enough nor strong enough to express the faith of the Church in a way that would completely rule out any Arian interpretation. So the decision was made to employ two technical terms not found in Scripture: *ousia* ("being" or "substance") and *homoousios* ("consubstantial" or "of the same substance"). The point was to make utterly clear that Jesus was not some inferior being to God the Father, but that the Father and Son are equally divine. For Arius, the terms "begotten" and "created" were synonymous. For the council, they were not. The Father begets or generates the Son from all eternity; he assuredly did *not* create him out of nothing at some moment in time.

All but a few of the council fathers were eager to completely rule out Arianism as an acceptable form of Christianity. So they agreed to the use the term *homoousios* because it helped them to accomplish this mission. Nevertheless, even many of those who consented to the use of this term had reservations about it. These concerns can be reduced to four principal ones:

---

224. Leo Davis, *The First Seven Ecumentical Councils*, p. 60.

(1) Even though Origen, the great Alexandrian, had used *homo-ousios* to help clarify the doctrine of the Trinity, he had apparently borrowed the term from the Gnostic heretics. Another condemned heretic of the third century had also used the term and done so in a completely heterodox sense. So the term was tainted by heretical associations.

(2) In Greek, *homoousios* could mean "of the same stuff" as if divinity were a material sort of thing that was divvied up between Father and Son.

(3) *Homoousios* could also be used to imply that the Father and Son were the same exact individual, in the sense of the Modalist heretics. One of the bishops who championed the use of the term did have strong Modalist tendencies. This only confirmed the suspicions of several other bishops that the use of the term was inadvisable.

(4) *Homoousios* was not a scriptural term. This probably was the most troubling thing to many of the conservative bishops.

Only eighteen of the bishops hesitated to sign the creed. In the end, everyone but Arius and two of his most ardent supporters put their signature on it. After leaving Nicaea, Constantine wrote to all the churches of the empire encouraging obedience to the council:

> That which has commended itself to the judgment of three hundred bishops cannot be other than the judgment of God; seeing that the Holy Spirit dwelling in the minds of persons of such character and dignity has effectually enlightened them respecting the Divine will. Wherefore let no one vacillate or linger, but let all with alacrity return to the undoubted path of truth; that when I shall arrive among you, which will be as soon as possible, I may with you return due thanks to God, the

inspector of all things, for having revealed the pure faith, and
restored to you that love for which we have prayed.[225]

Arius and the two diehards were exiled. Within a year, the politically astute Arian ringleader, Eusebius of Nicomedia, found himself
in exile with them. Constantine and most of the bishops were jubilant—the Holy Spirit, through the council fathers, had spoken. Case
closed.

---

225. Quoted in Leo Donald Davis, *The First Seven Ecumenical Councils* (Wilmington,
Del.: Michael Glazier, 1987), p. 69.

CHAPTER 17

Athanasius against the World

It wasn't just emperors and bishops who had occupied the council chambers at Nicaea. Several bishops had brought along personal assistants who attended council sessions with their bishops. Bishop Alexander of Alexandria brought a youthful secretary named Athanasius who also served as his advisor. This lad, still in his twenties, did not have the right to vote. After all, he was just a deacon. But he undoubtedly left his mark upon the council, emerging as a champion of the Nicene cause. He was a precocious young man who had something in common with the great sculptor Michelangelo: Each had created a famous masterpiece soon after the age of twenty. In the case of the Italian sculptor, it was his renowned Pietà. In the case of the deacon Athanasius, it was a short treatise called *On the Incarnation,* reckoned as one of the great theological classics of all time.

A Youthful Masterpiece

Athanasius's little book was not written as an argument against Arianism; it makes no reference to it.[226] Instead, it was a positive statement of the faith in Christ he had received from his martyred teacher, Bishop Peter, and a tribute to the divine Word who became man in order to lay down his life for us. For the most part, this treatise was addressed to his fellow believers, but Athanasius concludes with

---

226. Therefore, it had to have been completed before 318, when the Arian storm arose.

a passionate plea for unbelievers to accept the person of Jesus Christ and the victory of his cross.

As it was written before Arius's heresy began in A.D. 318, it is possible that this treatise helped incite it. For over and over again this little book repeated that the Son was divine. Throughout the book, Athanasius refers to Christ as "God the Word." Athanasius definitely admits the difficulty of conceiving how the infinite God could unite himself to a finite human body. But rather than resisting this utter paradox, Athanasius revels in it, marvels at it, and celebrates it. One of the properties of God is that he can be present everywhere at the same time, something no finite creature, not even an angel, can do. This omnipresent divine Word, in uniting himself with the flesh of Jesus of Nazareth, is nonetheless simultaneously present in all creation, holding it all together, said Athanasius:

> Even while present in a human body and himself quickening it, he was, without inconsistency, quickening the universe as well, and was in every process of nature.... He was not bound to his body, but was rather himself wielding it, so that he was not only in it, but was actually in everything.[227]

That the Immortal One should come to die, and to die the most shameful of all deaths, naked on the cross, this is a marvelous paradox. That the cross, symbol of disgrace and torture, should become his symbol of victory is the glorious irony of the Gospel:

> He made even the creation break silence: in that even at his death, marvelous to relate, or that at his actual trophy over death—the cross I mean—all creation was confessing that he who was made manifest and suffered in the body was not man

---

227. *On the Incarnation*, 17.

merely, but the Son of God and Saviour of all. For the sun hid his face, and the earth quaked and the mountains were rent; all men were awed. Now these things showed that Christ on the cross was God, while all creation was his slave, and was witnessing by its fear to its master's presence. Thus God the Word showed himself to men by his works.[228]

Over the course of the ages, some have asked, as they do today, what real difference it makes whether or not Jesus is truly God. Constantine, for example, when he first heard about the Arian controversy, wondered what all the commotion was about. But Athanasius understood that the deity of Christ is actually the linchpin of our salvation. If Christ were only a creature, the Gospel would not truly be such good news after all.

In the New Testament Scriptures, salvation is not simply presented as the erasure of the legal judgment against us because of sin. Moreover, sin is not just an offense on God's record book. For Athanasius and the Catholic tradition he represents, sin has caused in us, beginning in this life and accelerating in the next, "dissolution… ruin…nonexistence…corruption…wasting."[229] Sin had corrupted the glorious image of God in us and horribly marred God's magnificent creation. But as Athanasius points out, creation can only be renewed by its Creator, and only the One who made us in his image and likeness is fit to restore that image in us.[230]

Yet, salvation entails even more than just healing our wounded humanity. It also involves elevating us mere creatures to partake in the divine nature (see 2 Peter 1:3–4). This divine nature that we are

---

228. *On the Incarnation*, 19.
229. *On the Incarnation*, 6.
230. *On the Incarnation*, 6–7.

to share even now is the self-giving, creative energy called *agape* or charity. To put it another way, the eternal life won for us is not eternal in the sense that it is an unending experience of the human existence that is all too familiar to us. No, it is a qualitatively different kind of life, eternal in the sense that it is a participation in the life of the Eternal One. Salvation causes the same love that created the universe and raised the dead to reside in human hearts. Only one who is God and is in full possession of the divine nature can impart that nature to us by means of grace. If Christ is going to divinize us, he must certainly be divine. Only one who is God can make us godlike. A century and a half earlier, Irenaeus said that Jesus had become as we are so that we could become as he is. Athanasius, echoing this tradition, states it in an epigram that has become classic: "God has become man so that man might become God."[231]

If Christ is simply a demigod, an intermediary who is something less than God, he is not really Emmanuel, God with us. Rather, he is an emissary sent by a God who is so remote and so transcendent that he prefers to keep us at arm's length. And since the emissary conveys the orders of the Sovereign but does not himself know the Sovereign intimately, he cannot reveal God to us as he really is. We are condemned to obey God but to never really know him. We may be saved from the fires of hell, but we are never really admitted to the beatific vision of heaven where we see him face to face in all his splendor and beauty.

Athanasius is vividly aware that the salvation that is offered to us includes true intimacy with and knowledge of the Father. He also

---

231. Irenaeus, *Against Heresies*, Book 5, preface. Athanasius, *On the Incarnation*, 54. Of course neither author means that we become God by nature, but rather that, by grace, we become godlike.

realizes that it actually begins here and now, even if it only blossoms fully in eternity. This could only be possible if the Word who became man were himself truly God. For Athanasius, life would not be worth living if we had no hope of knowing God:

> Inasmuch as he is good, he [God] did not leave them destitute of the knowledge of himself, lest they should find no profit in existing at all.... Why did God make them at all, as he did not wish to be known by them? Whence, lest this should be so, being good, he gives them a share in his own image, our Lord Jesus Christ, and makes them after his own image and after his likeness: so that by such grace perceiving the image, that is, the Word of the Father, they may be able through him to get an idea of the Father, and, knowing their maker, live the happy and truly blessed life.[232]

Nicaea Unravels

Athanasius's book illustrates the continuous tradition of the Church from the New Testament down to his day, which was subsequently crystallized in the Nicene Creed, the first defined dogma in Christian history. Sadly, it did not take long for what seemed to be a decisive consensus to come apart at the seams.

Exiled or not, Eusebius, the fox of Nicomedia, had a few special cards left to play. There was his blood relation to Constantine's family. Then there was Constantine's mother, Helena, who had a great devotion to Lucian, the martyred mentor of Arius and Eusebius. Finally, there was Constantia, Constantine's half-sister, who looked to Eusebius as her spiritual mentor. Three years after the council, most probably under the influence of Helena and Constantia, Constantine

---

232. *On the Incarnation*, 63.

declared an amnesty that restored Eusebius and other Arians to their episcopal sees. They had learned their lesson, thought Constantine naively, and now everyone just needs to forgive and forget and get along. The unity of the Church and the empire demanded it.

In the very same year, the bishop of Alexandria died, and his deacon, Athanasius, barely thirty years old, was elected to replace him. A few years later, the emperor recalled Arius from exile and ordered Athanasius, his new bishop, to accept him back. Athanasius, convinced that his contrition was a sham, flatly refused. Rebuffed in Alexandria, Arius went to Constantinople. Ironically, the night before he was to be reconciled, his bowels ruptured, and he bled to death. He had long since been replaced as the leader of the party that bore his name, however, so the rebellion continued to simmer without him.

Eusebius, reestablished as the emperor's chief ecclesiastical advisor, remembered the damage Athanasius had done to the Arian cause at Nicaea and began to plot his downfall. For good measure, he planned the demise of all those who were, with Athanasius, champions of the Nicene faith. Within a few short years, employing innuendo and trumped-up charges, Eusebius managed to get all the key Nicene leaders deposed and exiled. Athanasius found himself on his way to Trier,[233] Germany, where he was received warmly by the local bishop.

Two years later in A.D. 337, Constantine died. He was buried not in the imperial purple but in the white garments of the newly baptized, having been christened by the Arian Eusebius. Athanasius and other exiles were able to return. But Constantine's successor in the East, his son Constantius, had not been at Nicaea. The new emperor quickly

---

233. The actual Latin name of this city was Augusta Treverorum, rendered in English today as "Trier."

fell under the spell of his cousin Eusebius who convinced him that the "narrow" Nicene Creed was politically inexpedient; the unity of the empire was best assured by a vague creed that was inclusive enough to encompass everyone, including Eusebius and his Arian friends. So Athanasius soon found himself exiled once more. This time he was invited by Pope Julius to take refuge in Rome, where he was sheltered for the next six years.

The Egyptian people loved Athanasius and wanted him back. The famous hermit, Antony, even wrote a letter to the emperor protesting Athanasius's exile. So when Constantius needed the military support of the Western emperor, who was a fan of Athanasius, he decided to invite the great Alexandrian to return to his see. Throngs went out to greet Athanasius before he even arrived in the city, rejoicing to have their father back. Constantius, meanwhile, bided his time.

The Western emperor, friend of the Nicene faith, died in A.D. 350, leaving Constantius as sole ruler of the entire empire. A couple of years later the resolute pope who had protected Athanasius was succeeded by the more mild-mannered Liberius. Constantius now saw his chance. He incited eighty Eastern bishops to sign a letter condemning Athanasius, which was then sent to the new pope, who simply ignored it. Constantius and the Arian party realized that Athanasius's strong support in the West had to be undermined before they could eliminate him. So Constantius called synods in Gaul and Italy and dispatched Arian bishops from the East to control them. These imperial representatives pressured the attending bishops into signing a condemnation of Athanasius, which implied a repudiation of Nicaea. Those who resisted were deposed and exiled. Pope Liberius, who refused to cooperate, was seized by force and put under house arrest in Thrace with an Arian bishop as his jailer. The elderly advisor of Constantine, Ossius of Cordoba, was also commanded to sign. In A.D. 356, Ossius told Constantius:

> I was a confessor at the first, when persecution arose in the time of your grandfather Maximian; and if you persecute me, I am ready now too to endure anything rather than shed innocent blood and betray the truth…. Do not intrude into ecclesiastical matters, and do not give commands to us concerning them; but learn from us. God has put into your hands the kingdom; to us he has entrusted the affairs of the Church; and as he who would steal the Empire from you would resist the ordinance of God, so likewise fear on your part lest, by taking upon yourself the government of the Church, you become guilty of a great offense.[234]

Constantius's response to his father's friend was to put him under arrest. With bishops of both East and West cowed into submission, Constantius was at last in a position to go after Athanasius. On the evening of February 8, 356, while Athanasius was engaged in a vigil service singing psalms with the faithful, imperial forces broke into the cathedral, and let loose a hail of arrows. Amidst the cries of the wounded and bodies of the dead, Athanasius was somehow hustled out of the cathedral by members of his clergy. The bishop immediately disappeared into the Egyptian desert, sheltered by monks who were among his most ardent supporters.

For the next six years, Athanasius was hidden by the monks who shuffled him from one remote place to another, always one step ahead

---

234. Ossius, quoted by Leo Donald Davis, *The First Seven Ecumenical Councils* (325–787): *Their History and Theology* (Wilmington, Del.: Michael Glazier, 1987), p. 93. Maximian was the emperor who presided over the persecuton of Diocletian in the Western part of the empire beginning in A.D. 303.

of the police. Meanwhile, Athanasius waged guerilla warfare against the Arians, issuing a constant barrage of writings condemning them and explaining the faith of the Church as defined at Nicaea.

The Life of Antony

Who were these men who successfully harbored the renegade bishop for six long years? From New Testament times, there had been Christians who opted to live a life of prayer, celibacy, and self-denial for the sake of the kingdom of God. There were consecrated virgins and widows who lived in the cities and participated in the life of the local churches. There were also celibate men, like St. Paul and Origen, who lived an active life of preaching and teaching. But from at least the third century, there is record of men who withdrew from everyday life to dwell on the outskirts of Egyptian towns to pursue a more contemplative life of prayer. Some called them "ascetics" from the Greek word for discipline. Since they withdrew from the organized life of the towns, others called them "anchorites" (from a Greek word that means "to withdraw outside the city"). Others called them "monks," or those who live alone (from *monos* in Greek).

The most renowned of these was a monk named Antony. Borne by word of mouth, stories about him were circulating all over the empire. Athanasius had certainly met him as a young bishop and had developed a deep and warm relationship with the holy man by the time he found himself on the run from Constantius. Sometime in that first year of Athanasius's desert exile, Antony died, at the ripe old age of 104. Shortly thereafter, Athanasius decided to write a biography of Antony, which, smuggled out of the desert, was translated into Latin and quickly became a sensation in both East and West. Despite the importance of *On the Incarnation* and his later anti-Arian works, it was this biography that has been Athanasius's most influential and most widely read work. It ranks among the most popular Christian books of all time.

This book, the very first life of a saint written in Christian history, became the paradigm of a whole new genre of Christian literature. It popularized the monastic life and contributed to countless conversions over the course of history,[235] as well as many monastic reforms. St. Basil, a decade or so later, called it a monastic rule of life in narrative form.

But the *Life of Antony* was about more than the monastic life, per se. It also provided an example of the meaning of that faith in God the Word that Athanasius had written about in *On the Incarnation* and that Nicaea had defined as dogma. For Antony's life illustrated the power of Christ that could be nothing short of divine. In the case of Antony, this power had transformed a young, illiterate man into a Christian sage whose intimacy with God continued to deepen until the very end of his life. In the course of his spiritual journey, Antony frequently triumphed over demons, conscious that it was Christ's power working in him that gave him the victory. Through him, Christ worked many healings and exorcisms, but Antony repeatedly tells others that they too can win the same battles over evil and disease, since the same divine Word will also work in and through them. The book tells the story of pagan Greek philosophers who come to dialogue with the unlettered Antony only to find their rationalistic syllogisms no match for his simple, straightforward wisdom that was a fruit of humble faith. In Antony, we see embodied the divinization that Athanasius had described in *On the Incarnation*, something that the Christ of the Arians could never produce.

---

235. Including that of Augustine, as he recounts in his *Confessions* and as we discuss below in chapter twenty-one.

Athanasius tells us that when Antony learned that Arians were claiming his support for their teaching, the normally calm monk was so outraged that he left his seclusion and came into the city of Alexandria to set the record straight. There, he publicly condemned the Arians as no better than the pagans who "serve the creature rather than the Creator."[236]

A Dream and a Prophecy

Athanasius recounts a dream experienced by Antony in the last years of his life that left him weeping. When his brother monks asked him what was wrong, he replied:

> "Wrath is about to overtake the Church and she is about to be handed over to men who are like irrational beasts. For I saw the table of the Lord's house, and in a circle all around it stood mules kicking the things within, just like the kicking that might occur when beasts leap around rebelliously. Surely you knew," he said, "how I groaned for I heard a voice saying, 'My altar shall be defiled.'" The old man said this, and two years later the current assault of the Arians began, and the seizure of the churches took place during which, forcefully taking the sacred vessels, they caused them to be carried off by pagans.[237]

But as soon as he recounted this horrible spectacle and saw the look of dejection on the faces of his comrades, Antony went on to issue this prophecy:

> Children! Do not lose heart! For just as the Lord has been angry, so again he will heal. And the Church will again quickly

---

236. See Romans 1:25 as quoted in *Life of Antony*, 67–68. The chapters and verses of biblical books had not been invented yet and so the text appears in the *Life of Antony* without the citation.
237. *Life of Antony*, 82.

regain her proper beauty and shine forth as before. You will see those who are persecuted restored, and impiety withdrawn once again to its own hiding places, while the holy faith declares itself openly everywhere with complete liberty. Only do not defile yourselves with the Arian, for that teaching is not from the apostle, but from the demons, and from their father, the devil; indeed, it is infertile, irrational, and incorrect in understanding, the senselessness of mules.[238]

Athanasius wrote down these words most probably in A.D. 357, the year following Antony's death. The bishop had been exiled three times already, and an Arian usurper was occupying his cathedral as he wrote. So it was natural that he thought that he had already seen what was described in Antony's alarming dream. Unbeknownst to Athanasius, the worst was yet to come. In the next few years, radical Arians were to gain the upper hand and force many to sign a creed, called "the Blasphemy" by St. Hilary of Poitiers, which essentially contradicted Nicaea:

Since some of many persons were disturbed by questions concerning substance, called in Greek *ousia*...of *homoousion, or what is called homoiousion*...there ought to be no mention at all.... No one can doubt that the Father is greater than the Son in honor, dignity, splendor, majesty...the Father is greater, and that the Son is subordinated, together with all things which the Father has subordinated to him; that the Father has no beginning and is invisible, immortal, and impassible, but that the Son has been begotten of the Father.[239]

This power play of the radicals led to outrage on all sides. Some moderate bishops had been concerned about the use of *homoousios*

---

238. *Life of Antony,* 82.
239. Davis, quoting *Creed of 2 Sirmium,* p. 95.

because it could be misinterpreted to mean that the Father and the Son were exactly the same person. They instead favored another term, *homoiousios* (of a *similar* substance rather than of the *same* substance).[240] By this new creed, both the diehard Nicenes like Athanasius and a very large group of Eastern moderates were equally condemned. Because of this, the aroused "moderate" camp convinced the emperor that this creed was even more inexpedient than that of Nicaea so both a new council and a new creed were needed. However, the creed that the bishops of both East and West were forced to sign at the resulting council[241] was little better than "the Blasphemy":

> But whereas the term essence (*ousia*) has been adopted by the Fathers in simplicity, and gives offense as being unknown to the people, because it is not contained in the Scriptures, it has seemed good to remove it, that essence be never in any case used of God again, because the divine Scriptures nowhere refer to the essence of Father and Son. But we say that the Son is like (*homoios*) the Father. [242]

Constantius was thrilled. Here was a creed that was vague enough so that virtually anyone could sign it. It prohibited the use of the controversial word of Nicaea and positively affirmed virtually nothing, for it totally failed to address in what way or to what degree the Son is like the Father. Virtually every bishop in attendance from both East and West was either tricked or forced into signing this creed. Two generations later, looking back on the approval of this creed, St. Jerome said,

---

240. The addition of an *i* (the Greek letter iota) after the "homo" was a serious change. To change the creed "one iota" was to guard against Modalism, but to create an opening for Arianism. The words could end in either "ion" or "ios," depending on their position in a sentence. Hence, *homoousion* means exactly the same as *homoousious*.
241. This was a local, not ecumenical, council of the same weight as Nicaea.
242. Davis, p. 97 quoting what came to be known as "the Dated Creed" of Rimini-Seleuca, A.D. 359.

"the world groaned to find itself Arian."[243] Meanwhile, Athanasius railed against it from his desert hideout and urged resistance.

Relief from an Unlikely Source

Constantius, stricken with a fever in A.D. 361, died shortly after he was baptized by an Arian bishop. Before he breathed his last, he named his cousin Julian as his successor. Having been tutored as a boy by Eusebius of Nicomedia, Julian had been instructed in Arian Christianity and had even been baptized. But after taking over the empire, he publicly renounced Christ and announced his determination to restore Rome to its pagan greatness. Athanasius and all other exiled bishops were recalled to their sees; Julian hoped that, unrestrained, the Arians and Nicenes would soon be at each other's throats and quickly destroy one another.

However, Athanasius, back in Alexandria, used his new freedom in a way that took Julian by surprise. Athanasius realized that the radical Arians had made a tactical error in ramming through the creed known as "the Blasphemy," for this had clearly unmasked them, revealing their true agenda. The reason they had gotten so far is that they had skillfully fooled moderates, beginning with Emperor Constantine, into believing that they really did not deny the divinity of Christ, but rather they simply wanted to express it in a different way. Their blatant extremism had rattled former allies, those for whom "*homoiousious*" (of like substance with the Father) was the watchword.

Some hardline Nicenes would not think of dealing with these bishops, whom they considered in the Arian camp. But Athanasius understood a principle not always sufficiently appreciated in

243. Jerome, *Dialogue Against the Luciferians*, 19

discussions on Christian doctrine—that orthodoxy is not a matter of terminology. It is not the term itself, but the intended meaning, which is either true or false. Words are inherently equivocal—the same words can be employed by different people in a very different sense.

Therefore, he invited "old" Nicenes, who favored *homoousios,* and moderates, who preferred the term *homoiousios,*[244] to come together for a "peace conference" in Alexandria. There, he asked each of the old Nicenes what they meant by their preferred term. If they made clear that they were not Modalists who denied the distinction in person between Son and Father, he accepted them into communion. Then he asked the "Semi-Arians" why they preferred their term. If they made clear that they did not deny the equality of the Father and Son, he accepted them into communion. The formerly antagonistic groups, hearing each other's explanations, came to understand that they were all fighting for the same truth using different words and embraced each other as allies. This was a monumental accomplishment, for it created the beginnings of a solid coalition against the Arian minority that, under the apostate emperor, no longer enjoyed imperial backing.

As soon as Julian realized what Athanasius was up to, he flew into a rage and banished him for the fourth time as "a disturber of the peace and an enemy of the gods." This time the bishop hid out not far from the city. On one occasion, as he was traveling up the Nile by boat, one of his friends informed him that an imperial barge was closing in on them from behind. Athanasius ordered his boat to be turned around and sailed directly toward the police vessel. As the two boats drew nearer, the police hailed the bishop's boat and asked, "Have you seen

---

244. Some refer to these "moderates" as Semi-Arians.

Athanasius, that enemy of the emperor?" Athanasius himself shouted back, "Yes, he is near. If you row quickly you can overtake him!" They thanked him for the tip, and immediately sped past Athanasius's boat, which then safely returned to port.[245]

The End of the Story?

When Julian died in A.D. 363, victory seemed at hand for the Nicenes. The new emperor, Jovian, was solidly in their camp. Athanasius was once again restored to his see, but within the year, Jovian was dead. Alas, the new emperor of the East, Valens, proved to be even more pro-Arian than Constantius. Athanasius was once again exiled, but this time, after a legal battle lasting several months, he was restored back to his see. Valens was even more brutal than Constantius had been, however. When the See of Constantinople became vacant, Valens promoted to this prominent post the Tracian bishop who had been the pope's jailer. When eighty churchmen protested, Valens had them burned alive.

As for Athanasius, during the forty-five years he was a bishop, he was banished five times for a total of seventeen years in exile. By the time he died in A.D. 373, he had outlasted most of his enemies. He had fought tirelessly, sometimes almost singlehandedly, for the truth of the Catholic faith as taught at Nicaea. But after every triumph, a new enemy appeared that seemed worse than the previous one. Few in Christian history have battled so long against such tremendous odds. Yet, like Moses who wandered for forty years in a hostile desert, Athanasius was not chosen by the Lord to be the one to lead the people of God into the Promised Land. At least Moses, however, had

---

245. See *Butler's Lives of the Saints, Complete Edition*, Herbert Thurston and Donald Attwater, eds., vol. II (New York: P.J. Kenedy and Sons, 1956), p. 215.

been able to see the land of milk and honey with his own eyes, even if it was from the top of Mount Nebo. To the contrary, all Athanasius could see on the eve of his death was his faithful Church in Egypt menaced by the darkness that shrouded the Eastern Empire.

After his death, the Egyptians immediately elected Anthanasius's brother Peter to replace him. Valens, however, would not stand for this. Instead he had the Arian Lucius installed by force. Police and rabble from the gutter invaded the cathedral. The sad spectacle that followed brought Antony's bad dream fully to life. A young man, dressed as a woman, danced obscenely on the altar while a naked pervert recited mocking, pornographic sermons while seated in Athanasius's episcopal chair. It was as if the demons, as well as the Arians, were wreaking vengeance on Athanasius. A reign of terror fell upon the faithful of Egypt—twelve bishops and over one hundred priests were sent into exile while the true bishop, Peter, fled to Rome, retracing his brother's steps.

Antony's nightmare had come true. But when would the Church see the subsequent restoration prophesied by the man of God?

CHAPTER 18

Basil the Great

If there was to be a doctrinal confrontation in the early Church, Alexandria would be the likely battlefield. And as an intellectual center both of pagan and Christian learning, it was always churning with theological ferment.

But Cappadocia was entirely different. It was a largely rural province in what is now eastern Turkey. Even St. Paul, who went just about everywhere, did not reach this out-of-the-way place. When a famous student of Origen was sent there to become its first bishop around A.D. 250, there were only seventeen Christians in the provincial capital. By the time of the Great Persecution, the Christian community in this largely backwoods province had grown to encompass most of the population and include even some families belonging to the landed gentry.

A Country Gentleman

Two of these noble Christian families united in marriage shortly after the persecution was over. The parents of the groom had been punished for their faith by the confiscation of all of their property, which was considerable. The father of the bride had lost not only all of his possessions, but his life as well. The mother of the bride was herself a confessor and a saint.

In a short time, the young husband, a renowned orator and professor of rhetoric by the name of Basil, managed to restore the family's financial fortune, which was providential, since he and his bride, Emmelia, were blessed with ten children. The eldest son, also named Basil, was born the year after Athanasius began his episcopal ministry. He was bright, strong-willed, and competent. Hoping he would follow in his father's footsteps, his parents procured for him the best possible education. His schooling began at home, where learning, both Christian and classical, was a normal part of daily life and conversation. The young Basil then pursued studies in the capital, Neocaesarea, then in Constantinople, and finally in the heady atmosphere of Athens. There, he was reunited with Gregory Nazianzen, an old schoolmate from Cappadocia, who now became his very best friend. Later on, these two remembered how one particular classmate in Athens had irked them with his pompous pseudo-intellectualism. The tiresome young man happened to be a nephew of Constantine. A few years later, he became the neo-pagan emperor known to history as Julian the Apostate.

Basil was in his mid-twenties when he returned to Cappadocia and embarked upon his career as a rhetorician.[246] He enjoyed immediate success and was quite impressed with himself. But there was someone who was not so impressed. His older sister Macrina had been one of Basil's first teachers. In her teenage years, Macrina had dedicated herself to the ascetic life, forswearing marriage and dedicating her life to prayer, self-denial, and tireless service to the family as well as to the poor. For her, as for Justin Martyr, philosophy meant the love of *true* wisdom—Christ crucified. Gregory of Nyssa, another of her brothers, tells of Macrina's impact on the up-and-coming orator:

---

246. A rhetorician was a teacher of both writing and public speaking. A good rhetorician could do quite well, since aspiring lawyers and politicians lined up to study the techniques of persuasion.

Basil returned after his long period of education, already a prac-
tised rhetorician. He was puffed up beyond measure with the
pride of oratory and looked down on the local dignitaries, excel-
ling in his own estimation all the men of leading and position.
Nevertheless, Macrina took him in hand, and with such speed
did she draw him also toward the mark of philosophy that he
forsook the glories of this world and despised fame gained by
speaking, and deserted it for this busy life where one toils with
one's hands.[247]

Basil himself tells the story this way:

I had wasted much time on follies and spent nearly all my youth
in vain labors, and devotion to the teachings of a wisdom that
God had made foolish (I Cor. 1:20). Suddenly I awoke as out of
a deep sleep. I beheld the wonderful light of the Gospel truth,
and I recognized the nothingness of the wisdom of the princes
of this world that was come to naught (I Cor. 2:6). I shed a
flood of tears over my wretched life, and I prayed for a guide
who might form in me the principles of piety.[248]

Basil the Lawgiver

If he had been willing to travel in pursuit of the worldly wisdom, it
was now only fitting to travel in search of spiritual wisdom. Basil had
heard tales of the holy men in the desert of Egypt, so he set out for
the land of the Nile. He arrived there while the renegade Athanasius
was hiding among the monks, writing the *Life of Antony*. Whether or
not he met the battle-hardened bishop during this visit to the desert,
one thing is sure: Besides a vision for the monastic life, Basil took

---

247. Gregory of Nyssa, *Life of Macrina*, 27ff. It is important to note that there are two
different Gregorys in Basil's life—his younger brother is referred to as Gregory of
Nyssa and his best friend is called Gregory of Nazianzus.
248. Basil, *Letter 223*, 2.

away from Egypt a lifelong admiration for Athanasius, whom he would ever after consider his spiritual father.[249]

Upon his return to Cappadocia, Basil and his youngest brother, Peter, withdrew to a remote place to live like the monks he had met in Egypt. Their sister Macrina, along with her widowed mother and several other women, established a convent nearby. Women flocked to Macrina, and a steady stream of men joined the brothers. Though he had met some hermits living in complete solitude in the Egyptian desert, Basil had also encountered a more communitarian style of monastic life there, under the direction of St. Pachomius. He prudently discerned that the cenobitic, or community, model would be much more stable and duplicable, so he designed his monastery after this pattern. Natural-born leader that he was, Basil also realized that without written instructions on how to practically live out the monastic ideal in the concrete circumstances of everyday life, it would be very difficult to keep monastic life consistent from monastery to monastery as the movement grew. Accordingly, he crafted a Rule of Life for his monks. This was the first written monastic rule in history and was destined to provide the fundamental blueprint of religious life in Eastern Christianity down to this day. In fact, the Rule of Basil had such a determinative impact on the future of monasticism that subsequent ages called its author "Basil the Lawgiver."

Basil the Pastor

Basil's extraordinary leadership skills could not go unnoticed for long. He had enjoyed his monastic vocation for only five years when Gregory Nazianzen, his friend and fellow monk, was sent to fetch him back to the provincial capital. The bishop and the Catholic

---

249. He calls Athanasius this in a letter he addresses to him. Basil, *Letter 82.*

community there were committed to resisting the Arianizing agenda of Emperor Valens and desperately needed Basil's help. The bishop was getting older and feebler, so Basil essentially ran the diocese for the next five years, though he was only a priest.

There were two pastoral priorities for Basil as he set to work to fortify the Catholic community. First and foremost was the reform of the liturgy. Based on his knowledge of Scripture and Church tradition as well as a masterful command of the Greek language, Basil took the old Eucharistic liturgy of Cappadocia and revised the prayers and ceremonies. The result was a work of such grandeur and beauty that it has been preserved down to this present day by not only the Greek Church, but the Coptic and Russian as well. The Liturgy of St. Basil is still celebrated in the Orthodox and Catholic churches of Byzantine heritage during Lent and certain special occasions of the Church year.

The liturgical life of the Church is centered on the Sunday Eucharist yet includes much more. Basil and the Christians of Neocaesarea received communion on Sunday, Wednesday, Friday, and Saturday, and they assembled each day before sunrise and again before the evening meal to sing psalms and hear the word of God. Basil preached at each of these services, twice daily, to crowds that grew so large over time that they overflowed into the streets.

His preaching was not always mild. He had been a country gentleman of a very prosperous family and recognized people of similar social standing in his congregation. In A.D. 368 when Cappadocia was stricken with a dire famine, the suffering was intense. Basil distributed the entirety of his inheritance to the poor. He also used Church funds to open soup kitchens where he was often found serving food, girded with an apron. Some of the people in his social class, however, both held on to their money and enjoyed profit from the higher prices resulting from decreased supply and increased demand. We are fortunate to still possess the text of a homily he preached to his peers during this crisis:

> You refuse to give on the pretext that you haven't got enough for your own need. But while your tongue makes excuses, your hand convicts you—that ring shining on your finger silently declares you to be a liar! How many debtors could be released from prison with one of those rings! How many shivering people could be clothed from only one of your wardrobes? And yet you turn the poor away empty-handed.[250]

Basil the Statesman

In A.D. 370, when his bishop died, Basil was elected to succeed him, to the delight of Athanasius and the chagrin of the emperor. Valens immediately made plans to visit Basil to bring him into line. He decided to send his right hand man, Modestus, ahead of him so as to procure Basil's advance submission to the emperor's Arianizing agenda. Modestus came armed with threats of the confiscation of property and exile for bishops who resisted. He was used to dealing with flatterers whose supreme desire was to protect their positions and curry the emperor's favor. He was not quite prepared for a personal confrontation with the likes of Basil who stood up to his bullying with these words:

> "Where God is endangered and exposed, there all other things are considered to nothing. Him alone do we look to. Fire, swords, beasts and instruments for tearing the flesh are wished for by us as delights more than horrors. Afflict us with such tortures, threaten, do all that you can now devise, enjoy your

---

250. Basil, *Sermon to the Rich*, 4. c. A.D. 369.

power. Also, let the Emperor hear this, that at all events you will not persuade us nor win us over to the impious doctrine [Arianism], though you threaten with cruel deeds." When Modestus, taken aback, remarked that no one had ever spoken to him like that, Basil responded, "Perhaps you have never met a bishop before."[251]

Modestus returned to Valens and reported: "Nothing short of violence can avail against such a man." For whatever reason, violence was ruled out by the emperor who planned instead to banish Basil. However, when Valens came to Neocaesarea and experienced the dignified beauty of Basil's liturgy, the power of his preaching, and the wide range of his relief efforts for the poor, Valens not only quietly dropped his plans to exile the bishop, but he even made a contribution to Basil's charities.

Though Basil won this battle, there was a war left to fight. Athanasius still occupied the see of Alexandria, thank God, but most churches in the East were in the grip of government-sponsored Arians. Thankfully, Neocaesarea was the capital of a province, which meant that Basil had fifty or so bishops under his jurisdiction. He quickly set to work appointing new bishops loyal to the Nicene faith. First, he insisted that his best friend, Gregory Nazianzen, accept episcopal consecration. Next, he consecrated his brother Gregory as bishop of Nyssa.

The Arians had been able to gain and keep ascendency for forty years through several tactics: (1) imperial sponsorship, and (2) keeping the larger Nicene party divided from Rome and each other through a variety of terminological and jurisdictional squabbles. If the Arians could use divide-and-conquer as their strategy, Basil knew

---

251. Gregory Nazianzen recounts this dialogue in his *Oration* 43, 49–50.

that the Nicenes must unite to conquer. His attempts to mediate a dispute over who was the lawful Catholic bishop of Antioch did not meet with success. But one of his efforts toward theological unity was so successful that it laid the groundwork for ultimate victory.

Athanasius had recognized that semantics were a major cause of misunderstanding among those truly faithful to Nicaea. Some favored *homoousios* (same essence) as the best way to express the relationship of the Son and the Father; some favored *homoiousios* (similar essence). Athanasius helped them see that though they used different words, they meant the very same thing. This began the work of building a new consensus.

Basil recognized another terminological muddle that, if ironed out, would carry along Athanasius's project and pave the way to a still broader consensus. In Greek, the terminology available to express the oneness of God and the three-ness of Father, Son, and Spirit was problematic, to say the least.

The Latin-speaking West did not have the same problems. In Latin, the classic formula, since Tertullian, had been "one substance, three persons." But this did not easily translate into Greek, since the Greek word *prosopon* (person), derived from the word for the mask worn by actors on the stage, carried a much stronger association than the Latin word did with the idea of impersonation, masquerade, or stage costume. In fact, that is exactly the way the Modalists had used the term, denying that there was any true, abiding, individuality of the three divine persons. Hence, Basil preferred to speak not of three persons but of three *hypostases*—this term conveyed a clearer sense of true and abiding individuality.

But there was a further problem. The word *hypostasis* (being or substance) was generally considered a synonym for another Greek word, *ousia*. Both terms could refer either to a common essence (such as "human nature") or to a concrete, individual entity (such as "Joe"). This had caused tremendous confusion among Christians trying to use these terms to describe the Trinity. Basil was the first to distinguish the two terms clearly and define them in the following fashion: *ousia* refers to the one being or nature of God, *hypostasis* refers to the distinctive way that Father, Son, and Holy Spirit participate in and express that one divine nature. The only acceptable Trinitarian formula, for Basil, is "one *ousia*, three *hypostases*." Thanks to Basil's explanation, this proved to be a formula around which virtually all the Nicene bishops of the East could rally. It also had the merit of being easily recognizable as orthodox by the Latin bishops of the West. Hence, over the course of the next few years, even while Emperor Valens was still pushing his Arian program, momentum was building for a reaffirmation of the faith of Nicaea by an increasingly broader base of churchmen from both halves of the empire. Basil's acumen as both statesman and theologian had borne great fruit.

Scripture, Tradition, and the Holy Spirit

Having consolidated the allied forces, Basil then proceeded to repel yet another theological attack. One of the new problems that had arisen since Nicaea was that of the proper understanding of the Holy Spirit. Since the Council of Nicaea had been preoccupied with the battle over the Son's divinity, it never really developed its teaching on the Holy Spirit. However, even before the council, Arius had denied not just the divinity of the Son, but that of the Spirit as well. Besides those who held this classic Arian position, there were others who conceded the divinity of the Son but refused to affirm the divinity of the Spirit. Macedonius, the Semi-Arian bishop of Constantinople, was the primary spokesperson of all those who denied that there was any biblical basis for calling the Holy Spirit "God." His followers came to be known as "Macedonians" or "Spirit-fighters."

In his later years, Athanasius, aware of this problem, had begun to address it. After the hero's death in A.D. 373, Basil realized that he now bore the responsibility to confront this problem head-on and deal with it once and for all. And so, around A.D. 375, he wrote the treatise *On the Holy Spirit.*

In this little book, Basil examines the claim that Scripture does not teach that the Holy Spirit is God. He addresses this objection in two ways. First of all, he concedes that there is no place in the New Testament that *explicitly* says, "the Holy Spirit is God." But he shows that there are countless places where the Scriptures teach the divinity of the Holy Spirit *implicitly.* For example, Jesus said that the only unforgivable sin is blasphemy against the Holy Spirit. Blasphemy is a sin against the divine name. Does not this teach the divinity of the Spirit? he asks.[252] Also, the Spirit is spoken of as filling the world. No created being can be everywhere at once, points out Basil, only God. "If wherever God is, the Spirit is present also, what nature shall we presume him to have?"[253] Next, the Spirit is called "Lord," clearly a divine title.[254] Scripture, says Basil, shows the Holy Spirit to be:

> An intelligent being, boundless in power, of unlimited greatness, generous in goodness, whom time cannot measure. All things thirsting for holiness turn to Him; everything living in virtue never turns away from Him. He waters them with His life-giving breath and helps them reach their proper fulfillment. He

---

252. Basil, *On the Holy Spirit*, 46.
253. Basil, *On the Holy Spirit*, 54.
254. Basil, *On the Holy Spirit*, 52.

perfects all other things, and Himself lacks nothing; He gives life to all things, and is never depleted. He does not increase by additions, but is always complete, self-established, and present everywhere. He is the source of sanctification, spiritual light, who gives illumination to everyone using His power to search for the truth—and the illumination He gives is Himself.[255]

Only God can sanctify, says Basil. Only God is the giver of life. So Scripture *does* actually teach the divinity of the Holy Spirit without using the words "the Holy Spirit is God."

However, we also can be sure that the Spirit is equal in nature to the Father and the Son, because, in the unwritten tradition of worship passed on to us by the Church, we are taught to adore and glorify the Holy Spirit along with the Father and the Son. Basil notes that in his church of Neocaesarea, the traditional doxology used to conclude prayers is "Glory to the Father, with the Son and with the Holy Spirit." He personally traced this usage at least a hundred years back to the beginning of the Church in Cappadocia, but he knows it goes back much further than that. Scripture teaches us to baptize in the name of the Father and of the Son and of the Holy Spirit. The unwritten tradition of the Church teaches us, when we are baptized, to profess our faith in the Father and in the Son and in the Holy Spirit. The object of our faith is God alone. So this evidence, from both the Church's doxology and its tradition of baptism, proves the divinity of the Holy Spirit. Basil's opponents say, "If it is not in Scripture, we can't do it." Basil attacks this *sola scriptura* approach as totally alien to both Scripture and Christian experience:

---

255. Basil, *On the Holy Spirit*, 22.

Concerning the teachings of the Church, whether publicly proclaimed (*kerygma*) or reserved to members of the household of faith (*dogmata*), we have received some from written sources, while others have been given to us secretly, through apostolic tradition. Both sources have equal force in true religion. No one would deny either source—no one, at any rate, who is even slightly familiar with the ordinances of the Church. If we attacked unwritten customs, claiming them to be of little importance, we would fatally mutilate the Gospel, no matter what our intentions—or rather, we would reduce the Gospel teachings to bare words. For instance (to take the first and most common example), where is the written teaching that we should sign with the sign of the Cross those who, trusting in the Name of Our Lord Jesus Christ, are to be enrolled as catechumens? Which book teaches us to pray facing the East? Have any saints left for us in writing the words to be used in the invocation over the Eucharistic bread and the cup of blessing? As everyone knows, we are not content in the liturgy simply to recite the words recorded by St. Paul or the Gospels, but we add other words both before and after, words of great importance for this mystery. We have received these words from unwritten teaching. We bless baptismal water and the oil for chrismation as well as the candidate approaching the font. By what written authority do we do this, if not from secret and mystical tradition? Even beyond blessing the oil, what written command do we have to anoint with it? What about baptizing a man with three immersions, or other baptismal rites, such as the renunciation of Satan and his angels? Are not all these things found in unpublished and unwritten teachings, which our fathers guarded in silence, safe from meddling and petty curiosity? They had learned their lesson well; reverence for the mysteries is best encouraged by silence.[256]

---

256. Basil, *On the Holy Spirit*, 66.

Basil then cites 2 Thessalonians 2:15, where Paul says, "Hold fast to the traditions you received from us, either by word of mouth or by letter."[257] He regards these apostolic traditions, as did Hippolytus nearly two centuries earlier, to be, for the most part, a pattern of worship going back to the apostles. And he recognizes a principle we have already seen: The doctrinal teaching of the apostles is implicitly expressed by the way they taught us to worship. *Lex orandi, lex credendi*—the way we pray reveals what we believe. The fact that we end virtually every prayer with equal worship to the three persons means that they are equal in nature and dignity. If in the celebration of baptism we have been taught to profess faith equally in the three persons, that means the three are equally divine.

First Rays of Dawn

Basil had accomplished much by the time he finished his work on the Holy Spirit. He had established a sound framework for monastic life, reformed the liturgy, been a champion of charity, and finally clarified the doctrine of both the Trinity and the Holy Spirit. He accomplished so much in fact, that history remembers him as St. Basil "the Great."

Nonetheless, this valiant warrior, like his hero, Athanasius, did not witness the final victory over Arianism before he died. Still, he was allowed a glimpse of the first light before dawn: On his deathbed in December 378, he received the news that the defender of the Arians, Valens, had died in the battle of Adrianople and that Gratian, an orthodox Nicene, was now at the helm of the empire. The finish line was within sight.

---

257. Basil, *On the Holy Spirit*, 71.

CHAPTER 19

Two Gregorys and a Council

O ut further in the country, west of Caesarea, lay the Cappadocian town of Nazianzus. While Basil's parents were beginning their family near Caesarea, two young lovers outside of Nazianzus were launching their life together as a married couple. The wife came from one of the prominent Christian families of the region. The husband, though a man of character and ability, was a pagan. The example and wise words of his saintly wife began to work on him, however, and he eventually became a Christian. That he was consecrated bishop of Nazianzus within a year after his baptism is a testimony to the ardor of his faith and the depth of his virtue.[258] It was A.D. 325, the year of the Great Council of Nicaea.

This bishop's son, Gregory, born around the same time as Basil, was, like Basil, being groomed for greatness. The two boys met briefly while in primary school in Caesarea and then went their separate ways. When they met again in Athens, during their university years, they became inseparable. Many years later, Gregory reflected on their friendship:

> Basil and I were both in Athens. We had come, like streams of a river, from the same source in our native land, had separated from each other in pursuit of learning, and were now united again as if by plan, for God so arranged it.

---

258. The ordination of married men to the episcopate as well as to the priesthood was allowed in the Eastern Church in the fourth century. Eventually, the Eastern Church required celibacy of bishops though it has always allowed married men to be ordained to the priesthood.

Such was the prelude to our friendship, the kindling of that flame that was to bind us together. In this way we began to feel affection for each other. When, in the course of time, we acknowledged our friendship and recognized that our ambition was a life of true wisdom, we became everything to each other: we shared the same lodging, the same table, the same desires, the same goal. Our love for each other grew daily warmer and deeper.

The same hope inspired us: the pursuit of learning. This is an ambition especially subject to envy. Yet between us there was no envy. On the contrary, we made capital out of our rivalry. Our rivalry consisted, not in seeking the first place for oneself but in yielding it to the other, for we each looked on the other's success as his own.

We seemed to be two bodies with a single spirit. Though we cannot believe those who claim that everything is contained in everything, yet you must believe that in our case each of us was in the other and with the other.[259]

Though these two young men had common interests, their personalities were quite different. Basil was by far the more outgoing and action-oriented of the two. Gregory, on the other hand, was much more comfortable alone with a book than in a room full of people. When Basil aggressively launched his career as an orator, it seemed as if they were going their separate ways once again. Gregory's desire was not to plunge into the world, but to shun it. He was determined to pursue a quiet life of prayer and learning.

So imagine his delight when Basil recovered his senses, abandoned his career, and told him of his plans to begin a monastery. Their friendship deepened. Gregory beat a path to Basil's monastery,

---

259. Gregory Nazianzen, *Oratio* 43, *in laudem Basilii Magni*, 15–17, 19–21; PG 36, 514–423. Translation by ICEL.

helped him write his Rule, and worked with him to edit a collection of Origen's words called the *Philocalia*, which became something of a classic for the Eastern Church.

The Reluctant Pastor

Gregory's serenity was shattered by a call to duty. His father, by now in his eighties, desperately needed help in the care of his diocese. After much wrangling, the elderly bishop prevailed upon his son to submit to priestly ordination. Gregory received the anointing, much against his will, and then promptly imitated the response of Jonah to the call of God—Gregory ran in the opposite direction. Taking refuge at Basil's monastery, Gregory wrestled with God, as Jacob had done. Finally, forgiving his father and recognizing his duty, he not only returned to his post in Nazianzus, but then proceeded to write a treatise on the dignity and responsibility of the priesthood, which is one of the greatest treatments of the subject in Christian history.

A few years later, Gregory convinced Basil that duty was calling him to leave his beloved monastery and serve the bishop of Caesarea as a priest. Gregory was proud to see Basil eventually succeed the bishop a few years later. But he was horrified when Basil, in need of orthodox bishops, imposed on him just as his father had, pressing him to accept consecration as a bishop. Once again, Gregory yielded under protest. He was sent to lead the church in a dusty, one-horse town on the border between provinces. The problem was that there really *was* no church to speak of in this miserable place. So Gregory once again ran away, this time to his father's diocese where he resumed helping his dad and ultimately succeeded him. But poor health drove him from Nazianzus after only a year as its bishop. He again took refuge in the quiet of the countryside and enjoyed several years of what he liked best, extended monastic retreat.

It was not long before duty called once again. In A.D. 379, Basil had died. A new emperor had arisen in the West who seemed friendly to the Nicene cause. Yet, the capital of the Eastern empire had been Arian for forty years. Several orthodox leaders told Gregory that someone needed to go to Constantinople and rally the troops, or at least what remained of them. These bishops were convinced that Gregory was the only man up to the task. Gregory was appalled at the prospect of leaving the beauty of monastic solitude to walk unarmed into enemy territory. He would be descending from the serenity of heaven into a hellish maelstrom. The reluctant prophet flatly refused, at least at first. But God ultimately prevailed, so off he went.

All the churches of Constantinople were solidly in the hands of its Arian bishop, the former jailer of Pope Liberius. Given that it was the seat of the imperial court, people were used to seeing prominent people who looked like prominent people. They heard that a great bishop would be coming to them, a wise and famous champion of sound doctrine. Then into town hobbled Gregory—poorly clad, bald, sickly, and prematurely bent over. Imagine their first impression. This unimpressive man was not even the bishop of the capital city but, rather, the opponent of the lawful bishop—he not only had no official standing, but he was a *persona non grata*. Since church property was controlled by the heretical bishop, Gregory had nowhere proper to preach and celebrate the liturgy. So he borrowed the home of a relative and consecrated it as a chapel. He had come to awaken the true faith in the city, so he named the chapel the *Anastasia,* or the Chapel of the Resurrection.

Gregory simply began preaching to anyone who would listen. As soon as he opened his mouth, people remembered what Paul had said about the treasure of Christ being given to us in earthen vessels (see

2 Corinthians 4:7). For despite his appearance, this man's preaching was more compelling than any churchman they had ever heard. The crowds coming to hear him swelled to an unmanageable size. Forty-three sermons, or orations, that he preached over the next couple of years have survived. Five of them, called his *Theological Orations*, were his attempt to teach this crowd the Nicene doctrine of the Trinity. These orations were so masterful and had such an impact on the universal Church's understanding of God that tradition has given Gregory a special title: "the Theologian." Only one other in Christian history has been honored with this title—the evangelist John.

As more and more people came to unlearn heresy and be schooled in true doctrine, Gregory had to correct many mistakes and confront many objections. He had to address the old denials of the Son's divinity. Then he had to deal with the more recent objections to the divinity of the Spirit. Some had said that if the Spirit was God, then Jesus was not the only-begotten Son. In his response, Gregory advanced Trinitarian doctrine. Noting the expression used by Jesus in John 15:26, he said the Spirit comes forth from the Father in an entirely different sort of way—he is not begotten of the Father, as is the Son, but *proceeds* from the Father. Gregory was the first to talk about "the procession" of the Holy Spirit and contrast that with the generation of the only-begotten Son.

Some also objected that, if the Holy Spirit too is God, why was this doctrine being clearly formulated for the first time more than three hundred years after Pentecost? Gregory's answer underlines the progressive nature not only of God's revelation over the course of salvation history, but also the development of doctrine, that is, the gradual development of our understanding of that revelation as time goes on:

The Old Testament proclaimed the Father clearly, but the Son more darkly; the New Testament plainly revealed the Son, but only indicated the deity of the Spirit. Now the Holy Spirit lives among us and makes the manifestation of Himself more certain to us; for it was not safe, so long as the divinity of the Father was still unrecognized, to proclaim openly that of the Son; and so long as this was still not accepted, to impose the burden of the Spirit, if so bold a phrase may be allowed.[260]

There was yet another heresy circulating at the time, and it had to be addressed. Apollinaris was a bishop who at first seemed to be a great supporter of the orthodox faith in the divinity of the Son, as taught by Nicaea. But his defense of the divinity of Christ proved to be a denial of his true and complete humanity. For Apollinaris, the Word united himself to a human *body* alone, so that he could die for us. He did not unite himself to a human mind, but instead substituted himself, who is the mind of God, for the human mind of Jesus.

In combating this error, Gregory expressed a deeper and clearer insight into how the human and divine are related in Christ than those who had taught before him. He made clear that, in contrast to the Trinity in which there is only one nature but three distinct persons, in Jesus Christ there is one person and two complete natures, human and divine. The incarnation took place not just, as Apollinaris would have it, to furnish the Son with a body to sacrifice on Calvary and so reconcile God and humanity. No, for Gregory, the reconciliation of God and man began to take place at the moment of the incarnation itself. God overcame the gulf between himself and us in the person of the babe of Bethlehem, for in this baby he united to himself a complete and entire human nature, thereby healing it

---

260. *Oration 31, 26.*

and ennobling it. It is the mind, not the body, that leads us into sin. So it is the human mind that is most in need of being healed and restored. If God had declined to assume a human mind when he assumed a human body, then our minds would remain unredeemed. He expressed this in a famous phrase that became classic: "what is not assumed is not healed."[261]

Gregory, considered an even greater orator than his friend Basil, so poignantly preached this teaching to those who came to his chapel that these simple people came to a profound appreciation of the meaning of the mysteries of the Trinity and the Incarnation. They became deeply attached both to the preacher and to his preaching. As could be expected, the Arian clergy of the city were not amused. Heretical mobs attacked Gregory, and on one occasion, they nearly succeeded in killing him at the altar.

Basil had been a natural scrapper. Gregory was not. When he announced his plans to flee the city in the face of the threats on his life, the people begged him not to take the Trinity away from them. So once again, Gregory restrained his inclination to run away and, standing his ground, did his duty.

The Nicene emperor of the West finally appointed a new emperor for the East. This man, a Spanish general by the name of Theodosius, proved to be a Nicene Christian. When he finally arrived in Constantinople in A.D. 380, he found Arians in possession of the city's churches, but no longer in possession of the people's hearts. The reluctant prophet, Gregory, had fulfilled his mission. The way had been prepared. The new emperor gave the Arian bishop a choice: accept the orthodox and catholic faith of Nicaea or leave town. The bishop

---

261. *Letter 101*, 4–6.

chose the latter. As his replacement, Theodosius chose Gregory. Of course, Gregory wanted no part of it. But as had Gregory's father and then Basil, the emperor, too, ultimately prevailed. Gregory moved from a makeshift chapel in someone's home to the great cathedral of the imperial capital.

The Unconsciously Ecumenical Council

Basil had helped rally the bishops around the faith of Nicaea; Gregory had rallied the people. Since the Nicene Creed was the orthodox faith of the Catholic Church, Theodosius restored all Church property to those confessing it. Deprived of government support, Arianism began to collapse like a house of cards. Nonetheless, Theodosius recognized that various forms of Arianism had prevailed for so long in the East that a new council was needed to repudiate the various Arian creeds that had weakened Nicaea or denied it outright. So, in A.D. 381, one hundred and fifty Eastern bishops assembled in Constantinople to reaffirm the creed of Nicaea and take care of a few housekeeping details. Their first act was to ratify the election of Gregory Nazianzen as bishop of Constantinople. And then, when the first president of the council died almost as soon as the council began, they chose Gregory as president.

Of course, Basil had not lived to see this triumphant day. But his teaching was in the forefront of the minds of the bishops as they assembled. This statement of Basil's evidently had a significant impact on them: "We can add nothing to the Creed of Nicaea, not even the slightest thing, except the glorification of the Holy Spirit, and this only because our fathers [at Nicaea] mentioned this topic incidentally."[262]

---

262. Basil, *Letter 258*, 2.

As the Fathers of this new council discussed the reaffirmation of Nicaea, they decided that rather than simply restating it in exactly the same words, they would carry it to its logical conclusion and complete what the Nicene Fathers had taken for granted but not had time to develop: the doctrine of the divinity of the Spirit. There were thirty-six Macedonian bishops present whom they very much wanted to reconcile to the orthodox majority, so they took the rather diplomatic tack that Basil had taken. Rather than saying bluntly "the Holy Spirit is God" or in the technical fashion of Nicaea, that the Holy Spirit is consubstantial (*homoousios*) with the Father and the Son, they preferred to state the doctrine clearly but implicitly, according to the logic of Scripture and Tradition. Nearly each phrase regarding the Holy Spirit which the Council added to the creed either came directly from the points made by Basil in his book on the Holy Spirit or expressed Gregory Nazianzen's[263] insight on the procession of the Holy Spirit:

> And [we believe] in the Holy Spirit,
> the Lord and Giver of life,
> Who proceeds from the Father,
> Who with the Father and the Son is jointly worshiped and jointly glorified,
> Who spoke through the prophets.[264]

---

263. Gregory's hometown was Nazianzus. He is sometimes referred to as Gregory of Nazianzus and other times Gregory Nazianzen, with Nazianzen used as a sort of surname. We will follow this second practice for the remainder of this book.

264. Biblical references: 2 Corinthians 3:17 calls Holy Spirit "Lord"; Romans 8:2 associated the Holy Spirit with life; 2 Corinthians 3:6 and John 6:63 call the Spirit "Life-giver"; in John 15:26, Jesus says the Holy Spirit proceeds from or comes forth from the Father; 2 Peter 1:21 associates the Spirit with prophecies. Text of the Creed from Davis, p. 122.

Alas, despite the majority's efforts, the thirty-six Macedonian bishops walked out and refused to sign the creed. Within a few years, these "Spirit-fighters" had faded into the oblivion of history.

The actual text of this creed might have also been forgotten, for this council did not regard itself as a new ecumenical council writing a new creed. They saw themselves as a local Eastern synod just reaffirming and clarifying the creed of Nicaea, the traditional and orthodox faith of the Catholic Church. Thus, the creedal statement of the bishops was placed in the archives and forgotten for seventy years. When, at the Council of Chalcedon, it was again retrieved from the episcopal archives, the bishops acclaimed it as an extraordinary achievement, guided by the Spirit. The Council that wrote it came to be considered as truly, though unconsciously, ecumenical, and the Creed itself was recognized as such a masterful exposition of the Nicene faith that from that moment on it became known simply as "the Nicene Creed."

The council lasted several months and also dealt with several practical matters of Church discipline. Since no official chronicle of the Council of Constantinople survives, we are not sure of the exact sequence of events. But we do know that, not long after Gregory was elected to the presidency of the council, some new delegates arrived who, on point of canon law, disputed Gregory's standing as bishop of Constantinople. The discussion of this matter grew quite heated. In response, Gregory gave an emotional speech to the assembled bishops:

> If my tenure of the see of Constantinople is leading to disturbance, I am willing, like Jonas, to be thrown into the waves to still the tempest, although I did not raise it. If all followed my example, the Church would enjoy tranquility. This dignity

I never desired; I assumed the charge much against my will. If you think fit, I am most ready to depart.[265]

This time, his offer to resign was accepted by the emperor, though not without regret. Gregory at last got his wish—he went from the hubbub of the council to the quiet beauty of the Cappadocian countryside. There, he lived out the remainder of his life in prayer and austerity, writing poetry and taking great delight in his garden while he prepared for his next and ultimate adventure, the final journey into the arms of God.

The Other Gregory

In the history of the Church, when people refer to "the Cappadocians," they are most certainly thinking of Basil and his friend Gregory. But also included in this designation is one more figure who is an integral part of the story. He is the "other Gregory,[266] "Basil's younger brother. In personality, he was much more like Gregory Nazianzen than he was like his brother—mild, withdrawn, more a man of letters than a warrior. He had not received the extensive formal education that Basil had enjoyed. The principal teachers of this "other Gregory" were his mother, his sister Macrina, and Basil, whom Gregory would always regard as his mentor. It was perhaps Basil who imparted to him the desire to follow in their father's footsteps as a professor of rhetoric. Gregory began the pursuit of success in his career and married. Spiritual pursuits were of little interest to him.

---

265. Cited in *Butler's Lives of the Saints,* complete edition, vol. II, p. 258.
266. History will later refer to him as Gregory of Nyssa after the town he served as bishop. He was a few years younger than both his brother Basil and Basil's best friend, Gregory Nazianzen, who later became his close friend as well.

On one occasion, Gregory's pious mother prevailed upon him to attend a family vigil service in honor of the forty martyrs of Sebaste.[267] Bored, Gregory fell asleep in the middle of the service. He woke up in a panic; he had dreamed that he was trying to enter a beautiful garden, but as he made his way through the gate, the forty martyrs drove him out with rods. Convicted of his indifference toward the martyrs and toward God generally, he repented and resolved to mend his ways, only to lapse into lukewarmness once life settled back to normal. It seems to have been the rebuke of Gregory Nazianzen that finally brought him to a realization that Basil and Macrina had chosen the better portion. So off went this "other Gregory" with Gregory Nazianzen for an extended stay at the monastic retreat of his siblings. There Basil schooled him in Scripture and theology, with special emphasis on the works of Origen.

Once Basil was bishop, he drafted his brother into service. Gregory was named bishop of the hamlet of Nyssa, a hotbed of Arianism. He proved a great preacher, and the people loved him. But he was particularly ill-suited for practical affairs and did not navigate conflict and intrigue very well. He was soon exiled on trumped-up charges and wandered the countryside sick and depressed for two years before being recalled after the last Arian emperor died in A.D. 378. The very next year, tragedy struck twice: First, he lost his brother Basil and then, a few months later, Macrina.[268]

---

267. The forty martyrs of Sebaste were all Roman soldiers who were some of the last martyrs before Constantine enforced religious liberty in the East. They were killed on the southern coast of modern Turkey around A.D. 320, and devotion to them in Cappadocia was great.

268. Around this same time, Gregory Nazianzen wrote a letter of condolence (*Letter 197*) to Gregory of Nyssa on the occasion of the death of a woman who Nazianzen refers to as "your sister Theosebia" and "true consort of a priest." Many think that she was Gregory of Nyssa's wife. Others think it was one of his blood sisters. Either way, her loss would have been a third tragedy for the bishop of Nyssa.

The short *Life of Macrina,* which Gregory later wrote, revealed the impact Macrina had had on him, Basil, and so many others. He was privileged to be with her in her last moments. Ironically, rather than him comforting her, he found himself unloading upon his dying sister the tale of all the troubles he had experienced with the Arians, the emperor Valens, and his years of bitter exile. We can hear the strength of the older sister, the spiritual pillar, as she exhorts her younger brother, the bishop and scholar, in these words:

> "Will you not put an end," she asked, "to your failure to recognize the good things which come from God? Will you not compare your lot with that of your parents? And yet it is true that according to the standard of this world, we can have great pride most of all in this, that we were well born and from noble stock.
>
> "Our father was very well thought of in his day for his education," she continued, "but his reputation only extended to the law courts of his own land. Later on, although he was a long way ahead of everybody else in his mastery of rhetoric, his fame did not reach outside Pontus, but he was glad to be widely recognized in his own country. But you," she said, "are known in the cities, the townships and the provinces. Churches send you forth and call upon you as ally and reformer, and you do not see the grace in this? Do you not even realise the true cause of such great blessings, that our parents' prayers are lifting you on high, for you have little or no native capacity for this?"[269]

The prayers of his deceased parents, and most likely of his saintly grandparents, the example of his older siblings and their friend Gregory Nazianzen all had a quite powerful effect indeed. For this

---

269. Gregory of Nyssa, *The Life of Saint Macrina,* trans. Kevin Corrigan (Eugene, Ore.: Wipf & Stock, 2005), p. 39.

"other" Gregory, the shy, melancholy, sickly man with the humble, home-based education, wrote more extensively and deeply than the other two Cappadocians combined.

When it came to classical literary and philosophical heritage, he integrated it into the Christian tradition more successfully than had his two Athens-educated colleagues, and even more successfully than the incomparable Origen. He was especially successful in synthesizing the profound classical concept of virtue together with the biblical idea of holiness.

Speaking of Origen, no one since the brilliant Alexandrian had even attempted anything like a systematic, comprehensive exposition of Christian theology. This Gregory of Nyssa did in his *Catechetical Oration*, which, though more a practical handbook for the catechist than Origen's book *De Principiis*, nonetheless advanced some very creative explanations of both the Eucharist and the theology of salvation.

If Gregory Nazianzen was orator and "Theologian," and Basil, the monk, was the "Lawgiver," the other Gregory was before all else "the Father of Mysticism." In his *Commentaries on Ecclesiastes*, his *Life of Moses*, and his treatise *On Virginity*, Gregory of Nyssa elaborated a theory of the stages of the mystical life that had a profound impact on the future of Christian spirituality. Although he identifies three stages of purification [*katharsis*], illumination [*gnosis*], and contemplation [*theoria*], this could convey the wrong impression that when a person reaches the third stage of contemplative or unitive prayer that he or she "has arrived." No, for Gregory, the spiritual journey is a dynamic adventure of progressively deeper union with God that can never stagnate or get boring, since our created nature can never contain or comprehend the fullness of the infinite God. Since God surpasses our intellect, Gregory identifies a certain darkness that characterizes the mystical experience, a theme that would be developed by many subsequent writers over the centuries.

Ironically, though he began his adult life as a married man, Gregory had as serious an impact on Eastern monasticism as did his brother. If Basil gave monastic life its abiding structure, his brother, Gregory of Nyssa, left an enduring mark on its spirit.

With regard to the Trinity, Gregory of Nyssa built on the work of his comrades and put the finishing touches on Cappadocian Trinitarian theology. First of all, this man, called "the Father of the Fathers" by the seventh ecumenical council, clarified how the procession of the Holy Spirit is different from the generation of the Son. The distinctiveness of the divine persons has everything to do, said Gregory, with their interpersonal relationships of origin. The Father is uncaused. The Son is eternally caused directly by the Father. The Father causes the Spirit eternally as well, but does so through the Son. Knowing the analogy to be, of course, inadequate to the reality, he uses the example of Adam, Eve, and their son Seth. Eve's being comes forth from Adam directly. Adam also causes Seth's being, but only through Eve.

But Gregory also explains the unity of the three persons in a deeper way than his comrades. In answering why there are not three Gods, he makes clear that the three are not independent, separate entities as three men would be, though we commonly say each equally possesses human nature. The three divine persons, to the contrary, actually share in one, single, indivisible divine nature. This means that it is incorrect to see the Father as Creator, the Son as Savior, and the Spirit as Sanctifier, each acting separately and independently. No, says Gregory: One nature means one will and one operation.

If one Divine Person wills something, it really means that the three are simultaneously willing it. If one acts, all three are simultaneously acting. The Father creates through the Son in the Holy Spirit. The Holy Spirit sanctifies according to the will of the Father and the Son. Although it is only the Son who dies on the cross, he is never for a moment separated from the Father and the Spirit. This dynamic process of triune willing and acting is called *perichoresis* in Greek, which has come into English through the Latin as *circumincession*. It becomes an integral part of the orthodox Christian understanding of the Trinity from Gregory onward.

All the Cappadocians emphasize the dignity of the human person, who has been made in the image and likeness of God. But in Gregory of Nyssa, man as image of God takes a central place in his theology in a striking way. It would seem that his extensive meditation on the equality and unity of the three persons caused him to see the implications for the equal dignity of each individual human person. One such implication is the recognition of the institution of slavery as being totally inconsistent with the revealed truth of human dignity. In one of his sermons on Ecclesiastes, Gregory boldly denounces an institution that is inherently evil:

> "I got me slave-girls and slaves." For what price, tell me? What did you find in existence worth as much as this human nature? What price did you put on rationality? How many *obols* did you reckon the equivalent of the likeness of God? How many *staters* did you get for selling that being shaped by God? God said, "Let us make man in our own image and likeness." If he is in the likeness of God, and rules the whole earth, and has been granted authority over everything on earth from God, who is his buyer, tell me? Who is his seller? To God alone belongs this power; or, rather, not even to God himself. For his gracious

gifts, it says, are irrevocable. God would not therefore reduce the human race to slavery, since he himself, when we had been enslaved to sin, spontaneously recalled us to freedom. But if God does not enslave what is free, who is he that sets his own power above God's?[270]

The Original Seminary

Reading about the three great Cappadocians, one may ask what seminary they attended. The question would have stumped them, for there existed neither formal academic seminaries in their day nor universities as we know them today. Yet, they were all holy priests, amazing scholars, and world-class preachers.

The word *seminary* means greenhouse, the place of ideal growing conditions where seeds can sprout and seedlings can be nurtured before being transplanted into the harsher conditions of the outdoors. Clearly, it was two Cappadocian families and the friendships that united them which provided the fertile soil for the germination of sanctity, genius, and priestly vocation in each of these three great men. Behind these Fathers of the Church stand holy parents, grandparents, brothers, and sisters who clearly played a decisive role in all they accomplished. The pastoral implications of the Cappadocian experience are considerable: the family as the domestic church, parents as primary educators of their children, the urgent need to recover and deepen the ideal of the Christian family even as society seeks to dismantle it.

But the personal experience of the Cappadocians has still greater significance. It is no accident that their profound insights into

---

270. Gregory of Nyssa, *Homilies on Ecclesiastes*, Stuart G. Hall and Rachel Moriarty, trans. (New York: Walter de Bruyter, 1993), p. 74.

God as Trinity—a creative and loving dynamism of interpersonal relationship—flowed out of a profound interpersonal life of Christian community beginning in their families. Gregory used the family of Adam to illustrate the unity in diversity of the three persons. But the Cappadocian insight flows both ways: If God, the ground of all being, is essentially a dynamic communion of irreducibly unique, distinct, and equal persons, then what are the implications of this for our understanding of human beings who are made in the image and likeness of God?

CHAPTER 20

Ambrose of Milan: The Jonah of the West

When Diocletian reorganized the empire, a second capital of the Western Empire was needed that would serve as the headquarters of the Caesar, the junior emperor of the West. Located on the western border of what is now Germany, Trier appeared the perfect choice. It had been Roman since Julius Caesar conquered it more than three hundred years earlier. When Athanasius was exiled there in A.D. 335, the Caesar lived there along with the Roman governor of Gaul, a man named Ambrose. The governor had died at an early age, but not before he and his wife had been blessed with a daughter and two sons, one of whom was named in his honor.

The widow brought her children back to Rome where the eldest daughter, Marcellina, saw to it that her brothers, Ambrose and Satyrus, pursued virtue as well as the education that would make them successful lawyers and statesmen like their father. As for herself, from a very young age, Marcellina had dedicated herself to the life of the spirit. When the boys were teenagers, they witnessed their sister receive the veil of a consecrated virgin in St. Peter's basilica from none other than the pope himself.

Ambrose and Satyrus applied themselves to their studies in the classics and in rhetoric. At a time when the knowledge of Greek was disappearing from the Western empire, Ambrose achieved a level of proficiency in the language of Homer and Plato that distinguished him from his peers. His eloquence and energy also set him apart; it was not long after passing the bar that his talent was noticed by the powers that be. He soon found himself appointed to a political post in Rome. A much greater honor was soon bestowed on him: The emperor, Valentinian I, called him to Milan[271] to serve as governor of Northern Italy. He was still not much more than thirty.

His father would have been proud. In A.D. 303, the imperial court of the West had been moved from Rome to Milan. Rome was still the historical heart of the empire. But Milan was now its political head, and as governor of the region, Ambrose had one of the most important posts in the West.

Immediately, Ambrose set himself to governing in a way that won the respect of the people. He hadn't been in Milan even two years when the first serious crisis arose. Unfortunately, twenty years earlier, the Emperor Constantius had appointed a bishop who had worked to make the imperial city a bastion of Arianism. But this bishop had just died. An assembly had gathered at the cathedral to elect his replacement, but the crowd was evenly divided between Arians and Catholics, and they were at each other's throats. The governor, in an effort to forestall a riot, immediately rushed to the cathedral to calm the crowd. As he made an impassioned speech to all about the duty of Christian charity, someone blurted out, "Ambrose for bishop!" Soon both Arians and Catholics were chanting, "Ambrose! Ambrose!" Dissension had become unanimity. Ambrose was appalled. Like his siblings, he was a devout believer, but according to the convention of that age, he had postponed his baptism. A decree of Nicaea prohibited the newly baptized from being ordained. "Emotion has overruled canon law," he quipped.

---

271. The actual Latin name of this city was Mediolanum, rendered in English today as "Milan."

His election had to be ratified by the bishops of the province. Surely, he thought, they will reject it as uncanonical. On the contrary, the bishops all thought Ambrose was the perfect candidate. But there was still hope, thought Ambrose. The emperor must ratify it, and he could hardly want to lose his governor to the Church. Surprisingly, Valentinian I said he was honored that one of his governors should be considered worthy of the office of bishop. Ambrose felt as if he had no choice but to emulate the prophet Jonah and run away. He literally hid in the home of his friend, a prominent senator. When the senator found out that the emperor had approved of Ambrose's election, he promptly turned him in.

Finally, Ambrose relented. He was quickly baptized and, one week later on December 7, 374, ordained bishop.

The Lingering Heresy

A gargantuan task lay ahead of the new bishop. After twenty years of Arianism, much work needed to be done. His brother Satyrus, aware of what his brother was facing, resigned his position as governor of another province and came to Milan to help. He took care of the administrative details of the diocese so Ambrose could entirely devote himself to his pastoral duties. The brothers had come from a prominent senatorial family of considerable means. Yet Ambrose, after providing for the support of their sister, Marcellina, gave all of his remaining assets away to the poor. He then set himself to acquiring a deeper knowledge of Scripture and Tradition. For this purpose, he engaged a wise priest name Simplicianus to tutor him in the Bible and the Fathers. His knowledge of Greek now came in handy, for it enabled him not only to read the New Testament in the original language, but also Athanasius, Origen, and Basil, whose works had not, for the most part, been translated into Latin. Ambrose became one of the main conduits channeling the stream of Greek Christian thought into the Latin tradition of the West.

The bishop won the hearts of the people by his inspiring preaching and his exemplary generosity. This generosity went beyond the gift of his property to the gift of his time. Ambrose made himself personally available to an extraordinary degree. He instituted an open-door policy—any member of his flock, regardless of social standing, could come and talk to him, though he did lay a few firm ground rules: He would engage neither in matchmaking nor recommendations to posts in the imperial court. Nonetheless, the stream of visitors was relentless. One of his many visitors, a young orator named Augustine, recounts how Ambrose would sneak in a few minutes of prayer and study between visitors. This hectic pastoral schedule explains why most of the writings we have from him are not lengthy treatises or extensive biblical commentaries, but rather collections of forceful homilies.

Soon after his election, Ambrose received a congratulatory letter from Basil, bishop of Caesarea, who urged him to press the battle against Arianism. In response, Ambrose set himself to what proved to be a lifelong program of eradicating the remnants of Arianism in Italy. In this agenda, he encountered a serious setback only a year after his ordination. The Catholic emperor, Valentinian I, was killed in battle along the northern frontier. His older son, Gratian, was also Catholic and had been named by Valentinian as co-emperor. Nevertheless, the army acclaimed not Gratian, but his younger half-brother, Valentinian II, as the new Augustus of the West.[272] Gratian

---

272. Gratian was son of Valentinian I's first wife. Valentinian II was son of his father's second wife, Justina.

retained control of Britain, Spain, and Gaul, leaving nominal control of Italy to his half-brother. Since Valentinian II was only four years old at the time, this new emperor was nothing more than a puppet in the hands of his manipulative mother, Justina, who happened to be an Arian. The empress even invited a renegade Arian bishop to reside as a member of the imperial court, putting Ambrose in a rather difficult position. But as long as her stepson Gratian was the real power in the West, she dared not promote her Arian faith openly. Rather, Justina bided her time.

Gratian meanwhile looked to Ambrose as his spiritual leader. Duty called him to bring an army to the relief of his uncle Valens, the Eastern emperor, who was menaced by a rebellion on his northern frontier. Wary of the aggressive proselytism he might encounter while in the company of his Arian uncle, Gratian turned to Ambrose before he embarked on his mission and requested instruction in the Catholic faith. In response, Ambrose wrote two of his more extensive works: *To Gratian, Concerning the Faith* and, a few years later, *On the Holy Spirit*.

However, Gratian and Valens were never to meet. When Gratian's army was still a few hundred kilometers away, Valens, thinking he had the barbarians cornered and outnumbered, decided to seize the glory for himself. But he miscalculated. His premature and overconfident attack on the Gothic forces at Adrianople resulted in the worst Roman defeat in a century. Valens lost not only two-thirds of his men, but his own life as well.

Gratian, now left with the entire empire to defend, appointed the Spanish general Theodosius, also a Catholic, as emperor of the East. Five years later, Gratian was treacherously murdered in Gaul. When Maximus, the rebellious general behind the assassination, threatened to swoop into Italy, Justina pleaded with Ambrose to go as an ambassador to persuade the usurper to content himself with the northern provinces and leave Italy in peace. Ambrose was successful in this mission, the first occasion in history whereby a bishop endeavored to mediate a major political and military dispute.

Ambrose's aim had been to avert bloodshed. But his efforts inadvertently secured Justina's control over Italy. With Gratian gone and the Catholic emperor Theodosius far away, the empress finally saw her chance to work for a resurgence of Arianism in Milan. Many of the Gothic barbarians had been converted to Christianity by Arian missionaries sent from Constantinople. Some of these Arian Goths were now serving in the Roman army and were stationed in Milan. Under the pretext of providing these soldiers a place to worship, Justina induced her son to demand that Ambrose hand over one of his churches. The plan was for the Arian bishop living in the imperial court to celebrate his first Eucharist there on Easter of A.D. 386. Ambrose flatly refused. When threatened with force, he replied: "I have said what a bishop ought to say; let the emperor do what an emperor ought to do. Naboth would not give up the inheritance of his ancestor, and shall I give up that of Jesus Christ?" [273]

Justina sent soldiers to seize the basilica, but Ambrose and his flock got there first. On Palm Sunday, they barricaded themselves inside the church. Soldiers surrounded the basilica hoping to starve them out before they were ordered to storm the building. But the congregation remained inside, fasting and praying, day after day, with the nervous soldiers ringing the basilica, poised to attack. A participant in this sit-down strike happened to be a woman named Monica, the mother of Augustine, the imperial rhetorician.

---

273. Ambrose, *Sermon against Auxentius on the Giving Up of the Basilicas.*

Ambrose made use of this extended retreat with his flock to teach them a new style of singing. Up till now, music in the Latin Church was limited to psalms sung by a choir with the people just singing no more than a short response between the verses. Ambrose wanted to get the congregation more engaged, so he taught them a new style called "antiphonal" singing, where the congregation was divided in two, with half singing one verse and the other half singing the next. He also taught them melodies that he had composed himself. His lyrics took their departure from biblical themes but were not simply quotes from the psalms or other scriptural texts. Rather, they were Ambrose's own creative, poetic compositions. Such hymns were common in the East but were relatively unknown in the Latin West. This Ambrosian hymn, reflecting on Peter's denial, was most likely taught to the people during this lock-in prayer vigil:

> Now the shrill cock proclaims the day,
> and calls the sun's awakening ray,
> the wandering pilgrim's guiding light,
> that marks the watches night by night.
> Roused at the note, the morning star
> heaven's dusky veil uplifts afar:
> night's vagrant bands no longer roam,
> but from their dark ways hie them home
> The encouraged sailor's fears are o'er,
> the foaming billows rage no more:
> Lo! e'en the very Church's Rock
> melts at the crowing of the cock.
> O let us then like men arise;
> the cock rebukes our slumbering eyes,

bestirs who still in sleep would lie,
and shames who would their Lord deny.[274]

The singing went on for a week before the soldiers finally stood down, but not before a eunuch of the imperial household had a few words with the recalcitrant bishop. In a letter to his sister Marcellina, Ambrose tells the story of the encounter: "The eunuch, Calligone, an imperial Chamberlain, said to me: 'You despise Valentinian. I will cut off your head.' To which I replied: 'May God permit it. Then I shall suffer as a bishop should, and you will act according to your kind!'"[275]

The fruit of this week-long standoff was long-lasting: The melodies and lyrics composed by Ambrose and his followers spread and quickly became the dominant music of the Western Church until Gregorian chant was popularized by Charlemagne and his heirs a few centuries later. In fact, this Ambrosian chant is the earliest surviving written music of Western civilization.

Father of the Catholic Emperor

But Justina was undaunted. The following year she pushed her son to issue a formal decree legalizing Arian assemblies and making it a capital offense to interfere with them. She then demanded once again that Ambrose hand over churches for Arian use, according to law. Ambrose called her bluff:

> If you demand my person, I am ready to submit: carry me to prison or to death, I will not resist; but I will never betray the church of Christ. I will not call upon the people to protect me; I will die at the foot of the altar rather than desert it.[276]

---

274. *Aeterne rerum conditor*, or "Maker of All, Eternal King," a hymn which Augustine identifies has having been written by Ambrose. Latin from the *Liturgia Horarum*, and Latin Hymns, F.A. March, 1894, W.J. Copeland, trans.
275. Ambrose, *Letter 20 to Marcellina*.
276. Ambrose, *Letter 20*.

Justina knew better than to lay a hand on the beloved bishop. Perhaps she realized the precariousness of her position when a troop of soldiers sent to enforce the decree decided to go inside the church to pray with the Catholics.

The constant warfare with the barbarian Goths and Huns during these years resulted not only in casualties but in numerous captives. The barbarians would either release their prisoners for a ransom or sell them into slavery. After Ambrose ran out of family and church funds to redeem as many captives as possible, he had golden chalices melted down to free even more people. The Arians, ironically, accused him of sacrilege. Ambrose responded that they had forgotten the meaning of the Eucharist; those vessels were golden because they contained the blood of Christ that had been poured out as a ransom. He declared, "If the church possesses gold it is in order to use it for the needy, not to keep it."[277]

A few years later Justina and her son fled to the East ahead of the usurper Maximus who decided it was finally time to invade Italy. They returned in the company of the Eastern emperor, Theodosius, who defeated the usurper and restored Valentinian as nominal head of the Western empire. In reality, Theodosius was in total control. And rather than return to Constantinople, he decided to stay in Milan where he could ensure no more trouble broke out in the West.

Soon after his arrival, the Catholic emperor who had distinguished himself as the champion of Nicene orthodoxy, appeared at Ambrose's Eucharist. It was a special feast, and Theodosius, having brought his offering to the altar, remained within the sanctuary. Ambrose asked if he wanted anything. The emperor responded that he stayed to assist

---

277. Ambrose, *On the Duties of the Clergy*, 2.28.136–139. Here he mentions the example of St. Lawrence, the deacon, who saw the poor as the riches of the Church.

at the holy mysteries and receive communion. Ambrose sent a deacon to him with this message: "My Lord, it is lawful for none but the sacred ministers to remain within the sanctuary. Be pleased therefore to go out and stand with the rest. The purple robe makes princes, but not priests." Theodosius apologized that he was unaware of the difference in custom between Constantinople and Milan. Thanking the bishop for explaining the proper protocol, the emperor humbly took his place among the laity.[278]

Theodosius and Ambrose developed thereafter a warm and cordial relationship. Theodosius, later called "the Great," had done much to end the Arian stranglehold on the East and to protect the rights of the Catholic Church. He was, in fact, a sincere believer. So Ambrose was stunned when news reached him of an unspeakable atrocity committed by this Christian emperor. The populace of Thessalonica had rioted, killing the imperial governor and some troops. In his rage, Theodosius ordered his remaining forces to surround the circus while the townsfolk were assembled for a chariot race, and to cut them all down without mercy. Seven thousand men, women, and children were butchered in the ensuing massacre. Ambrose wrote the emperor privately and urged him to repent publicly for this crime. Indeed, Ambrose made clear that, should the emperor appear in church, Ambrose would have to stop the liturgy. His words were firm, but in the text of this confidential letter, which has fortunately come down to us, we can hear the grieved voice of a loving spiritual father:

---

278. Ambrose was known for his great respect for legitimate diversity of custom that existed in the church catholic. In Milan, Saturday was traditionally a festive day while it was a fast day in Rome. Ambrose's advice to Augustine to follow Roman customs while in Rome has come down to us in Western culture as the dictum: "When in Rome, do as the Romans do."

What has been done at Thessalonica is unparalleled in the memory of man.... You are human, and temptation has overtaken you. Overcome it. I counsel, I beseech, I implore you to penance. You, who have so often been merciful and pardoned the guilty, have now caused many innocent to perish. The devil wished to wrest from you the crown of piety which was your chiefest glory. Drive him from you while you can.... I write this to you with my own hand that you also may read it alone.[279]

What Ambrose required was that the emperor submit to the public, canonical penance that was the custom of the time for the case of notorious, public sin. The sinner, dressed in sackcloth, would stand outside the church, begging the intercession of those entering to worship. The emperor did exactly this for several months before being admitted back into communion at Christmas. Augustine said that the faithful entering the church, at the sight of his imperial majesty abasing himself, were moved to tears. As Ambrose recounted in the sermon he preached at Theodosius's funeral:

> He stripped himself of every sign of royalty and bewailed his sin openly in church. He, an emperor, was not ashamed to do the public penance which lesser individuals shrink from, and to the end of his life he never ceased to grieve for his error.[280]

Theodosius, who could, of course, have banished or executed Ambrose, instead declared that Ambrose was the only bishop he'd ever met who was truly worthy of his office. A few years later, Theodosius died in the arms of his bishop.

---

279. Ambrose, *Letter*.
280. The entire funeral oration by Ambrose in honor of Theodosius, Roy J. Deferrari, trans., can be found in *Funeral Orations, Fathers of Church, vol. 22* (Washington, D.C.: Catholic University of America Press, 1953).

....

Legacy

Ambrose is known as the "Father of Hymnody" in the Western Church. But first and foremost, Ambrose the bishop was a spiritual father who left his imprint on the Church and on Western civilization not only through his powerful writings and music but through his spiritual sons. Two of them, Gratian and Theodosius, were emperors who helped restore the Creed of Nicaea to the church. Another spiritual protégé would go on to become the most influential Christian teacher in the West until Aquinas.[281]

While Ambrose did not make decisive new contributions to the understanding of the Trinity, the Holy Spirit, or the Incarnation, as had the Cappadocians, he did bring out clearly the implications of the dogma of Nicaea for the understanding of the Church, the state, and their interaction.

As we have seen, theology that, at first glance, seems remote and theoretical has, in reality, very serious implications for everyday life. Athanasius, to his credit, recognized how Arianism imperiled and impoverished our idea of salvation. And Gregory of Nyssa saw the implications of Trinitarian theology for our idea of human dignity and what it means to be made in the image and likeness of God.

In Ambrose's interactions with the emperor, we see how Arian and Nicene theology led to radically different visions of church and state. For the Arians, God is not community but rather a solitary and remote monarch. The role of the Son is relativized by Arian theology. He is merely a creature, God's prime minister so to speak, who served as the instrument of the King in the creation and salvation of the world. But God can use different instruments; the same King can

---

281. This convert of Ambrose's will be the subject of our next chapter.

have a succession of prime ministers. In the present time, it is the Christian emperor who is the acting prime minister through whom God governs both his Church and his world. The bishops of the Church, according to this Arian vision, primarily receive their legitimacy from imperial selection and appointment and could be moved to whichever see the emperor wishes. They are the spiritual officers in the imperial bureaucracy. It is no wonder that the Arian bishops in the East, to a man, had fawned ceaselessly on the emperors from Constantine to Valens and that such emperors found Arianism quite congenial to their tastes.[282] This explains why, in Constantinople, where Arianism held sway for forty years, it had become customary for the emperor to stand with the priests in the sanctuary.

For the orthodox Catholics of the Nicene Creed, the Son is not a mere temporary instrument of God but is himself eternally the King of kings and Lord of lords. He chose apostles, who in turn founded churches where they ordained bishops who succeeded them. The ground of the bishops' authority is not the favor of the emperor but rather the unbroken apostolic succession going back to the Lord himself.

For Nicene Christians, even the emperor who is the champion of the Catholic faith is not himself the law but is, instead, *under* God's law. Or as Ambrose put it so succinctly, "The emperor is in the Church, not above it."[283]

---

282. For an example of this, see *The Life of Constantine*, written by the Arian Eusebius of Caesarea.
283. Ambrose, *Sermon Against Auxentius on the Giving up of the Basilicas.*

CHAPTER 21

Augustine and Amazing Grace

I n the fourth century, Italy was the center of the civilized universe, as it had been for centuries. All roads still led to Rome. Milan, however, strategically located at the foot of the Alps, served as a secondary epicenter of political intrigue and intellectual fashion.

In contrast, Roman North Africa, the homeland of Cyprian and Tertullian, was far off the beaten track. It was provincial in the worst sense of the term. And the further you went from the main city of Carthage, the more provincial things got.

Under the African Sun

Around the time Ambrose was launching his political career in Rome, a teenager named Augustine was finishing his primary schooling in North Africa. He was born and raised in a little farming town called Thagaste.[284] It was in the interior, about 150 miles from Carthage. His mother, Monica, a daily communicant in the Catholic Church, did her best to raise the boy as a Christian. The pagan father, Patricius, did his best to provide the boy a decent education. This meant getting him out of their dead-end town and sending him to university. So at age seventeen, Augustine was packed off to confront the challenges of the big city on his own. Patricius died soon after.

The new widow was comforted to find out that her son was at least going to catechism class while away at school. What she didn't

---

284. Modern-day Souk Ahras, Algeria.

know was that his main motivation was to meet a girl. Augustine found what he was looking for and immediately moved in with her. In his autobiography, he writes, "I came to Carthage and all around me hissed a cauldron of illicit loves."[285]

His father had recognized his intellectual gifts and planned for him to become a lawyer. His mother recognized his spiritual promise and prayed for him to find God. In his second year, as he sought to honor his father, he appeared poised to bring joy to his mother. For in his quest to improve his rhetorical style, Augustine had picked up a book called the *Hortensius*, written by the great Roman orator Cicero. In it, the author includes an appeal to abandon the superficial quest of money and pleasure and instead pursue wisdom. Augustine, jolted into recognizing the vanity of his career ambitions, abandoned his plans to study law and dedicated himself instead to the search for truth. To find it, he went to the Christian Scriptures, as Monica had hoped. But he was quickly disillusioned. To a young man schooled in the classics, the Bible was frankly unimpressive in style and filled with crude stories that seemed unworthy of God. Augustine was desperate to find wisdom to shed light on the mysterious battle he observed in his own soul between good and evil. Yet, the Old Testament held up heroes like David and the patriarchs who seemed as much victims of passion as he was himself.

At about this time, he made the acquaintance of missionaries who claimed to be representatives of the authentic and pure form of Christianity. These Manicheans, disciples of a Persian prophet called Mani, were eminently logical. They were dualists who, like the Gnostics centuries before, rejected the Old Testament since its God,

---

285. Augustine of Hippo, *The Confessions*, Henry Chadwick, trans. (New York: Oxford University Press, 1992), 3.1.1.

they taught, was none other than the source of the evil in the world. Matter was evil; spirit was divine. Augustine's inner struggle, they explained, was simply a symptom of the cosmic war between good and evil, matter and spirit, playing out in his own person. There was no reason to be ashamed of his lust—it was just what the evil body produces. His real self was the spiritual part of himself. One day, they assured him, his body would die, and he'd be free from it. Finally, Augustine had answers that explained himself to himself and would give him inner peace—or so he thought.

For many years, Augustine remained a Manichaean "hearer." He admired the "perfect" members of the inner circle of this sect on account of their austere life of celibacy and self-denial. But, of course, he could not become one of them, because he did not have the inner resources to part with bodily pleasures, especially sex. But at least, he thought, he was monogamous; he had remained faithful to his concubine[286] and with her was raising their son, Adeodatus (meaning "given by God"). Meanwhile, Augustine was acquiring a reputation as a professor of rhetoric. As year followed year in his Manichaean group, questions kept piling up, and frustrations were mounting. He desired progress in this Manichaean way, but he saw no progress. He had problems to resolve, but there were no answers.[287] He had never had a spiritual father and desperately needed one. The "perfect" did not have the solutions for him but kept telling him that if only he could meet their leader, the great Faustus, all his questions could be answered. He could be the spiritual father Augustine was searching for.

---

286. Nowhere in his writings does Augustine ever name his mistress.
287. Augustine gives one example: He had noticed discrepancies between what Mani says about the heavenly bodies and what the science in his day knew about astronomy. See Book 5 of his *Confessions*, 3.3–5.13.

At last, Faustus came to town. Alas, this proved to be a total letdown for Augustine. Faustus was a charming, eloquent, old man but really had nothing to say. He honestly admitted he could not answer Augustine's questions. Augustine quickly realized that the sect no longer had anything to offer him. In fact, neither did Carthage. The students there were unruly and undisciplined. The people were boorish and small-minded. Augustine decided that his future was in cosmopolitan Italy, not the backwaters of North Africa. As he made preparations to depart for Rome, Monica came to Carthage and pleaded with him either not to go or, if go he must, to take her with him. One night, while she was occupied with a vigil at the shrine of St. Cyprian, Augustine secretly embarked on a late-night ship, giving her the slip. The next morning, realizing she had been deceived, she looked out to sea from the dock and wailed in grief.

Son of Ambrose

Augustine's experience in Rome was miserable. The students there were worse than in Carthage.[288] But then, what he thought was the break of a lifetime came his way. The emperor needed a rhetorician to be the official imperial orator, and the governor of Rome, who was impressed with the young African, secured the appointment for Augustine. So off he went to Milan. When the news got back to Africa, the proud mother set sail for the imperial capital as well.

As Augustine and his family got settled in Milan, Monica was immediately off to the cathedral. She told him that he'd be impressed with the bishop, who was himself a master of rhetoric and the former

---

288. Students in Rome had a racket going—they'd enjoy a professor's instruction until just before the tuition bill was due. At that point, they would leave the class, thus "stiffing" the teacher. *Confessions* 5.12.22.

governor of Northern Italy. So Augustine came to church on Sundays merely to study Ambrose's oratorical style. Years later, he would write about this experience in the form of a prayer addressed to God:

> By his eloquent sermons in those days he zealously provided your people with the fat of your wheat, the gladness of your oil, and the sobering intoxication of your wine. All unknowing, I was led to him by you, so that through him I might be led, while fully knowing it, to you. That man of God received me in fatherly fashion, and as an exemplary bishop he welcomed my pilgrimage. I began to love him, at first not as a teacher of the truth, which I utterly despaired of finding in your Church, but as a man who was kindly disposed towards me. I listened carefully to him as he preached to the people, not with the intention I should have had, but to try out his eloquence, as it were, and to see whether it came up to its reputation.[289]

As he came to hear Ambrose Sunday after Sunday, the beauty of the Ambrosian chant began to work on him, moving the young professor to tears. And the content of Ambrose's message began to work on him as well. As Ambrose explained the Scriptures, they suddenly began to make a lot more sense. Following the Pauline dictum that "the letter brings death, but the Spirit gives life." (2 Corinthians 3:6, *NAB*), Ambrose taught that beneath the literal sense of those troublesome Old Testament figures and events, there was a profound spiritual meaning that prepared for, prefigured, and predicted Christ, his Church, and the institutions of the New Covenant. Ambrose had learned, from the great Origen and other Eastern fathers, that the humble surface of the Bible concealed depths of meaning that

---

289. *The Confessions of Saint Augustine,* John K. Ryan, trans. (New York: Doubleday, 1960), 5.14.23.

were truly inexhaustible. Confronted by Ambrose's spiritual interpretation of Scripture, the rationalistic objections that Augustine and
his Manichaean friends had against the Bible and the Catholic faith
began to crumble. True, questions remained. But at least Augustine
was now ready to enroll himself as a catechumen. Perhaps he would
learn more from this bishop who personally instructed his catechumens.[290] Augustine had found the spiritual father for whom he had
been searching and for whom Monica had been praying.

Bishop Ambrose was learned in the philosophy of Plato. Augustine,
up to this point, had been more a student of literature than philosophy. Now he decided to explore the works of Plato and his disciple,
Plotinus. In them, he found two important things: a new idea of God
as pure spirit and of evil not as a dark entity opposed to God, as
the Manichaeans had taught, but as a nonentity, as the privation, or
absence, of good. These two insights were the intellectually necessary
steps he needed to bring him to the threshold of the baptistry. But
they did not give him the strength to step over that threshold. He
could not lawfully marry his mistress for they were not of the same
social class. But neither could he live without sex: "I was an unhappy
young man, wretched as at the beginning of my adolescence when
I prayed to you for chastity and said: 'Grant me chastity and continence, but not yet!'"[291]

Augustine was an intensely social person. One of his best friends
from Africa, Alypius, was living with him and his family. One day,
during the period Augustine was stalled in this no-man's-land of
indecision, another African friend dropped in to visit Augustine and

---

290. For an example of Ambrose's teaching to the newly baptized, see his treatises *On the
Mysteries* and *On the Sacraments* available at www.crossroadsinitiative.com.
291. *Confessions*, 8.7.17.

Alypius. As he sat down, he was surprised to see a book of the letters of St. Paul lying on the table. This visitor, Ponticianus, was a baptized Christian and so was delighted to see that Augustine and Alypius were reading Scripture. He went on to tell them about a new book so many people were talking about. By an Egyptian bishop named Athanasius, it told the story of Antony, the monk from Egypt who had abandoned everything after hearing God speak to him through the Scriptures. This simple monk, though illiterate, had gone on to work wonders and achieve great heights of holiness. Hearing about Antony, Augustine felt a sense of shame. He turned to Alypius, who also was unbaptized and said, "What is wrong with us?... Uneducated people are rising up and capturing heaven [Matthew 11:12], and we with our high culture without any heart—see where we roll in the mud of flesh and blood."[292] Augustine ran out to the garden clutching the book of St. Paul's letters. Alypius followed right behind him. In the garden, the friends sat in silence, side by side, as Augustine trembled with successive waves of agitation. Finally breaking into tears, he left Alypius to find a place further into the garden where, privately, he could give full vent to his emotions. As he sat alone under a fig tree, his weeping was interrupted by the singsong voice of a child chanting over and over again, "Take and read, take and read!" He could remember no childhood game that contained such a phrase. It suddenly dawned on him that this could be a message to him from on high. He remembered how God had spoken to Antony through a passage from Scripture, so he hastened back to Alypius, next to whom he'd left the volume of St. Paul's letters. Picking up the book, he opened it at random and read the first line his eyes ran across:

292. *Confessions*, 8.9.21.

"Not in riots and drunken parties, not in eroticism and indecencies, not in strife and rivalry, but put on the Lord Jesus Christ and make no provision for the flesh in its lusts" (Romans 13:13–14). "It was," he later writes, "as if a light of relief from all anxiety flooded into my heart."[293] Mysteriously, he knew he now possessed the strength to do what he must do.

The following Easter vigil, Augustine, his son, Adeodatus, and Alypius were baptized by St. Ambrose and received for the first time the "bread of heaven." Their plan was to return to Thagaste and live a quiet life of contemplation in Monica's humble house. They made their way to Ostia, the port of Rome, to prepare for the long voyage back to Africa. But there, Monica fell ill. Seeing her son baptized as a Catholic was the one thing for which she had been living. Having witnessed that miracle, she was now ready to depart for her heavenly homeland. She died and was buried at Ostia. Augustine wrote: "I cannot speak enough of the love she had for me. She suffered greater pains in my spiritual pregnancy than when she bore me in the flesh."[294]

Drafted into Service

Augustine and his band of brothers eventually made their way back to Thagaste to carry out their plan. They became known as the *Servii Dei*, or the Servants of God. For several years, Augustine enjoyed the community life of contemplation with his spiritual family. But the tranquil happiness was not to last. Both Nebridius, one of Augustine's two best friends, and his young son Adeodatus, fell sick and died.[295] Shortly thereafter, in 391, Augustine made a journey sixty miles

---

293. *Confessions,* 8.12.29.
294. *Confessions,* 5.9.16.
295. Augustine, in his *Confessions,* does not provide us with any more information than this.

north to the port of Hippo Regius.[296] His mission was to convince a friend who was lodged there to come back to Thagaste with him to join the Servants of God community. While in town, doing his best to maintain a low profile, he quietly slipped into church to attend the liturgy, standing inconspicuously at the back of the church. He evidently was recognized by both bishop and congregation. At the time of the homily, the elderly bishop lamented how badly he needed a priest to assist him, but alas, candidates were lacking. At that moment, Augustine found himself being literally dragged forward by a shouting mob of churchgoers until he was before the bishop's chair. Thus, Augustine, much like his hero Ambrose, was pressed into service as a priest.

Augustine could not live alone. So the old bishop, grateful for his help, agreed to give him a house adjoining the cathedral garden, where what was left of the Servants of God could reside with Augustine. Their program was to carry on the apostolic life described in Acts 2 and 4, and they planned to share all property and carry out together a common life of prayer, study, and service to the Church. For the next forty years, the dining room of this house would host many guests from all over the empire. The diet was strictly vegetarian; the true feast was the daily conversation that took place around this table. Augustine had a prohibition against gossip, which he strictly enforced. He even had these verses carved into the table to remind his guests:

---

296. Modern-day Annaba, Algeria. It was called "Regius" because it had once been the residence of the kings of Numidia.

Whoever thinks that he is able,
To nibble at the life of absent friends,
Must know that he's unworthy of this table.[297]

This house would be a literal seminary: Augustine would cultivate fruitful vines here that would be transplanted to bear fruit in other dioceses. His best friend Alypius, for example, would become bishop of their former hometown of Thagaste.

Within a few years, Bishop Valerius saw to it that Augustine was consecrated coadjutor bishop.[298] By A.D. 397, Valerius had died and Augustine was the sole bishop of Hippo. From this moment on, a crushing weight of demands would press upon the man who had once sought a life of contemplative serenity. It was customary at that time in history for Catholic bishops to be called upon to arbitrate everyday disputes between citizens. They were what everyone, even non-Catholics, desired in such circumstances: impartial, honest mediators who judged cases swiftly and without cost. So, much like Moses and the judges he selected in the Bible (see Exodus 18), Augustine spent a good part of each day listening to disputes between landowners, children fighting over their parents' wills, and the like. Then, there was the task of frequent preaching and pastoral care. Finally, there was the difficult business of responding to heresy and crisis.

Amidst all this, Augustine sought time for personal prayer, friendship, and writing. Now he understood what his hero Ambrose had had to contend with.

---

297. Possidius, *Life of Augustine*, 22. 6–7. Possidius was one of the residents of Augustine's house who wrote this biography after Augustine's death.
298. Assistant bishop with the right of succession once the principal bishop died or retired.

The Revolutionary Confessions

Ten years after his conversion, in the first few years of his episcopacy, Augustine wrote a book about his life entitled *The Confessions*. By "confessions," Augustine meant the confession of his own sinfulness, the confession of his praise for God's astounding mercy, and testimony of the miracles that God has done in his life. Nothing quite like it had ever appeared before in Latin or Greek literature. Its uniqueness is what has distinguished it as a classic of Western civilization. However, its uniqueness has also bewildered and put off many people. This is sometimes because people expect it to be a biography. But it is not really a biography, at least not in the conventional sense of the term. It is really the history of Augustine's heart, the recounting of his inner experience, the evolution of his will and feelings.

Up till this point, most stories of conversion in the early Church had followed a standard pattern: sin, conversion, baptism, all is made new. End of story. But Augustine's spiritual odyssey is far more complicated. The conversion starts with Cicero, detours with the Manichaeans, gets back on track with Ambrose, and proceeds through Plato, Plotinus, Antony of the desert, and St. Paul. It is not a straight line but a meandering path with twists and turns. Moreover, despite having experienced the critically important moment of baptism, the process is still not over. Augustine's conversion is an ongoing journey of progressive healing, of continual combat. Now a Catholic bishop, Augustine is still confessing his temptation, vulnerabilities, and his faults, to the glory of God. The pathos and depth of feeling in the story are most extraordinary. Augustine's passion for sexual union, the biggest obstacle to his freedom, is not extinguished, but is rather redirected to a passion for union with God. His prayers to God are imbued with a red-hot intensity and employ the love-language of the heart:

Late have I loved you, O Beauty ever ancient, ever new, late have I loved you! You were within me, but I was outside, and it was there that I searched for you. In my unloveliness I plunged into the lovely things which you created. You were with me, but I was not with you. Created things kept me from you; yet if they had not been in you they would not have been at all. You called, you shouted, and you broke through my deafness. You flashed, you shone, and you dispelled my blindness. You breathed your fragrance on me; I drew in breath and now I pant for you. I have tasted you, now I hunger and thirst for more. You touched me, and I burned for your peace.[299]

This reminiscence of the stages of his inner life that Augustine undertakes at the beginning of his episcopal ministry launches an entirely new genre of Christian literature. The *Retractations*, which he wrote toward the end of his tenure as bishop, launched another new genre. In this book, he goes back over his works and corrects them, noting where he has changed his mind or enlarged his perspective. But these two works at the beginning and end of his career have something in common: The *Retractations* show that Augustine's journey does not end with his fig tree experience, or his baptism, or his election to the episcopacy. The *Retractations* are necessary because Augustine never stopped developing. It was natural for him to admit that his earlier statements needed to be amended, corrected, and qualified.

During Augustine's life as a bishop, he seldom had the leisure to write on a topic simply according to his intellectual interest. First and foremost, his efforts had to be directed toward the pressing pastoral and doctrinal problems that confronted his church in given moments during his episcopacy. And dominating Augustine's landscape in

---

299. *Confessions*, 10.27.38.

North Africa loomed two heresies that occupied him for most of his life as a bishop. The issues facing the West at this time did not pertain to the Trinity and the Person of Christ, as was the case in the East. Rather, they had more to do with the Church, its sacraments, and the interplay between grace and free will.

True Church, True Sacraments

Africa had always been the seedbed of rigorism. Tertullian had become the spokesman of the Montanists, a rigorist sect. Cyprian had struggled with a rigorist schism of great proportions. But these movements were dwarfed by the movement that rent the African church in two after the Great Persecution. First of all, there was significant difference of opinion as to what made a person an apostate or, in other words, one guilty of denying Christ. Everyone agreed that those who offered the required sacrifices to the gods were included in this category. But how about those who handed over the Scriptures to the police? How about those who, when asked for the Scriptures, had handed over heretical writings or Greek medical texts? Were these also traitors (from the Latin *traditor*, meaning "one who hands over")?

A very large group of North African churchmen saw all of these acts as equally guilty. They accused Caecilian, who became the bishop of Carthage in A.D. 311, of having been ordained by one such "traitor." In their view, not only did the traitor fail to transmit the grace of ordination to Caecilian, but he instead infected Caecilian with the guilt of his filthy sin. Caecilian therefore could not bestow sacramental grace. Instead, he contaminated all who were in communion with him.

The rigorist bishops who leveled this accusation therefore ordained a "true" bishop for Carthage to provide the true Church with valid sacraments. The group came to be known as the Donatists after

Donatus, one of the bishops who led the movement. The bishop of Rome recognized Caecilian as the authentic Catholic bishop as did Emperor Constantine. The Donatists appealed the ruling, and a council was convened in France which upheld the decision of the pope and emperor. Still, the Donatists persisted in identifying themselves as the only true Church, since it was the only Church that was truly holy. The so-called "Catholics," claimed the Donatists, were an anti-church, a church of Judas, who compromised with the world. When Augustine arrived in Hippo, the Catholics were in the minority in the city, as they were in most of North Africa.

There was the pastoral and political problem of reconciling the Donatists. Augustine was certainly involved in this process. But the more important issues were theological in kind: What does it mean that the Church is holy, and on what do the sacraments depend for their authenticity?

Augustine provided answers that clarified the apostolic Church's long-standing tradition relative to the Church and the sacraments.

First of all, the Donatists saw themselves as the true "Catholics" (from the Greek word meaning "whole") because they alone kept the "whole" Law of God in its purity. Because of the compromise of the so-called Catholics with the world through entanglement with the empire, the true Church of the martyrs was reduced to the faithful little sect of Donatists in Africa. For Augustine, the Catholic Church was destined by God to spread over the whole world and offer Christ's salvation to everyone. A sectarian mentality for him never could be authentically Catholic. In commenting on one of the psalms, he alludes to the Donatists who had a cathedral down the street from his: "The clouds roll with thunder, that the House of the Lord shall be built throughout the earth; and these frogs sit in their marsh and croak—'we are the only Christians!'"[300]

The Donatists were content for the Church to be the ark where the select few could ride out the flood in safety as they watched the mass of humanity perish in the waves. For Augustine, the Church Catholic was the new family of God, called to restore to humanity the unity it had lost through Adam's sin. It had been born in Pentecost where the preaching in many tongues (see Acts 2) was a symbol that Babel had been undone through this gathering of men from every tribe, tongue, people, and nation. This new universal family of God was to spread everywhere and reach out to everyone. The Church was holy because it is the body of Christ, the Holy One. The head communicates his objective holiness to his members, who each subjectively appropriate it progressively more deeply though a dynamic journey of conversion. This journey often involves detours and mishaps, as Augustine's did. The Church, for Augustine, was a hospital for sinners, not an exclusive club for saints.

The sacraments, for the Donatists, communicated a holiness that was a personal property of the minister. If he was a sinner, he could not possibly be a conduit of God's grace. Augustine responds that if the sacrament's validity is dependent on the unknowable moral purity of the minister, we find ourselves in a quite impossible situation. The sacraments are not really works of the minister at all (*ex opere operantis*) but, rather works of Christ, who instituted them, and so have their own intrinsic efficacy (*ex opere operato*) that is independent of the personal holiness of the minister or lack thereof. The priest or bishop who is ordained receives a permanent charism to function in the place of Christ (*in persona Christi*) for the good of

---

300. Augustine, *Exposition on Psalm 95*, 11.

others. While the minister may lose his own soul through unrepentant, serious sin, he cannot lose this charism, even should he go into schism or heresy. In this way, Augustine helped the Church in his own day to understand the apostolic tradition it had lived and passed down for centuries. Since ancient times, there had been a widespread custom not to require rebaptism of those coming into the Church who had been previously baptized by schismatics, like the Donatists. Now the Church could finally explain the reason for this practice.

Grace, Free Will, and Original Sin

When Augustine published *The Confessions* around A.D. 397, the book made its way rather quickly around the empire. It caused a sensation. But not all the reactions were positive. A lay ascetic named Pelagius, who had settled in Italy, was troubled by Augustine's contention that he was helpless and needed grace to change. To Pelagius, this sounded like an excuse. God gave us his law; he would not require of us what was not within our nature to do. Jesus never would have told us to be perfect as our Heavenly Father is perfect (see Matthew 5:48), if it were impossible to do so. He gave us free will and expects us to use it. It is not a matter of whether you can or can't obey God; it is a matter of whether you will or won't. Perfection is possible, and if it is possible, it is obligatory. As far as Pelagius is concerned, it's just that simple. Grace is a wonderful thing, but it is not necessary. It is a sort of bonus God gives a person for good behavior. In other words, for Pelagius and his followers, God helps those who help themselves. A fitting motto for Pelgianism would be "Just do it!"

For Augustine, God helps those who *can't* help themselves. From the time we are born, we find our freedom is impaired by a sort of downward tug, whereby we are drawn to prefer lower things, even sordid things, to God. This tendency Augustine calls "concupiscence." It is often mistakenly interpreted as sexual desire, but concupiscence is not natural appetites at all, but rather their perverted, inordinate, and twisted expression. This tendency toward self-gratification at the expense of others we can discern in ourselves even as children, prior to committing deliberate sins, which of course further inflame this tendency. Such concupiscence is one of the consequences of the sin of Adam that is passed on to each of us through birth. The other thing that is passed on through original sin is the state of separation from God caused by this sin. We are born needing salvation, which is the reason, says Augustine, that infant baptism has been practiced in the life of the Church.[301]

The point is that our wills need to be healed, and this can only be a free gift of God's grace. This grace comes through the sacraments, of course; to step into the baptismal waters, we need grace. To even want to enroll in the catechumenate, we need grace. To even begin to think about the things of God and attempt to please him, we need grace. We need grace, says Augustine, to take the very first step toward God.

For Pelagius, we not only can take the first step toward God, but after receiving baptismal grace, whatever weakness that had come to us through our own sin and ignorance is completely and totally healed, leaving us no excuse for further sin.

For Augustine, though the guilt of sin is totally and completely wiped away in baptism, the newly baptized is just beginning a long

---

301. Infant baptism was the earlier tradition witnessed to by Cyprian and Hippolytus. After the edict of Milan, the new custom arose of postponing baptism out of fear of sinning gravely after receiving baptism. The sacrament of penance was much more arduous in those days, as the public penance of Theodosius attests.

and precarious convalescence in the "inn" of the Church.[302] The process will only be completed in that final and total healing which is the resurrection of the dead.

For the Pelagians, total freedom of choice and the power of complete self-determination are simply assumed. Pelagius's disciple Celestius puts it this way: "It is the easiest thing in the world to change your will by an act of the will."[303] For Augustine, on the other hand, freedom is something that is progressively achieved. Augustine, as one biographer points out, will "always speak of freedom in comparatives, of 'greater freedom,' 'fuller freedom,' 'perfect freedom.'"[304] The Christian life, for Augustine, is a lifelong process of the recovery of freedom and of healing and transformation of the will that is initiated by grace, sustained by grace, and brought to completion by grace. Against the Manichaeans, he had argued that human beings are responsible for their actions and have free will. Against the Pelagians, he argues that grace is necessary if that free will is ever to become fully free.

Pelagius himself visited Carthage briefly, then moved to Palestine. He soon faded from the picture, as Arius had a century earlier, but his thought lived on and was developed by several of his disciples who found in Augustine their archenemy. The Church, through successive popes and councils in Carthage, Ephesus, and Orange (in Gaul, or modern France), rejected the teaching of the Pelagians and recognized the voice of the apostles in the words of Augustine.

---

302. Augustine, *Sermon 131,* 6 and *Sermon 151,* 4–5 alluding to the story of the Good Samaritan in Luke 10:25–37.
303. Quoted by Augustine, *On Nature and Grace,* 30, 34.
304. Augustine, *Letter 157,* 2, 8, analyzed by Peter Brown, *Augustine of Hippo* (Berkeley, Calif.: University of California Press, 1967), p. 373.

....

A Severe Mercy

When Ambrose was on his deathbed, a prominent general prophesied, "The day that this man dies, destruction hangs over Italy."[305] The year was A.D. 397 and Augustine was writing *The Confessions* in the tranquility of North Africa. Thirteen years later barbarian hordes pillaged their way through Italy and sacked the ancient city of Rome. Pelagius and other prominent Romans came to Carthage as refugees. But in 430, the destruction finally reached North Africa. A barbarian tribe of Arian faith crossed the Strait of Gibraltar and headed straight to Hippo, destroying everything in its path. So brutal was their marauding that their very name, the Vandals, has come to signify those who deface and destroy for the perverse pleasure of it. After pillaging the small towns and estates in the countryside, they surrounded Hippo and laid siege to the city. By the mercy of God, Augustine, who had remained with his flock, did not live to witness the city's tragic destruction. In the third month of the siege, he took ill. He knew it was the end. He asked his brothers to write the penitential psalms on the walls in his room and leave him alone as much as possible. For several days, he prayed those psalms and wept for his own sins and those of his people. His last letter was to the clergy of the diocese, urging them to stay with their people no matter what might come. A few days later, he was gone. Ten months later, the city's walls were breached, and it was destroyed.

Augustine's decisive intervention in the debate provoked by Pelagius earned him the title "the Doctor of Grace." But Augustine's legacy is not limited to his teaching on grace and free will, nor his teaching on the sacraments and the Church. For despite the arduous pastoral

---

305. Spoken by Count Stilicho, the guardian of Emperor Honorius.

schedule that he kept up for forty years, Augustine had nevertheless managed to write on just about every aspect of Christian doctrine and culture. *The Confessions* includes a philosophy of time, and his book *The City of God* lays out a philosophy of history. His book on the Trinity provides new ways of looking at the procession of the Holy Spirit and the understanding of the Three Persons. We could go on and on. No Church Father except Origen produced anything remotely resembling Augustine's work in breadth, depth, and impact on posterity. It is estimated that Augustine preached three to four thousand homilies in his years in Hippo. Only about five hundred survive. But when you put these surviving homilies together with his extant letters and treatises, the corpus of Augustine's work numbers over four million words! Possidius, his friend and biographer, put it well: "He who says he has read all of Augustine…lies."

In an amazing act of divine providence, the Vandals, though they did not spare Hippo, somehow, for some reason, spared the cathedral library.[306] This invaluable corpus of writing became the lifeline of the Western Church throughout the subsequent dark ages of chaos and barbarian domination. Over the course of the next six or seven hundred years, the monasteries in Western Europe were the only places where the light of learning was kept burning. And what were the monks reading and copying? The Bible, of course. And the works of Augustine.

---

306. Of course, many of Augustine's writings had already been copied and were in homes and libraries all over the empire by now. So much would have survived even if the Vandals had destroyed all that they found.

The Preacher with the Golden Tongue

The Christian pedigree of Antioch is impressive indeed. Paul and Barnabas had made Antioch their missionary base. Peter and Ignatius had led the Church there before dying in Rome. But in the middle of the fourth century, a baby was born in Antioch who would add another gem to the city's crown.

This child, named John, was the son of the city's military commander, who died a few months after his son was born. Given the family's noble status, the mother had the resources to pay for the best education. The instructor chosen for the boy was a rhetorician named Libanius, the most famous rhetorician of his day. But by the time John was a teenager, Libanius had to concede that his student had surpassed him in both eloquence and power of persuasion. The pagan professor only had one misgiving about his student. "It is a pity," he remarked, "that the boy is a Christian—otherwise he could be my successor."

Despite his rosy prospects for success, before the age of twenty, John had lost his enthusiasm for a life in law or public service. He had met some hermits outside the city and, inspired by their example, decided to join them. For four years, he was mentored by wise, experienced monks. Finally, he set out to live in complete solitude. For two years, he practiced extreme self-denial, spending all his time in prayer. However, the severity of his austerities took a toll on his health, and he was forced to return to the city to convalesce. As he was regaining his strength, he was noticed by the bishop, who promptly ordained him to the diaconate. In A.D. 386, the bishop raised him to the priesthood and assigned him to preach in the most popular church in Antioch. John was about forty years of age.[307]

The following year, Emperor Theodosius, who had to fund a new war to repel an invasion of Italy,[308] increased taxes that already had been a crushing burden to many. A mob in Antioch, furious at the tax increase, defaced the city's statues of the emperor and the imperial family. Theodosius announced his intent to punish the city severely for this outrage. Everyone knew what this could mean: Bloodshed was probable, total destruction of the city was likely. The bishop immediately rushed to Theodosius's palace in Constantinople to plead for mercy. John was left with the people of the city, who were beside themselves with fear. In the face of impending disaster, he led the people in prayer and preached a series of powerful sermons. In these twenty-one homilies, *On the Statues,* John consoled the people but also upbraided them for the vices that had led to the crisis. Fortunately, he received good news, which he was privileged to announce to the people: The emperor had accepted the town's apology and would relent, canceling the planned punishment. By means of his efforts throughout this crisis, John had won the hearts of the people, and his reputation as a preacher was now soundly established.

The Preacher of Antioch

For the next ten years, John continued to preach daily in Antioch, sometimes twice a day. Stenographers committed these sermons to

---

307. Augustine, ten years his junior, was a catechumen in Milan at this time.
308. The foe was Maximus Magnus, whose invasion of Italy was delayed for a season by the appeal of St. Ambrose. See chapter 20 above.

writing, and a vast quantity of his work survives today. In fact, we have more writings from John than from any other writer of the early Greek Church. One of the most notable themes struck by John is the centrality of the Eucharistic sacrifice in the life of the Church. He insisted that the consecrated elements truly become the Body and Blood of Christ:

> It is not man who causes what is present to become the Body and Blood of Christ, but Christ Himself who was crucified for us. The priest is the representative when he pronounces those words, but the power and the grace are those of the Lord. "This is my Body," he says. This word changes the things that lie before us; and as that sentence "increase and multiply," once spoken, extends through all time and gives to our nature the power to reproduce itself; even so that saying "This is my Body," once uttered, does at every table in the Churches from that time to the present day, and even till Christ's coming, make the sacrifice complete.[309]

In a Christmas homily, John reminded his hearers that he whose birth is celebrated on this feast is given to them in the sacrament which therefore must be approached with fear and trembling: "Reflect, O man, what sacrificial flesh you take in your hand! To what table you will approach. Remember that you, though dust and ashes, do receive the Blood and the Body of Christ."[310]

John most often preached a series of homilies on given books of the Bible. His sermons on the Psalms are the highlight of his preaching on the Old Testament. His sermons on the Gospel of Matthew form the earliest complete commentary on the first Gospel. But where John

---

309. *Homilies 1 and 2 on the Betrayal of Judas* (*de proditione Judae*), PG (*Patrologiae Gracea*) 49, 393–418, n. 6.
310. *Homily on the Birth of the Lord*, 7. See also *Homily 46 on John*, 3.

shines the most is in his work on St. Paul. Nearly half of the writings we have from him were sermons on the writings of the apostle to the Gentiles. He preached on first and second Corinthians, Galatians, Ephesians, Colossians, Titus, and Timothy. But his greatest work of all was on the Letter to the Romans, by far the best commentary on this book from the days of the early Church. He began and ended his commentary with exuberant praise for this apostle who was truly his model and his hero. Though he was born in the city where Paul began his ministry, he had a special devotion to city where Paul's life ended. He concludes his commentary with this tribute to Rome, the city of both Peter and Paul:

> I love Rome even for this, although indeed one has other grounds for praising it, both for its greatness, and its antiquity, and its beauty and its populousness, and for its power, and for its wealth, and for its successes in war. But I let all this pass, and esteem it blessed on this account, that both in his lifetime he [Paul] wrote to them, and loved them so, and talked with them while he was with us, and brought his life to a close there. Wherefore the city is more notable upon this ground, than upon all others together. And as a body great and strong, it has as two glistening eyes the bodies of these Saints. Not so bright is the heaven, when the sun sends forth its rays, as is the city of Rome, sending out these two lights into all parts of the world.[311]

John perhaps was attracted to Paul most especially because John himself was so much like him—tender, sincere, yet fiery, even severe at times. He was as bold as Paul in calling out sin and challenging people to change. His preaching, like Paul's, was eminently practical. Though a monk and committed to an intense life of prayer

---

311. John Chrysostom, *Homily 32 on Romans.* The second light was, of course, Peter.

and self-denial, he was uncommonly in touch with the challenges and temptations of the everyday life of the lay people to whom he preached. Though celibate, he highly prized marriage and family life and devoted much of his preaching to the subject. He recognized that many mores of his society regarding marriage, love, and family were contrary to Christian values. A double standard existed for men and women regarding marital fidelity. Sexual abuse of female slaves by their masters was an accepted occurrence. Wedding receptions, even of Christians, often featured drunkenness, bawdy shenanigans, and hymns in honor of the pagan goddess Aphrodite. John was not afraid to confront these established features of the culture of the day and challenge people to abandon them and create a new, authentically Christian culture of love, marriage, and family. This ruffled feathers then as such an appeal would do today. John responded to those who thought he was being unreasonable:

> I know that some people think I am burdensome and difficult, giving advice like this and uprooting ancient custom. But I do not care at all about their objections. I do not seek your favor but your benefit. I do not ask for the applause of praise, but the profit of wisdom. Let no one tell me that this is the custom. Where sin is boldly committed, forget about custom. If evil things are done, even if the custom is ancient, abolish them. If they are not evil, even if they are not customary, introduce them and establish them.[312]

The Intrepid Patriarch

While John was exercising his priestly ministry in Antioch, things were changing in the imperial city of Constantinople. The council

---

312. *Sermon on Marriage*, in *John Chrysostom on Marriage and Family Life*, trans. Catharine P. Roth (Crestwood, N.Y.: St. Vladimir's Seminary Press, 1986), p. 82.

that had met there in A.D. 381 had passed a law vastly increasing the influence of the bishop of the new capital, making him first in honor among Eastern bishops, a patriarch[313] second only to the pope in Rome. Gregory Nazianzen had resigned his post as the city's bishop, so Emperor Theodosius chose an officer in the imperial bureaucracy to replace him. Nectarius was a good man but a mild and rather unremarkable successor to the great Gregory. Theodosius also had a lackluster successor. When he died in A.D. 395, his son Arcadius, a shy and somewhat spineless boy of eighteen, took over rule of the East.

In A.D. 398, the patriarch of Constantinople died. Arcadius was advised to make the now-famous preacher of Antioch the new patriarch of Constantinople. John was not interested. So the emperor arranged for him to be, as it were, kidnapped and brought to Constantinople. When John arrived, he submitted to the wish of the youthful emperor and was consecrated bishop of the city.

John was taken aback at the laxity that he found among the clergy and high-ranking laity who filled the imperial court. He cut down the lavish spending of the bishop's household, abolishing the practice of his predecessor of treating the clergy and prominent laity to elegant banquets. The money saved was dedicated to the relief of the poor of the city. In one of his sermons, John indicated that there were about 100,000 Christians in the imperial city and over 50,000 people living in poverty. He was aghast at the great disparity between the haughty lifestyle of the wealthy Christians and the destitution of so many of their fellow Christians. Some of the wealthy were happy to give a chalice or marble statue to the Church, but would never think

---

313. The bishops of the historic Christian centers of Rome, Constantinople, Alexandria, Antioch, and Jerusalem had special status officially recognized by the first Council of Constantinople in 381 and subsequently came to be referred to as patriarchs.

of donating food or medical care to the poor. Again and again, John addressed the issue of almsgiving in his sermons:

> Do you want to honor Christ's body? Then do not scorn him in his nakedness, nor honor him here in the church with silken garments while neglecting him outside where he is cold and naked. For he who said: This is my body, and made it so by his words, also said: "You saw me hungry and did not feed me, and inasmuch as you did not do it for one of these, the least of my brothers, you did not do it for me" (Matt 25:34ff).... Let us learn, therefore, to be men of wisdom and to honor Christ as he desires. For a person being honored finds greatest pleasure in the honor he desires, not in the honor we think best. Peter thought he was honoring Christ when he refused to let him wash his feet; but what Peter wanted was not truly an honor, quite the opposite! Give him the honor prescribed in his law by giving your riches to the poor. For God does not want golden vessels but golden hearts.[314]

The year after John arrived in the city, there was a major uproar in the palace. Though the young Arcadius was technically emperor, the real power behind the throne had been his chief advisor, Eutropius. However someone within the palace accused Eutropius of a treasonous plot, and Arcadius was persuaded to have him executed. Soon after, the emperor's young but strong-willed wife, Eudoxia, gave herself the title "Augusta," the female form of Augustus. Next, she began wearing the purple vestments of an emperor. Her image even began to appear on coins minted in Constantinople. Everyone knew that this vain woman was now the real power behind the throne and had probably been the one behind the execution of Eutropius. The

---

314. *Homily 50, 3–4, On the Gospel of Matthew, PG* 58, 508–509.

elite of the city pandered to her conceit and avoided crossing her at any cost—the emperor's right-hand man had evidently gotten in her way and paid for it with his life.

Bishop John was not about to be intimidated by this display of ruthlessness. God had brought him to Constantinople because the city needed reform, and he would not back down. In light of the needs of the poor and vanity of the rich, John took aim at luxury while preaching on one of Paul's letters:

> Do you delight in expensive clothes, or golden jewelry? Remember Paul's bonds, and these things will seem to you as more worthless than a prostitute's filthy rags, or a handful of withered grass. Do you spend long hours adorning your hair, and painting your face with cosmetics, hoping to make yourself beautiful? Think of Paul's squalor in prison, and you will burn with desire for his beauty. You will then consider worldly beauty to be ugly, and will bitterly long to share Paul's chains. Think of his face streaming with tears. Day and night for three years he never ceased his weeping (Acts 20:31). Imitate his weeping. Make your face bright with tears. Weep for your sins: your anger, your loss of self-control, your love of revelry. Imitate Paul's tears, and you will laugh to scorn the vanities of this passing life. Christ blessed these tears, when He said, "Blessed are you that weep now, for you shall laugh" (Lk. 6:21). Nothing is sweeter than these tears; they are more to be desired than any laughter. Pray earnestly for these tears, so that when others sin, your heart may be broken for them.[315]

---

315. *Homily 12 on Colossians*, 4:18, in St. John Chrysostom, *On Marriage and Family Life*, 74.

The common people cheered such preaching and loved their new patriarch. But many among the clergy and privileged classes resented him and resisted his call to reform. Some whispered in the ear of the empress that John's railing against women's adornments were directed at her. She was not amused. She needed to find an episcopal ally to take John down and was pleased to find one in the patriarch of Alexandria, Theophilus. Prior to the Council of Constantinople, Alexandria had been the greatest Christian see after Rome. The great city of Origen and Athanasius was now playing second fiddle to a city that had been no more than a fishing village seventy years earlier.[316] Hence, the bishop of Alexandria already had a reason to resent the patriarch of Constantinople. Theophilus's dislike of John turned to rage when he received a summons to Constantinople to answer charges that he had unjustly excommunicated a group of Egyptian monks. Since John was the chairman of the inquiry, Theophilus blamed John for the whole thing and vowed to turn the tables on him. Eudoxia met with him and gave him the opportunity to do so. The next year, the empress filed twenty-nine trumped-up charges against John and invited Theophilus back to be his judge. When John refused to appear before this kangaroo court, he was deposed and ordered into exile. His people were wild with outrage. The day before he departed for exile, he did his best to comfort his grieving people:

> The waters have risen and severe storms are upon us, but we do not fear drowning, for we stand firmly upon a rock. Let the sea rage, it cannot break the rock. Let the waves rise, they cannot

---

316. Constantine in 330 moved his capital from Nicomedia to a rather insignificant town strategically located on the Bosphorus, the strait between the Black Sea and the Sea of Marmara. The town formally known as Byzantium was renamed Constantinople. The Eastern Roman Empire from this time is hence referred to by historians as the Byzantine Empire.

sink the boat of Jesus. What are we to fear? Death? Life to me means Christ, and death is gain. Exile? 'The earth and its fullness belong to the Lord. The confiscation of goods? We brought nothing into this world, and we shall surely take nothing from it. I have only contempt for the world's threats. I find its blessings laughable. I have no fear of poverty, no desire for wealth. I am not afraid of death nor do I long to live, except for your good. I concentrate therefore on the present situation, and I urge you, my friends, to have confidence.

Do you not hear the Lord saying: Where two or three are gathered in my name, there am I in their midst? Will he be absent, then, when so many people united in love are gathered together? I have his promise; I am surely not going to rely on my own strength! I have what he has written; that is my staff, my security, my peaceful harbor. Let the world be in upheaval. I hold to his promise and read his message; that is my protecting wall and garrison. What message? Know that I am with you always, until the end of the world!

If Christ is with me, whom shall I fear? Though the waves and the sea and the anger of princes are roused against me, they are less to me than a spider's web. Indeed, unless you, my brothers, had detained me, I would have left this very day. For I always say "Lord, your will be done"; not what this fellow or that would have me do, but what you want me to do. That is my strong tower, my immovable rock, my staff that never gives way. If God wants something, let it be done! If he wants me to stay here, I am grateful. But wherever he wants me to be, I am no less grateful.[317]

The next day, John was gone, but not for long. That night an earthquake rocked the imperial city, and Eudoxia saw it as a warning from

---

317. John Chrysostom, *Ante exsilium* (Sermon before Exile), 1–3, PG 52, 427–430.

on high. She immediately petitioned her compliant husband to bring John back. So exactly one day after he departed, the beloved bishop returned to town, and the whole city went out to welcome him.

The favor of the vain empress lasted only a short while. Two months later, she had a silver statue of herself erected directly in front of John's cathedral. The dedication celebration deteriorated into raucous revelry and disrupted the divine liturgy that was taking place inside the cathedral. John could not remain silent in the face of this sacrilege. So a few days later, on the Feast of St. John the Baptist, he thundered from the pulpit: "Again Herodias raves; again she is troubled; she dances again; and again desires to receive John's head on a platter."[318]

John received a decree from the emperor disbarring him from preaching and celebrating the liturgy. He paid no heed. Next, he was forbidden to even set foot in a church building. He nevertheless continued to carry out his ministry. On Holy Saturday eve, as he baptized new Christians at the Easter vigil, troops broke into the church and mixed blood with the baptismal water. The frail old bishop found himself brutally dragged into remote exile in easternmost Turkey. Within a few months, the empress died from complications following childbirth. She was not yet thirty.

For the next two years, John, though broken in health, was comforted in his exile by a steady stream of pilgrims who had traveled all the way from Antioch to pay homage to one they considered a living saint. Fearful of John's influence over these visitors, the emperor in 407 determined to completely isolate him in the remote territory east of the Black Sea. But John's health finally gave out and he died on the way. His last words were "Glory to God for all things!"

---

318. Socrates, *Ecclesiastical History*, 18.

....

Chrysostom

Before he was sent off into his final exile, John had managed to send a letter of appeal to Rome. The pope wrote to the devious bishop of Alexandria stating that he did not accept the removal of John from his see. He demanded a synod be held with representatives from both West and East so that John's case could be impartially reviewed. When Bishop Theophilus refused, the pope excommunicated him as well as John's successor in Constantinople until such time as John's name was cleared and he was restored to a place of honor in the Eastern churches. Meanwhile, the popularity of this prophetic patriarch, who had stood up to Jezebel, increased by the day. His sufferings and unjust death only heightened his authority in the eyes of the people.

The hapless emperor Arcadius died only a few months after John. Thirty years later, John's remains were brought back to Constantinople in solemn procession. The new Emperor Theodosius II, son of Eudoxia, laid his head on the casket and begged forgiveness for the sin of his parents. John was buried in the Church of the Holy Apostles next to the remains of Saints Andrew, Luke, and Timothy, and Emperor Constantine.

John was later recognized as one of Three Holy Hierarchs of the Orthodox Church and, similarly, by Catholics as one of the four greatest Doctors of the Eastern Church.[319] Due to his great devotion to the sacrament of Christ's Body and Blood, he is also referred to by many in the West as "Doctor of the Eucharist." Within a century,

---

319. The Three Holy Hierarchs of Orthodoxy are Gregory Nazianzen, Basil, and John; the Catholic list of four Eastern Doctors adds Athanasius to these three.

an epithet was given him that has all but replaced his proper name. Acknowledging him as the greatest popular preacher of the East, it calls him "Chrysostom," meaning "golden-mouthed." To this day, the predominate liturgy celebrated in Eastern Churches, both Orthodox and Catholic, is known as the liturgy of St. John Chrysostom.

CHAPTER 23

Jerome and the Bible

D ioncletian's line dividing the Eastern from the Western Empire
passed right through the Balkan Peninsula. The Roman province of Illyricum,[320] across the Adriatic Sea from Italy, lay on the west
side of this line. So it was natural that, when it was time to send their
sons to university, Illyrians would look to Rome.

Thus, in the middle of the fourth century, a young man from
Illyricum arrived in Rome to learn the classics. Over the next few
years, this boy named Jerome picked up some Greek, for sure. But
what really distinguished this young scholar was the extent to which
he mastered the Latin language and its greatest authors, especially
Virgil and Cicero. By the time he finished his studies, he had developed a Latin style of extraordinary fluency and beauty.

From Cicero to Moses

His studies under a pagan schoolmaster, however, did not do much
to nourish the Christian spirit that his parents had tried to instill
in him. Though he customarily spent Sundays with some Christian
friends and would occasionally visit the tombs of martyrs, his devotion was not particularly deep. He did, however, submit to baptism
in Rome before relocating to Trier to pursue further studies. It was
there that Jerome encountered the monasticism that had begun to

---

320. Modern-day Slovenia, Croatia, and Albania.

spread like wildfire in the West thanks to Athanasius's *Life of Antony*. Jerome decided to dedicate himself to Christ as a monk and moved to Aquileia, Italy, not far from his hometown, where he spent several years in community with a number of equally zealous young friends.

The monastic light had come from the East, and it was to the East that Jerome was determined to go. So in A.D. 374 Jerome, accompanied by one of his friends, arrived in the historic city of Antioch. He soon found himself ill, and while in the throes of a fever, he had an alarming dream. He saw himself before the judgment seat of Christ. The question was put to him, "Who are you?" Jerome replied to the Lord, "I am a Christian." Jesus replied, "You lie—you are a Ciceronian. For where your treasure is, there is your heart as well." Jerome awoke from this dream badly shaken. Determined to detach himself from the Latin classics, he left the sophisticated atmosphere of Antioch and withdrew to the Syrian desert. There, he lived in solitude, doing penance and fighting temptations, especially those of the flesh. Near him lived another monk who was a converted Jew. In meeting him, Jerome had an inspiration: What better antidote to his attachment to Cicero than to learn the language of Moses? So he asked his fellow monk to tutor him and began the arduous work of learning a new alphabet, entirely new sounds, and a very different grammar:

> When my soul was on fire with bad thoughts,...I became a scholar to a monk who had been a Jew, to learn of him the Hebrew alphabet; and, from the judicious rules of Quintilian, the copious flowing eloquence of Cicero, the grave style of Fronto, and the smoothness of Pliny, I turned to this language of hissing and broken-winded words. What labour it cost me, what difficulties I went through, how often I despaired and left off, and how I began again to learn, both I myself who felt the burden can witness, and they also who lived with me. And I

thank our Lord, that I now gather such sweet fruit from the bitter sowing of those studies.[321]

Returning to Antioch after a few years of penance and study, the new Hebrew scholar was ordained a priest by the local bishop and taken by him to Constantinople where a council was about to begin. There, Jerome studied Scripture with the bishop, Gregory Nazianzen, and entered into discussions with another brilliant bishop, Gregory of Nyssa.

Secretary to Pope Damasus

Not long after the Council of Constantinople ended (A.D. 381), Jerome and his bishop sailed for Rome, where another council was to be held the following year. When they arrived, the aging pope, Damasus, took a liking to Jerome. Recognizing his great abilities, the pope insisted that Jerome become his personal secretary. As he went about his duties, Jerome found time to continue his Hebrew studies, tutored by a Roman rabbi. It was at this time that he began his first translations of the Bible. Since people in the West no longer, for the most part, knew Greek, it was necessary that they have a Latin translation of the Bible. From the time at least of Tertullian (c. A.D. 200), some rough Latin translations of the Bible had existed. But now, under Damasus, the liturgy had been translated from Greek to Latin.[322] That liturgy needed a Latin translation of the Gospels and the Psalms that was more dignified than the crude, choppy translation provided by the Old Latin version. Jerome's Latin style was

---

321. Jerome, *Letter 125*, 12.
322. The original language of the Roman liturgy had remained Greek for over three hundred years; bishops such as Damasus and Ambrose took the "liberal" step of translating the traditional liturgy into the new vernacular—Latin.

unsurpassed. And he, after his years in the East, knew Greek better than most and Hebrew better than any Christian in Rome. So Damasus either asked Jerome to begin a new translation or warmly encouraged the project when Jerome brought it to him. Jerome translated the Psalms and Gospels into a more accurate and refined Latin and, apparently, employed one of his students to translate the epistles.

Over the several years of service to Damasus, Jerome assumed a rather high profile in the city. He was an obviously brilliant scholar. And, as an expert in the new asceticism from the East,[323] he found an eager audience among a group of holy widows, including St. Marcella and St. Paula, who sought to make greater progress in the life of prayer and holiness.

Jerome, however, gained foes as well as fans. He was relentless in his condemnations of paganism and heresy, both of which existed in Rome, and as a result, he was disliked by pagans and heretics. But Jerome gained enemies among Catholic Christians as well, and the fault, in at least some cases, was Jerome's. Whereas John Chrysostom's tongue was golden, Jerome's was sharp. He was afflicted with an irascible nature that often got the better of him. Sincere and passionate as he was, it must be admitted that his words often lacked tact and, in some circumstances, charity. St. Marcella, who was his disciple and student, did not hesitate to rebuke him from time to time on this account.

When Pope Damasus died, Jerome expected to be elected as his successor. Instead, Siricius (who was not exactly Jerome's best friend) was chosen. When false and malicious rumors began to circulate about his relationship with his women disciples, Jerome decided

---

323. His several years as a hermit in the Syrian desert gave him firsthand experience with the Eastern monasticism that devout Christians wanted to know more about.

to return to his diocese in Antioch. His brother and several of his women disciples joined him. After arriving in Antioch, the troupe made a pilgrimage to Egypt where they visited the desert monasteries as well as the famous catechetical school in Alexandria. Then, in A.D. 386, they decided to settle in Bethlehem.

Community and Work in Bethlehem

The widow Paula, one of Jerome's companions, was from one of the wealthiest families of Rome. Her generosity made it possible for Jerome and his community to establish four adjacent monasteries, one for men and three for women. A hospital and a hostel for visitors were also constructed. They raised their own food, chanted the psalms in Hebrew, and prayed all together in a common chapel. Jerome took up residence in one of the natural caves adjoining the birth cave of our Lord. This put him directly next to the Church of the Nativity built over the place of Jesus's birth sixty years earlier by Constantine's mother. They were thrilled to be away from the tumult of Rome and able to concentrate on prayer in this center of pilgrimage. From the serenity of their Bethlehem retreat, Jerome wrote these words to St. Marcella, who had remained behind in Rome:

> The Armenians, the Persians, the peoples of India and Ethiopia, of Egypt, of Pontus, Cappadocia, Syria and Mesopotamia... they throng here and set us the example of every virtue. The languages differ but the religion is the same; there are as many different choirs singing the psalms as there are nations.... Here bread, and vegetables grown with our own hands, and milk, country fare, afford us plain and healthy food. In summer the trees give us shade. In autumn the air is cool and the fallen leaves restful. In spring our psalmody is sweeter for the singing of the birds. We do not lack wood when winter snow and cold

are upon us. Let Rome keep its crowds, let its arenas run with blood, its circuses go mad, its theatres wallow in sensuality.[324]

Here, Jerome was able to undertake his life's project: the translation of the Old Testament directly from Hebrew. The Old Testament of the Church had been the famous Greek translation of about 200 B.C. known as "the Septuagint."[325] But this translation, as Origen had realized, was not the only Greek translation and, so, could, in fact, be improved upon. Besides, all Greek translations needed to be compared to the Hebrew text. Origen had made parallel columns of the Hebrew Bible and all the Greek translations available to him. This work, called the *Hexapla*, along with Origen's entire library, was just seventy miles away in Caesarea. Jerome made the journey more than a few times to take advantage of this invaluable resource. He even consulted some rabbis in Bethlehem and utilized the Hebrew version of the Bible in current use by these rabbis. He finally finished this project in A.D. 405, nineteen years after his arrival in Bethlehem. The death of Paula in the prior year had dealt a heavy blow to Jerome and his community, but the life and the work went on.

Commentaries and Controversy

Jerome now set himself to tackle his next project—a commentary series on all the books of the prophets. He began his commentary on the book of Isaiah with these words:

> I interpret as I should, following the command of Christ: *Search the Scriptures,* and *Seek and you shall find.* Christ will not say to me what he said to the Jews: *You erred, not knowing the Scriptures*

---

324. Jerome, *Letter 43,* 3, to Marcella.
325. So called since legend had it that it was the work of seventy translators. It is often abbreviated as LXX.

and not knowing the power of God. For if, as Paul says, Christ is the power of God and the wisdom of God, and if the man who does not know Scripture does not know the power and wisdom of God, then ignorance of Scripture is ignorance of Christ.[326]

During this period, Jerome, who always relished a good fight, got embroiled in several theological disputes. He was already famous for the reply he made years earlier to a Roman layman named Helvidius. This man had alleged that, contrary to the Church's tradition,[327] Mary had borne other children after Jesus. Jerome could not believe that Helvidius, whom he called "an ignorant boor," had the nerve to insinuate that Joseph had "dared to touch the temple of God, the abode of the Holy Ghost, the mother of his Lord." Helvidius had adduced as evidence for his opinion that the Gospels referred to "the brothers of the Lord." Jerome responded by showing that in the Old Testament, the term "brothers" can refer to not only sons of the same mother, but also "countrymen" or, as it is in the case of brothers of the Lord, kinsmen. He pointed to the example of Abraham who said that, in truth, Sarah was his sister on the father's side, not on the mother's side (see Genesis 20:11).[328]

Next, Jerome had to defend another traditional practice of the Church. For centuries, Christians had honored the relics of the martyrs and sought the intercession of departed saints. A priest who had actually once availed himself of the hospitality of Jerome and his community in Bethlehem had returned to his native Gaul and written a pamphlet against vigils undertaken in honor of the saints.

---

326. Jerome, *Commentary on Isaiah*, 1.2 (CCL 73, 1–3).
327. The earliest written evidence for belief in Mary's perpetual virginity is the second-century document called the *Protoevangelion of St. James.*
328. Jerome, "On the Perpetual Virginity of the Blessed Virgin Mary" (*Against Helvidius*), 8, 16, 21. His opponent's name is also occasionally rendered Helvetius or Helvidius.

In his pamphlet, which reached Jerome in A.D. 406, this priest, named Vigilantius, claimed that the saints do not pray for the living, and since they are not omnipresent, like God, they cannot hear our requests for their intercession.

Amused at the irony that a man whose name means "vigilant" would condemn vigils, Jerome wrote his response in one night and suggested that the man should change his name from vigilant to "sleepy-head":

> All at once Vigilantius, or, more correctly, Dormitantius, has arisen, animated by an unclean spirit, to fight against the Spirit of Christ, and to deny that religious reverence is to be paid to the tombs of the martyrs.... For you say that the souls of the Apostles and martyrs have their abode either in the bosom of Abraham, or in the place of refreshment, or under the altar of God, and that they cannot leave their own tombs, and be present where they will.... Will you lay down the law for God? Will you put the Apostles into chains? So that to the day of judgment they are to be kept in confinement, and are not with their Lord, although it is written concerning them, "They follow the Lamb, whithersoever he goeth" [Rev 14:4]. If the Lamb is present everywhere, the same must be believed respecting those who are with the Lamb. And while the devil and the demons wander through the whole world, and with only too great speed present themselves everywhere; are martyrs, after the shedding of their blood, to be kept out of sight shut up in a coffin, from whence they cannot escape? You say, in your pamphlet, that so long as we are alive we can pray for one another; but once we die the prayer of no person for another can be heard, and all the more because the martyrs, though they cry for the avenging of their blood, have never been able to obtain their request. If Apostles and martyrs while still in the body can pray for others, when they ought still to be anxious for themselves, how much

more must they do so when once they have won their crowns, overcome, and triumphed?[329]

When Rome was sacked in A.D. 410, a great many refugees from Italy made their way to Palestine. Among them was the monk Pelagius. He received a congenial welcome from the bishop of Jerusalem who was unaware of the danger posed by Pelagius's teaching. Jerome collaborated with St. Augustine, with whom he corresponded, to resist the heresy of Pelagius. Pelagius's followers in Palestine did not appreciate this. In A.D. 416, a mob of Pelagian terrorists burned Jerome's monastery to the ground.

But nothing short of death could deter Jerome from his work. For the next three years, he continued to work feverishly. While the brilliant monk was working on his final commentary on the prophets, on Jeremiah, he breathed his last.

The Lion's Roar

During the thirty or so years of his sojourn in Bethlehem, Jerome had preached regularly to his community, on Sundays and feast days. Fortunately, one of the community members wrote these sermons down and we still have them today, a precious resource for the understanding of Scripture and its real-life application. We also still have most of the letters that Jerome wrote on a variety of topics to a wide variety of people. These have proved invaluable for understanding not only him, but the times in which he lived.

Yet, above all this stands the rigorous scholarly work done by Jerome to create the Latin translation of the Bible popularly known

---

329. Jerome, "Against Vigilantius," 1, 6, trans. W.H. Fremantle, in *Nicene and Post-Nicene Fathers*, series 2, vol. 6, Philip Schaff, ed. (New York: Christian Literature Company, 1889), pp. 417–419.

as the *Vulgate*, which comes from the word for the common language of the people. The sack of Rome, which occurred ten years before Jerome's death, was a sign of the fall of Rome and the imminent isolation of the Western world from the Greek East and from much of its own heritage. During the coming time of cultural darkness, the monks who preserved Western civilization would be studying the theology of Augustine while they chanted psalms whose Latin translation was given them by Jerome. The Bible translation that would be read, sung, and memorized in the liturgy and life of the Catholic Church for the next fifteen hundred years would be the *Vulgate* of Jerome. The Western Church owes an incalculable debt of gratitude to this man who is numbered as one of the four greatest teachers of the early Western Church.[330]

In iconography, Jerome is often depicted with a red hat of a cardinal. This symbolizes his valuable years of service as Pope Damasus's chief assistant and counselor. But he is also depicted with a lion at his feet. This is a result of an error: Jerome was early on confused with another saint who, according to legend, removed a thorn from a lion's paw. But in a sense, this image is most fitting. A lion is a perfect symbol of the vehement temperament of this Father who turned his wrath on those who attacked the truth. And the fact that he, at times, turned his wrath against even his friends ought to give hope to those of us who find ourselves beset with stubborn faults, as he was. For if God could so greatly use a character as flawed as Jerome and lead him even to sainthood, then there is hope for us all.

---

330. The others being Ambrose, Augustine, and Gregory the Great.

CHAPTER 24

Leo and Peter

After Theodosius the Great died in A.D. 395, the Western Roman Empire went into a death-spiral. The fifth century saw not a single great Roman emperor in the West. Instead, there was a succession of weak men who were emperors in name only. The real powers behind the throne were generals and warlords, some of whom were half-Roman, half-barbarian. Huge swaths of territory were lost as various tribes marauded through the empire, meeting little or no military resistance. Generals and emperors were too busy fighting each other to protect their people.

Rome Falls and Rises

Amidst this depressing situation, the Church in the West was growing enormously in maturity. As the Latin Empire dissolved into chaos, its Church produced some of its greatest teachers and leaders of all time. This was the Golden Age of the Latin Fathers—following Ambrose came the likes of Augustine and Jerome. These great men all spent time in Rome, but none of them served as Rome's bishop.

In A.D. 440, a man became pope who would bring a new luster to the chair of Peter. Leo had been in Gaul on a diplomatic mission to help reconcile feuding generals when he received news of his election. That he had been entrusted with such a delicate task while yet a deacon speaks volumes about his extraordinary leadership ability.

It is from what he did and the way he taught that we form a picture of this man who, unlike Augustine, declined to write much about himself. We don't know exactly when he was born, or the names of his parents, or how many siblings he had. In fact, we know few personal details about him, other than that he apparently was born in Rome. Though he left behind 143 letters, all of them were written after he had assumed his office as bishop of Rome. And once he stepped into his office, he always spoke from the perspective of his office. He was very conscious of the weighty character of this responsibility; for him, the bishop of Rome was the successor of Peter. His letters, then, were not private correspondence with friends, but expressions of his Petrine role as teacher, father, and judge.

This does not mean that he was stuffy, pompous, or bureaucratic. In fact, that is precisely what Leo was not. He was simple, zealous, energetic, fatherly, and unaffected. Nonetheless, he always carried himself with the noble dignity of one who speaks with Peter's voice.

After his resurrection, Jesus asked Peter three times to "feed my sheep" (John 21:15ff). Thus, this became the first priority for this pastor of the Roman church, to break open the bread of God's Word. There were forty-four popes between Peter and Leo, but there are no surviving sermons from any of them.[331] From Leo, we have preserved ninety-six homilies that are true gems. Take, for example, his homily on the occasion of the celebration of his own episcopal consecration. One would think he would expound on his own dignity as successor of Peter. But he does the opposite—he uses the occasion to remind the people of their own dignity:

---

331. There is a homily that came to be known as the *Second Letter of Clement*, although it was almost certainly not from him. However, it is a valuable example of early Christian preaching.

For all, regenerated in Christ, are made kings by the sign of the cross; they are consecrated priests by the oil of the Holy Spirit, so that beyond the special service of our ministry as priests, all spiritual and mature Christians know that they are a royal race and are sharers in the office of the priesthood. For what is more king-like than to find yourself ruler over your body after having surrendered your soul to God? And what is more priestly than to promise the Lord a pure conscience and to offer him in love unblemished victims on the altar of one's heart?[332]

Since, year after year, Leo preached on the feasts of the liturgical calendar, his ninety-six homilies cover the sadness of Good Friday and the glory of Easter, the Sermon on the Mount and the parables. But his words are most resplendent when they celebrate the wonder of Christmas. This excerpt is from one of many powerful sermons celebrating Christ's birth:

> Dearly beloved, today our Savior is born; let us rejoice. Sadness should have no place on the birthday of life. The fear of death has been swallowed up; life brings us joy with the promise of eternal happiness.
>
> No one is shut out from this joy; all share the same reason for rejoicing. Our Lord, victor over sin and death, finding no man free from sin, came to free us all. Let the saint rejoice as he sees the palm of victory at hand. Let the sinner be glad as he receives the offer of forgiveness. Let the pagan take courage as he is summoned to life....
>
> And so at the birth of our Lord the angels sing in joy: Glory to God in the highest, and they proclaim peace to men of good will as they see the heavenly Jerusalem being built from all the nations of the world. When the angels on high are so exultant at

---

332. Leo the Great, *Sermon 4*, 1–2 (*PL* 54, 148–149).

this marvelous work of God's goodness, what joy should it not bring to the lowly hearts of men?...

Christian, remember your dignity, and now that you share in God's own nature, do not return by sin to your former base condition. Bear in mind who is your head and of whose body you are a member. Do not forget that you have been rescued from the power of darkness and brought into the light of God's kingdom.

Through the sacrament of baptism you have become a temple of the Holy Spirit. Do not drive away so great a guest by evil conduct and become again a slave to the devil, for your liberty was bought by the blood of Christ.[333]

Controversy in the East

While Leo was still a deacon, trouble broke out in the Eastern capital that would eventually land on his doorstep. In A.D. 428, Constantinople had gotten a new patriarch named Nestorius, a former monk from Antioch who came to Constantinople accompanied by several of his monks and priests. One day, while preaching a sermon in the cathedral, one of Nestorius's priests proclaimed from the pulpit that the Blessed Virgin Mary should not be called *Theotokos* (the God-bearer or Mother of God). The people did not understand the explanation the preacher gave for this; all they knew is that they had been paying homage to Mary under that title for centuries; they were outraged, as people are when their mother is slighted. They expected the patriarch to correct the priest. Instead, Nestorius not only affirmed the priest's teaching, he widened the controversy by sending out pamphlets saying that Mary should not be called the

---

333. Leo the Great, *Homily 1 on the birth of the Lord* (*Sermo 1 in Nativitate Domini*) 1–3 (*PL* 54, 190–193).

"Mother of God" but rather the "Mother of Christ." He so sharply distinguished between the human and divine natures of Christ that his explanation made them appear to be only loosely conjoined. He made it sound as though Christ were a split personality, as if God were dwelling within the man Jesus much like he would in a temple.

Whatever Nestorius meant, he had violated a principle invoked by many Fathers up to that point—*lex orandi, lex credendi.* In other words, the liturgy of the Church is evidence of what the Church believes. Origen, Athanasius, and Cyril of Jerusalem, to name a few, had called Mary *Theotokos.* The oldest surviving written evidence of a prayer directed to Mary addresses her by this title in the third century. Gregory Nazianzen, predecessor of Nestorius fifty years earlier, had this to say regarding the serious issues involved in according or denying Mary this title: "If anyone does not believe that Saint Mary is the Mother of God (*Theotokos*), he is severed from the Godhead."[334]

The patriarch of Alexandria, Cyril, saw that what was at stake here was not principally Marian devotion, but proper understanding of the humanity and divinity of Christ. From the moment of his conception, the divine Word intimately united himself with a full human nature so that Jesus of Nazareth was indeed the divine Word made flesh. If he is God, then quite simply it is proper to call Mary the "Mother of God." Essentially, the title of *Theotokos* applied to Mary was simply a function of the Church's faith as professed at Nicaea. To deny it, then, was to deny Nicaea. A council called by the emperor to clarify this matter met at Ephesus in A.D. 431. It reaffirmed Mary as *Theotokos* thus, according to the intent of the council fathers, reaffirming Nicaea.

---

334. Gregory Nazianzen, *Letter 101,* 4–6.

But as often happens after a council, controversy continued. A monk named Eutyches alarmed people by teaching that Christ, after the incarnation, had only one nature and that his body was not consubstantial with ours. Pope Leo was notified of the problem by letter, and he responded quickly and decisively. His profound meditation on the incarnation, expressed in his homilies, helped him draft a short but poignant theological treatise intended to express the Church's faith in Christ's complete humanity and divinity and how the two are related. This letter, commonly called the *Tome of Leo*, was carried to a council that was called by the emperor in A.D. 449. Unfortunately, the powerful supporters of Eutyches had thoroughly rigged this council, even using force to make the bishops endorse the theology of Eutyches. The *Tome of Leo* was not even allowed to be read at the council. Leo promptly invalidated the whole affair, calling it the *Latrocinium*, or the "Robber Council." The emperor supporting Eutyches died and his successor called a new council intended to be truly ecumenical. This new council that assembled in the city of Chalcedon[335] included over four hundred bishops from all parts of the empire, papal legates included. In an effort to express the Church's Christological faith in a way that would win the allegiance of the bishops and people of both East and West, Leo's *Tome* was read. Here are a few salient words from the document:

> The proper character of both natures was maintained and came together in a single person. Lowliness was taken up by majesty, weakness by strength, mortality by eternity. To pay off the debt of our state, invulnerable nature was united to a nature that could suffer; so that in a way that corresponded to the remedies we needed, one and the same mediator between God and

---

335. Across the Bosphorus from Constantinople in what is now the Asian side of Turkey. It is now a district of Istanbul named Kadıköy.

humanity the man Christ Jesus, could both on the one hand die and on the other be incapable of death. Thus was true God born in the undiminished and perfect nature of a true man, complete in what is his and complete in what is ours.[336]

An Eastern bishop stood up at the conclusion and shouted: "Peter has spoken through the mouth of Leo!" There was widespread enthusiasm among the council fathers for Leo's eloquent explanation. While the final conciliar definition of faith also owed a great deal to the late Cyril of Alexandria, Leo's intervention had proved decisive, cementing the importance of the teaching role of the bishop of Rome for both East and West.

Filling the Vacuum

In this age of weak political leadership and ineffectual military protection, local leaders began leaving the vulnerable cities and taking refuge in fortified country estates. It was the precursor of the feudal era of castles and knights in the countryside, with little going on in cities.

In such a leadership vacuum, it was inevitable that strong pastors would have to stand in the breach and take over some responsibilities for statesmanship and charity that normally would be the province of the state. In A.D. 452, Attila and his Huns entered Italy unopposed. After laying waste to Aquileia and Milan, they were headed straight to Rome. The weak Emperor Valentinian III was in the city as the hordes approached. He turned to whom he could trust: Leo. Within days, Leo had organized an embassy around himself that included a few priests and two senators. Leo called for the people

---

336. Leo the Great, *Letter 28.*

to pray and then went out to meet Attila in a city outside of Rome. Reminiscent of what happened to Sennacherib when his army laid siege to Jerusalem, a devastating plague suddenly fell upon Attila's camp. Attila also got word from the Huns' homeland on the Danube that they were under attack and needed him to return. So Leo's intervention spared the city entirely; for the price of some tribute money, Attila turned around and left.

Three years later, the Vandals came from their new strongholds of Hippo, Carthage, and Sicily to attack Rome. This time Leo's embassy was not quite as successful. The Vandals had come at the invitation of one of the imperial princesses to rescue her from her own family! Thus, they were determined not to go away empty-handed. Nevertheless, Leo was able to get them to agree that there would be no killing and no burning. So after pillaging the city for several days, the Vandals returned to Africa, taking with them many captives. Leo sent priests to minister to the captives and alms to be taken by them to the prisoners. He also set to work raising money for the relief of still more captives and the restoration of ruined churches.

Greatness

One of the greatest challenges to Christian unity today is the office of the papacy. Both Protestants and Eastern Orthodox have been suspicious of this office and its tendency to be an instrument of domination and even tyranny. Some popes, notably John Paul II, have frankly acknowledged this difficulty and have asked their Eastern Orthodox and Protestant brethren to explore ways that this office might be exercised as a fruitful ministry of unity in the present age.[337]

---

337. See John Paul II, encyclical on ecumenism, *Ut Unum Sint* (Rome: Liberia Editrice Vaticana, 1995).

Perhaps the example of Leo has something to teach us here. He was an able administrator who was above all a pastor, a leader who reminded his followers of their dignity, and a doctrinal teacher who, in a time of crisis, built consensus. Leo believed that the Petrine authority had been passed on to Peter's successors whom he identifies as the bishops of the city in which Peter gave his witness. Some Christians would take exception to that line of reasoning. But what is beyond dispute is that Leo's example makes a persuasive argument that a strong papacy need not be exercised at the expense of the freedom and dignity of others.

Leo was not a creative theologian like Gregory of Nyssa or Augustine. But he was an extraordinary model of leadership. His combination of evangelical preaching, able administration, charity, diplomacy, and clear doctrinal teaching have earned him an epithet given to only one other pope in history. He is referred to most commonly not as Leo I, but as "Leo the Great." In light of this and his deep devotion to the prince of the apostles, it is only fitting that he was the first pope to be buried in St. Peter's basilica.

CHAPTER 25

Gregory the Great

The people of Rome were shocked when they heard the news. Gregory was one of the wealthiest men in the city. His great-great-grandfather had been pope. His father was a wealthy noble with vast estates in Sicily. He was heir to all the family's possessions and had been named prefect of Rome while still a young man. He had everything to live for, so they thought. Yet, here he was resigning his post, selling all he owned and giving it all away to the poor? History tells us nothing about what Gregory's father thought about this, but chances are that his mother's influence had something to do with it. We find her name in the Roman Martyrology as St. Silvia.[338]

One thing that Gregory kept was his family villa in Rome, located near the Circus Maximus.[339] This he turned into a monastery under the patronage of St. Andrew. Selecting an experienced monk as abbot, Gregory submitted himself completely to his spiritual direction and authority. The next several years of prayer and seclusion at this abbey were the happiest and most tranquil of Gregory's life. Unfortunately, this mayor-turned-monk was more zealous in fasting than his body could handle; for the rest of his life, he struggled with ill-health.

---

338. The Roman Martyrology is the official list of saints honored in the Roman liturgy, so called because for the first few hundred years they were all martyrs. As for Gregory's papal ancestor, Felix III—we do not know if his offspring were born before he became a cleric, as in the case of Augustine, or after. Married clergy, including bishops, were becoming increasingly rare in the West at this time.

339. The spot is still the site of a church and functioning monastery: San Gregorio Magno al Celio.

Gregory's serenity came to a screeching halt when the pope became aware of his talents and named him, much to his horror, as one of the seven deacons of Rome. Fortunately, he could still live with his brothers in the monastery. But not for long. Shortly after his ordination, he received a very uncongenial assignment. The pope needed an ambassador to the emperor in Constantinople, and he thought the former prefect of Rome was the perfect man for the job. The last thing Gregory wanted was to leave the spiritual atmosphere of St. Andrew's monastery to go to the worldliness of the imperial court. As a safeguard, he took a few of his monastic brothers with him. Somehow, despite the fact that he knew no Greek, he managed to hold his own. Nevertheless, he found shocking the corruption, intrigue, and vanity of the court. He saw clearly that the internal and external problems besetting the empire meant that Rome could not realistically expect much help from the emperor in defending itself from the barbarians.

After six long years in Constantinople, Gregory was called back to Rome where he became abbot of St. Andrew's monastery and continued in the pope's service.

A few years later, in A.D. 590, a destructive flooding of the Tiber led to a severe plague that claimed the life of the pope. Gregory organized a series of penitential processions from the major churches of the city beseeching God for an end to the horrible scourge. Tradition has it that, following the processions, St. Michael the Archangel appeared atop the Mausoleum of Hadrian, sheathing his sword as a sign that the plague would cease, which, in fact, it did. From at least the tenth century, the retelling of this tale led to Hadrian's tomb being renamed the Castel Sant'Angelo (Holy Angel), hence the statue of St. Michael that is perched at its summit to this day.

After the deceased pope was buried came the next shock for Gregory—the people acclaimed him as the new pope! He resisted vigorously, sending an official letter to the emperor begging him not to confirm this election. But, of course, the emperor agreed not with Gregory but with the people. A French bishop who knew Gregory wrote that he was planning to flee the city when the people came and carried him away to St. Peter's to be consecrated bishop.

The Bishop as Watchman

Gregory had inherited a mess. The devastating plague was only Rome's most recent problem. The city had been pillaged four times in a century and a half and conquered four times in twenty years. It was impoverished and largely in ruins. With no effective government, there was no one to repair the damage to streets and buildings caused by attacks, fires, and earthquakes. Soon after his election, he wrote:

> We see what has become of her who once appeared the mistress of the world. She is broken by all she has suffered from immense and manifold misfortunes…. Ruins upon ruins everywhere!… Where is the senate? Where are the people?… We, the few who are left, are menaced every day by the sword and innumerable trials…. Deserted Rome is in flames: her buildings also.[340]

But the deplorable condition of the city was not the reason he had wanted to run away. It was the dignity of the episcopal office that frightened Gregory. Quite frankly, he did not deem himself worthy of it. One of the treasures that has come down to us is his commentary on the book of Ezekiel, who had to deal with similar devastation to Jerusalem caused by the Babylonians. One of Gregory's homilies,

---

340. Quoted in *Butler's Lives of the Saints*, vol. 1, Alban Butler, et al. (New York: P.J. Kenedy & Sons, 156), p. 566.

given to the people of Rome, tells us much about Gregory's character. Here, he comments on the famous passage from Ezekiel 33:

"Son of man, I have made you a watchman for the house of Israel." Note that a man whom the Lord sends forth as a preacher is called a watchman. A watchman always stands on a height so that he can see from afar what is coming. Anyone appointed to be a watchman for the people must stand on a height for all his life to help them by his foresight.

How hard it is for me to say this, for by these very words I denounce myself. I cannot preach with any competence, and yet insofar as I do succeed, still I myself do not live my life according to my own preaching.

I do not deny my responsibility; I recognize that I am slothful and negligent, but perhaps the acknowledgment of my fault will win me pardon from my just judge. Indeed when I was in the monastery I could curb my idle talk and usually be absorbed in my prayers. Since I assumed the burden of pastoral care, my mind can no longer be collected; it is concerned with so many matters.

I am forced to consider the affairs of the Church and of the monasteries. I must weigh the lives and acts of individuals. I am responsible for the concerns of our citizens. I must worry about the invasions of roving bands of barbarians, and beware of the wolves who lie in wait for my flock. I must become an administrator lest the religious go in want. I must put up with certain robbers without losing patience and at times I must deal with them in all charity.

With my mind divided and torn to pieces by so many problems, how can I meditate or preach wholeheartedly?...

So who am I to be a watchman, for I do not stand on the mountain of action but lie down in the valley of weakness? Truly the all-powerful Creator and Redeemer of mankind can give me in spite of my weaknesses a higher life and effective speech; because I love him, I do not spare myself in speaking of him.[341]

When a neighboring bishop criticized Gregory for resisting his election, Gregory decided to write a book outlining the lofty calling of a bishop and high standards to which he should hold himself. It is hard to overestimate the impact made by this work, called the *Book of Pastoral Care* (*Liber Regulae Pastoralis*). The Byzantine Emperor Maurice was so impressed with it that he had it translated into Greek and distributed to every bishop in the empire. Several centuries later, the Anglo-Saxon King Alfred would dictate a preface for it, have it translated into Old English, and circulate it among English bishops. The great Charlemagne did the same. In short, this little book became the veritable textbook for bishops and popes for centuries to come.

Scripture and Preaching

Gregory ranked effective preaching as one of the supreme duties of the pastor. The pastor who does not preach or cannot preach well was, in his mind, not much of a pastor.

> Anyone ordained a priest undertakes the task of preaching, so that with a loud cry he may go on ahead of the terrible judge who follows. If, then, a priest does not know how to preach, what kind of cry can such a dumb herald utter? It was to bring this home that the Holy Spirit descended in the form of tongues on the first pastors.[342]

For Gregory, preaching was his number one priority. It should be noted that this Father of the Church was not an original theologian

---

341. *Homily on Ezekiel*, Book 1, 11, 4–6 (CCL 142, 170–172).
342. Gregory the Great, *Pastoral Care,* Book 2, 4 (PL 77, 30–31).

like Augustine or the Cappadocians. He is, above all, a pastor who is absorbed with the task of explaining the Scriptures to ordinary people. He expounded the Bible according to its threefold meaning: literal, allegorical, and moral (spiritual). One of his famous commentaries, called *Moralia in Job*, illustrates his method. The literal sense would be the story of Job itself and its meaning in its original context. The allegorical sense would see Job's sufferings as a type or prefigurement of Christ's sufferings. The moral or spiritual sense would be what we should learn and apply to our own lives today from the story of Job. As a monk and a pastor, this third moral or spiritual sense is Gregory's real preoccupation. That's why his commentary on Job is actually titled "Moral Reflections on Job." Notice here how he goes from the brief description of Job as simple and upright (Job 1:1) to a teaching on the nature of authentic Christian simplicity and how it differs from naïve simplemindedness:

> Some people are so simple that they do not know what uprightness is. Theirs is not the true simplicity of the innocent: they are as far from that as they are far from rising to the virtue of uprightness. As long as they do not know how to guard their steps by walking in uprightness, they can never remain innocent merely by walking in simplicity. This is why St. Paul warns his disciples: "I hope that you are also wise in what is good, and innocent of what is bad but also brothers, you are not to be childish in your outlook, though you can be babies as far as wickedness is concerned." Thus Christ our Truth enjoins his disciples with the words "be cunning as serpents and yet as harmless as doves." In giving them this admonition, he had to join the two together, so that both the simplicity of the dove might be instructed by the craftiness of the serpent, and the craftiness of the serpent might be tempered by the simplicity of the dove.

That is why the Holy Spirit has manifested his presence to mankind, not only in the form of a dove but also in the form of fire. For by the dove simplicity is indicated, and by fire, zeal. So he is manifested in a dove and in fire, because those who are full of the Spirit have the mildness of simplicity, but catch fire with zeal.[343]

Doves and Serpents

Gregory took his own advice relative to combining fiery shrewdness with gentle simplicity. He, a simple monk, was thrust into the chaos of pastoral care amidst a collapsing empire. He had been trained both in prayer and in diplomacy, Scripture and governance. He would shrewdly employ all his skills, both spiritual and temporal, for the good of the people.

Gregory had no naïve illusions; he realized that there was no help to be gotten from the emperor. If the poor were to be fed, the Church would have to feed them. If captives were to be freed, the Church would have to free them. If the cities' defenses were to be rebuilt, the Church would have to organize it. Into the vacuum left by an impotent state stepped the pope, seeking to use all the means at his disposal to fill the void. Thus, it is with Leo and Gregory that we see the beginning of the temporal power of the papacy that was to grow during the Middle Ages and last till the new state of Italy was formed in 1870. It all began not due to some desire for wealth and power, but because the pope, as the only effective leader in central Italy, was forced either to take over all the normal duties of the collapsed state or watch his people die.

---

343. Gregory the Great, *Moral Reflections on Job* (*Moralia in Job*), Book 1, 2, 36 (PL 75, 529–530, 543–544).

Assets were sold, including lands and sacred vessels of precious metals. A considerable number of captives were freed, and thousands were saved from starvation by the relief efforts of Gregory. In fact, he spent so much to relieve the temporal suffering of the people that his successor was left with an empty treasury.

Gregory beseeched the emperor to negotiate a peace with the Lombards, the latest barbarian tribe to afflict Italy. He got no response. So without any official permission, he took the initiative to carry out his own negotiations and secured a separate peace for Rome and surrounding cities, saving many lives.

To his credit, Gregory is notable for tolerating no persecution of the Jews. He demanded that their property and freedom be respected. He was a champion of the early Christian principle that God works through persuasion, not compulsion. When a Jewish community complained to him that a Jewish convert to Christianity had seized their synagogue and turned it into a church, he mandated that the synagogue be returned to its rightful owners.

Impact on Christian Culture

Gregory made an impact on the imagination and the culture of succeeding centuries in several notable ways. The first was through storytelling. Gregory himself had been inspired by the example of an Italian monk who had died while Gregory was still a child. This monk, St. Benedict, had grown up and been educated in Rome but left to live in the hills outside the city in pursuit of a prayerful life of penance and solitude. He had founded monasteries and, like St. Basil, had written a rule. But he also was a wonder-worker, and his story, which moved Gregory, needed to be told. So Gregory interviewed monks who had lived with Benedict and put together a popular book, written in the form of a dialogue between Gregory and his deacon, Peter, that could entertain and inspire the simplest of people as well as the greatest. Called the *Dialogues*, it also contained stories of other great Italian mystics and saints. With stories that were easy to hear, remember, and retell, the *Dialogues* became one of the classics of medieval Christianity in a society where all loved a good story but few could read. It was carried and popularized all over the continent and the British Isles by the Benedictine monks for whom Benedict was founder and hero. Since it inspired many to join the monasteries, as the *Life of Antony* had, it greatly affected the growth of the monasticism that would preserve Christianity in the West.

The second way that Gregory made a difference in culture was through his devotion to the improvement of the liturgy and his care to see that it was enriched with music. We know that Gregory was renowned, even in his own day, as a pope who loved music. We also know that he reorganized and strengthened a school for Christian music in Rome called the Schola Cantorum. Finally, it is clear that he at least collected and organized chant.[344] The whole tradition of chant that ultimately came to be known as "Gregorian" was probably not all written by him, but he had a significant role in its development and promotion.

It would be hard to imagine English history without Becket, Westminster Abbey, and the *Canterbury Tales*. But in the time of Gregory, while most barbarians of Europe, including the Goths and the Vandals, were at least Arian Christian, the Anglo-Saxons who had invaded England were totally pagan. Gregory had seen some

---

344. John the Deacon, biographer (c. A.D. 872) of Pope Gregory I, claimed that the saint "compiled a patchwork antiphonary." See the article on "Gregorian Chant" in the 1913 *Catholic Encyclopedia*, article by Heinrich Bewerunge.

Anglo-Saxon slaves in the marketplace in Rome and was shocked to find out that they and their land were still unevangelized. So he bought Anglo-Saxon slave boys, gave them their freedom, and educated them in letters and godliness. Next, he sent them back to England accompanied by forty monks from St. Andrew's, led by the monastery's abbot, a man named Augustine. This troop of missionaries established their center at Canterbury and planted the first church among the English. Canterbury remains the primatial see of the Church of England to this day.

Sunset and New Dawn

Gregory's pontificate marks the end of one era and the beginning of the next. The sun was setting on the ancient world and dawning on the new medieval world. A sophisticated urban culture was giving way to an illiterate, rough-hewn, feudal society. The barbarian tribes carving up Europe were nomads with no written language. With the exception of the barbarian nobles who lived in the Byzantine society of the East, even the kings would remain illiterate for centuries to come. The Frankish king Charlemagne, crowned Holy Roman Emperor in A.D. 800, was aware of this and sought to spur a revival of learning in his realm. But it is telling that he himself only learned to read haltingly and never mastered the art of writing.

But the age of the Fathers of the Church, which comes to an effective close in the West with Gregory,[345] had assembled a very rich legacy to be passed on to this new medieval world. This legacy included the Latin Bible of Jerome and the creed of Nicaea. Augustine's vast

---

345. The last Latin author traditionally recognized as a Father of the Church is Isidore of Seville who died approximately thirty years after Gregory's death. Isidore is a minor figure in comparison with Gregory.

theological commentary on the Bible and the creed was also part of the heritage. This tradition was celebrated in the Roman liturgy dating back through Hippolytus and Justin all the way to Peter and Paul. In the coming centuries, the monks of Benedict would sing of this patristic legacy in the chant of Ambrose and Gregory and would nourish the Christian community out of its storehouse of this same rich legacy.

It is no accident that the last of the Early Church Fathers in the West, the one who plays such an important role in bequeathing this heritage to the medieval world, happens to be the first monk ever to have become pope.

This monk-pope was a strong man who wrote about leadership and modeled it. Known as Gregory the Great, this man exemplified the philosophy of evangelical leadership taught by Jesus. This leadership style can be summed up by the new title Gregory developed for himself as pope, a title that has been used by every pope since: "Servant of the Servants of God."

CHAPTER 26

The Voice in the Voices

The lives of the various characters in our story span over five hundred years. They hailed from across the then-civilized world—Europe, Africa, and Asia. And they came from diverse walks of life as well. Some were priests like Hippolytus and Jerome, others laymen like Justin and Clement, still others bishops like Cyprian and Athanasius. Several, such as Tertullian and Ambrose, were even lawyers. A few were highly educated, like Origen and Basil. Others, such as Polycarp and Antony, were the kind of rough and simple men whom Jesus called by the lakeside.

The voice of each of these teachers is distinctive. You can hear their unique personalities resonating in their words—the down-to-earth freshness of Ignatius, the Platonist sophistication of Origen and Gregory of Nyssa, the severe, North African earnestness of Tertullian, the Roman sobriety of Clement. These are real people we meet in these pages, and this is one reason why their stories are so engaging.

Tradition, Consensus, and Authority

But there is another reason why, for centuries, the Church has considered these men, called the early Church Fathers, to be so vitally important. It is because, reverberating through these diverse voices, we can discern a single voice. That voice is the Word of God, coming to us through the apostolic Tradition.

The word *apostle* means "one who is sent." The original apostle is the one sent by the Father into the womb of a virgin. This apostle is also the Word, the Word made flesh. He chose a band of men whom he taught, commissioned, and sent forth. He lived with these apostles for three years before he received the baptism he longed for, the baptism that cast fire on the earth. That fire was at once the fire of truth and the fire of love. It was poured out upon the men he had chosen, who in turn passed it on.

What they passed on was not primarily a book, or a set of truths. It was a life. It was the truth. It was more than could be recorded in any one book, says John in the twentieth chapter of his Gospel. It is more than could be expressed in any number of written words, even inspired words. There are some things that you can only learn by absorbing them. You absorb such a thing by living with people who have it. And once absorbed, you can never fully articulate it. But you can live it, and you can pass it on to those you live with.

This is the apostolic Tradition, with a capital *T*. It is the entire life and teaching of the Messiah, the whole inheritance, our rich and inexhaustible patrimony, passed on from the Lord, to his first disciples, who in turn passed it to us by an uninterrupted succession of believers led by the successors of those first disciples. This Tradition is expressed in worship as much as it is in teaching, indeed, perhaps more. That's why documents like the *Didache*, and Hippolytus's *Apostolic Tradition* are so important. But the Tradition is most perfectly expressed by those who love as Jesus loved, to the end. And that's why the testimony of the martyrs is of such extreme importance.

Christians from all the major faith traditions today—Evangelical, Catholic, and Orthodox—agree that the Scriptures are inspired by the Holy Spirit and are therefore infallible, or inerrant. But in the centuries-old struggle to understand and apply them aright, teachers of all these Christian traditions have turned for guidance to the early Church Fathers.

As individuals, none of the Fathers, even the holiest or the most brilliant, has ever been deemed personally infallible. As we have seen, some, such as Tertullian and Origen, have come up with ideas that were later rejected. But it is no wonder, with such diverse backgrounds and personalities, that they would differ at times. That is natural. What is not natural is that they should so often agree! When we discern agreement or consensus among them, it is because, in these cases, what we are hearing from them is not something coming *from* them at all, but something coming *through* them, namely the voice of the Word borne by that apostolic Tradition to which they are irreplaceable witnesses.

It is actually striking how many areas of consensus we find among them. It would not be fitting to conclude this volume without attempting to identify at least some of these points of convergence.

Logically, the first thing we find in all of them who in any way touch upon the issue of authority is the very principle of apostolic succession itself. This is expressed in different ways by different authors. But all, from Clement to Irenaeus to Tertullian to Basil, are equally emphatic: The Church is an ordered community. It was founded by Christ upon Peter and the apostles. Our connection with the apostles depends upon a connection with those who serve as our personal link, through a family tree, that goes back to the apostles and, ultimately, to the Word himself. This living, family bond is made visible and concrete through communion with the apostle's successors, the bishops. This chain, anchoring us to Christ who is the cornerstone, existed prior to the writing of the books known as the New Testament and at least a hundred and fifty years prior to the assembling of all the twenty-seven books that make up that inspired collection.[346] Indeed, it was the principle of apostolic succession that enabled the Church to discern which scriptures were genuinely apostolic and which, like the Gospel of Thomas, were not.

The Person and Work of Christ

The most fundamental truth passed down by the Tradition is the answer to the question Jesus once put to his disciples: "Who do men say that I am?" The Fathers make clear that the one Peter identifies as the Christ, the Son of the Living God, is truly divine and truly human. Every effort to diminish either of these equally important affirmations is met with stern rebuke, from Ignatius down to Leo. Indeed, Tertullian goes beyond simply repeating this traditional double affirmation to provide new vocabulary to help the Church to express it more precisely as time goes on. The *Tome of Leo*, employing this terminology, helped to resolve the issue at the Council of Chalcedon.

Equally emphatic are the Fathers that this divine man, or "God-man" as Origen puts it, has come not primarily to teach or heal but to die. Throughout history there have been revisionist attempts to redefine who Jesus *really* was—a social reformer, the greatest of the prophets, a New Age guru, even a political zealot.[347] This is nothing new.

The Ebionites had said he was a great prophet, the Jewish leaders a zealot, the Gnostics an esoteric teacher. The Fathers slapped all these

---

346. The death and resurrection of Christ most likely occurred in A.D. 30. The first book of the New Testament, almost certainly Paul's First Letter to the Thessalonians, was written in A.D. 50, give or take a year. The first list including the New Testament books and the first writer to employ most of the books, as we have seen, dates only as early as about A.D. 185, with the first full list of the twenty-seven found in A.D. 367 in a festal letter of Athanasius.

347. See for example Reza Aslan, *Zealot: Life and Times of Jesus of Nazareth* (New York: Random House, 2013).

theories down. He was the God-man, they insisted, and he came to offer his life as a sacrifice. Those who passed on this story lived with him. Most later died for him. Many of the Fathers who passed on the apostolic message suffered and/or died for him as well. To those who dismissed Jesus's death as a mirage, Ignatius pointed to his upcoming execution as a compelling testimony to the death of Christ. Despite the use of several signs in the early Church such as the fish[348] and the Chi-Rho of Constantine, it was the sign of the cross that was traced, symbolically branded, onto the foreheads of the newly baptized. And it was the sign of cross, made at a pagan festival, which was the spark igniting the Great Persecution.

Eucharist and Baptism

This sacrificial love, stronger than death, was not only preached and taught, it was celebrated by the early Church in the Eucharist. There it was made visible, present again, so that Christians could feed on it, be transformed by it, and become consumed with it. It is significant that no author of the first six hundred years depicted the Church's Sunday worship as a service of singing and preaching. The Eucharist, understood not as a mere symbolic reminder but as bodily presence and sacrifice, is referenced everywhere in the writings of the Fathers. This "Bread of Heaven in Jesus Christ" is so important that, at least in Africa and Rome, it was understood as the "daily bread" we pray for in the Lord's Prayer. As such, it was reserved in homes to be solemnly consumed on a daily basis.

Baptism was also omnipresent in the teaching of the early Fathers. We see that it was given to infants as well as to adults and that this

---

348. In Greek, the letters of the word "fish" or ICTHUS, served as a confession of faith in an acrostic form: Jesus Christ Son of God Savior.

is believed to be a practice dating back to the apostles. For those old enough to answer for themselves, it was not some sentimental "christening" but a radical and dramatic act of commitment. It was the pledge of a life so wholly dedicated to God that it was hard for the Church to figure out what to do when someone fell from baptismal grace. Such a thing was not to be expected or taken lightly. The spiritual experience of conversion, the "born-again" experience that has been so important in evangelical Christianity since the nineteenth century, this is something known in the early Church, but most often described in the context of the experience of baptism itself, which was called the enlightenment.[349]

This enlightenment was followed by an episcopal anointing understood as an empowerment. The gifts of the Holy Spirit were expected to come as a result of these sacramental encounters, freely given at the Spirit's discretion. In the early Church, we see no separation between sacraments, charisms, and office. In fact, we see in Ignatius, "the God-inspired," a bishop who was a prophet, and in Polycarp, a bishop who received visions and dreams. And the greatest of all charisms, the love stronger than death, is a gift poured out as the Spirit wills on those of every rank and station of life.

Sacramental, Charismatic, Evangelical

For the early Fathers, the normal Christian life was at once sacramental, charismatic, and evangelical. It was evangelical first of all in its focus on the Word of God. There were three years of instruction in the Word of God before baptism. There was prayer multiple

---

349. We are reminded of Cyprian's recounting of his baptismal experience. But it should be pointed out that this subjective experience of initial conversion is not emphasized and widely noted in the early Church Fathers.

times a day with the Word of God. Origen's two thousand works are mostly biblical homilies that he preached on a daily basis. Hippolytus encouraged Christians to attend house church meetings on weekday mornings before work where there was teaching of the Word of God.

Moreover, the normal Christian life was also evangelical in the sense that it was truly catholic or universal—the Church is meant to extend universally, which means that the Gospel must be offered to everyone. All considered themselves bound to share the Gospel with people of every stripe—Roman or barbarian, slave or free, educated or simple. They considered themselves bound to share it, even at the risk of their lives. The decree of Septimius Severus in A.D. 202 was not against *being* a Christian—it was against *sharing* Christ with others. Origen's father died rather than keep the truth to himself. The Church grew in numbers during the first three hundred years of persecution not because of mass media advertising or specialized officers who were evangelists. There were specialized, official roles called "lector" and "exorcist" in the early Church. But not "evangelist." It was a normal part of the Christian life for everyone to engage in personal evangelism, to bring neighbors and relatives to take instruction in the catechetical schools run by people like Justin, Clement, and Origen.

Church as Family

The normal Christian life, however, is not the life of an academy. It is family life. Jesus taught his disciples to call God "Father." The early Christians were conscious of the fact that this was a key feature distinguishing the Church from the synagogue. It is no accident that Origen, Tertullian, and Cyprian each wrote a work entitled "On Prayer" that was largely about the "Our Father." Neither was it an accident that a tradition, traceable to the first century, directed Christians to pray this prayer at least three times per day.

Of course, it is God who is the heavenly Father of the community. In addition, the bishop was naturally understood as an instrument of God's fatherhood from the time of Ignatius forward. Indeed, the title "Pope" is nothing more than an English rendering of "Papa," the unofficial, affectionate name by which members of the Christian family initially called their bishop, the head of the household.

In this Church family, the members were understood to be brothers and sisters. Widows and orphans were supported financially by the community, as they would be in any family worthy of the name. This was a striking testimony to outsiders, indeed part of the evangelical draw of the Church during the time of persecution, as Tertullian shows us. This continues after the days of Constantine in the sermons of the Cappadocians and in the charitable work of Basil, Ambrose, Leo, and Gregory.

Every family needs to have a mother as well, and this family is no different. The mother was seen both as the Church, as in Tertullian and Cyprian, and, even more widely, beginning with Justin and Irenaeus, as Mary, the New Eve, the mother of a new creation. While devotion to the Virgin Mary certainly developed greatly in the golden age of the Fathers, it was noticeably present even in the first two Christian centuries in seed form.

This is actually the way that many orthodox Christian doctrines, later defined with precision by the first four Ecumenical councils, appear in this age of the earliest Fathers.

The Contribution of the Fathers

The Fathers of the Church were writers who witnessed to and helped clarify the apostolic Tradition over the course of nearly seven hundred years. The earliest of them, the ante-Nicene Fathers, are primarily important as witnesses to the basic elements of that Tradition, since they lived so close to the time of the apostles. However, a few of these Fathers also helped to clarify and develop that Tradition. Theology takes the data of revelation and reflects upon it so that we can grasp it more deeply, coherently, and comprehensively. Some of these earliest Fathers made masterful contributions along these lines. We think for example of Cyprian on the theology of the episcopate, Irenaeus on apostolic succession, and Tertullian and Origen on Christology and Trinitarian theology.

But the time was not yet ripe to weave all the strands together. Tertullian provided the words *Trinity* and *person* but failed to provide us with a finished Trinitarian tapestry. The same was true for Origen who first baptized the brilliant term *homoousios* (consubstantial) to describe the unity of divine nature possessed fully by both the Father and the Son.

It remained for the Fathers of Golden Age, the amazingly fertile period after Constantine, to take the baton and carry it further. They put together the bits and pieces contributed by these earlier witnesses and made of them a glorious mosaic of the face of Christ. And the ecumenical councils that relied on them discerned the voice in the many voices, clarifying the message of the divine Word to their age, to our age and to every age.

"When the Church Was Young"

The title of this book raises an important question. If the Church was young in the first eight centuries, does that mean that now it is old?

That depends what you mean by old. The Church has matured over the course of two thousand years. There are battles that have been fought and won't have to be fought again, thank God. Those of us who have made it to adulthood may look back to our teen years and smile wistfully. But probably, if given the chance, we wouldn't want to go through it all again, thank you very much.

So yes, the Church is old in that it is mature. For this, we should be grateful.

But aging has its unsavory side. There is the deterioration of body and mind. There is rigid attachment to old ways and the unwillingness, even inability, to live in a new and changing world. What is worse, there can be a loss of purpose, joy, and vitality. Roman society was experiencing exactly this sort of worn-out tedium in the days of the early Fathers, as attested by many pagan writers.

One of the biblical writers who best captured the somber bleakness that can accompany aging is Qoheleth, author of Ecclesiastes. He insists there is nothing new under the sun.

Writing before the coming of the Messiah, Qoheleth was right. His words are an abiding rebuke to all who place their hope in the things of this world. Vanity of vanities!

But with the coming of Christ, there *was* at last something new under the sun. The divine love that had made the universe in all of its loveliness had descended upon the earth and burned in a human breast. And then it spread to other human breasts. Agape. Charity. Self-giving love that is stronger than death—this was something radically new under the sun.

This something new gave rise to a new way of life and a new doctrine, a new perspective and a new community. If that community is true to itself, it will never grow old. But if that community, which is the Church, maintains the buildings and the organization and the ceremonies, but allows the flame of charity to die down, it becomes a museum. People visit museums from time to time. It is something that one should do. But one would never think of living there.

It must be admitted that many today have this sort of impression of the Church. Rather than dismissing them as skeptics and secularists, perhaps we should look at ourselves. Nietzsche, the atheist philosopher of the nineteenth century, once said, "If you Christians want me to believe in your Redeemer, you have to look more redeemed."

It would be hard to imagine a pagan Roman philosopher using this line on the Christians of his day. The Church was not perfect then. But it was alive. The early Church Fathers were the spokesmen of this youthful Church, so bursting with vitality that it literally brought to its knees history's mightiest empire. The voices of these spokesmen cry out to us still. They tell us that Jesus's love is still stronger than death and that he makes all things new!

Further Reading on the Early Church Fathers

I t is my sincere hope that reading this book will whet your appetite
to learn more about the early Church Fathers! The most important
thing is to read them directly. For more selections from the Fathers
discussed in this book and many others, visit my website at www.
DrItaly.com.

Still, there are translations of the Fathers as well as certain of their
works that are not available online at the time of this book's publica-
tion. Neither are most of the secondary sources and references works
available online. For this reason, we offer the following bibliography
that lists the translations of the Fathers that we've used in this work,
other translations and collections of patristic writings, and reference
works and secondary sources that we recommend as worthwhile.

Primary Sources: Writings from Early Christianity

Athanasius. *The Life of Antony and the Letter to Marcellinus.* Classics
of Western Spirituality Series. Translated by Robert C. Gregg.
Mahwah, N.J.: Paulist, 1979.

_____. *On the Incarnation.* Introduction by C.S. Lewis. Crestwood,
N.Y.: St. Vladimir's Seminary Press, 2012. Accessible, modern
translation.

Augustine of Hippo. *Confessions.* The recent translation by Henry
Chadwick is good (Oxford University Press World Classics paperback, 2009) but innumerable editions and translations are available.

Basil the Great. *On the Holy Spirit.* Translated by David Anderson.
Crestwood, N.Y.: St. Vladimir's Seminary Press, 2011.

Chadwick, Henry, and J.E.L. Oulton, eds. *Alexandrian Christianity* (Library of Christian Classics Series). Philadelphia: Westminster John Knox, 1954. Contains selections from Clement of Alexandria and Origen.

Deferrari, Roy et al. *The Fathers of the Church: A New Translation.* Washington, D.C.: Catholic University of America Press, 1947. This series consists of more than 120 volumes with two new volumes translated every year. Contemporary translation with excellent introductions.

Deiss, Lucien. *Springtime of the Liturgy: Liturgical Texts of the First Four Centuries.* Collegeville, Minn.: Liturgical, 1979. Contains Hippolytus's *Apostolic Tradition* and many other writings.

De Lubac, Henri. *Catholicism: Christ and the Common Destiny of Man.* Translated by Lancelot C. Sheppard and Sister Elizabeth Englund, O.C.D. San Francisco: Ignatius, 1988. Contains marvelous extracts from the Fathers.

Dix, Gregory, and Henry Chadwick, eds. *The Treatise on the Apostolic Tradition of St. Hippolytus of Rome, Bishop and Martyr.* New York: Routledge, 1995.

Eusebius. *The History of the Church: From Christ to Constantine.* Translated by G.A. Williamson. New York: Penguin, 1990. A key primary source on the history of the Church from the New Testament to Constantine, written by a bishop-historian of the fourth century.

Greenslade, S.L., ed. *Early Latin Theology: Selections from Tertullian, Cyprian, Ambrose and Jerome* (Library of Christian Classics Series). Philadelphia: Westminster John Knox, 1956.

Gregory of Nyssa. *The Life of Saint Macrina.* Translated by Kevin Corrigan. Eugene, Ore.: Wipf and Stock, 2001.

John Chrysostom. *On Marriage and Family Life* (Popular Patristics Series). Translated by Catharine P. Roth and David Anderson. Crestwood, N.Y.: St. Vladimir's Seminary Press, 1986.

Jurgens, William A., ed. *Faith of the Early Fathers* (3 vols.). Collegeville, Minn.: Liturgical, 1979. Very useful, since it organizes patristic teaching by topic.

Layton, Bentley, ed. *The Gnostic Scriptures: A New Translation with Annotations and Introductions.* New York: Doubleday Image, 1995. Forty-six heretical Gnostic texts including those of Valentinus, foe of St. Irenaeus.

Migne, J.-P., ed. *Patrologia Graeca.* Vols. 1–85. Paris, 1857–1866. Original Greek text of the Fathers who wrote in that language.

_____. *Patrologia Latina.* Vols. 1–73. Paris, 1844–1849. Original Latin text of the Fathers who wrote in that language.

Possidius. *The Life of St. Augustine: A Translation of the sancti Augustini Vita by Possidius, Bishop of Calama* (Christian Roman Empire Series). Translated by Herbert T. Weiskotten. Merchantville, N.J.: Evolution, 2008. A primary source on Augustine, written by a monk who had lived many years with him before himself becoming a bishop.

Quasten, Johannes, et al., eds. *Ancient Christian Writers: The Works of the Fathers in Translation.* New York: Paulist. Successive individual volumes have made their appearance in various years. Extremely careful and well done modern translation.

Richardson, Cyril C. ed. *Early Christian Fathers.* New York: Macmillan, 1970. Good paperback edition of most of the Apostolic Fathers.

Roberts, Alexander, and James Donaldson, eds. *The Ante-Nicene Fathers: The Writings of the Fathers down to A.D. 325* (10 vols.). Edinburgh: T. & T. Clark, 1900.

Rordorf, Willy, et al., eds. *The Eucharist of the Early Christians.* Translated by Matthew J. O'Connell. New York: Pueblo, 1978. Indispensable for study of Eucharistic practice and theology up till Origen. Contains primary source texts and commentary.

Schaff, Philip, and Henry Wace, eds. *The Nicene and Post-Nicene Fathers*: Series I and Series II (each 14 vols). Edinburgh: T & T Clark, 1867–1900. These translations are sometimes challenging in style for contemporary readers. Another problem is that the notes are often anti-Catholic. The collection is available online, however.

Socrates Scholasticus. *The Ecclesisastical History of Socrates, Surnamed Scholastitus, or the Advocate.* Translated by E. Walford. London: Samuel Bagster, 1853. Written by a Byzantine Christian historian around A.D. 440 to cover the history of the Church from Constantine up to the time the book was written. It picks up where Eusebius of Caesarea leaves off.

Sozomen. *The Ecclesiastical History of Sozomen.* Translated by E. Walford. London: Samuel Bagster, 1855. Written by a Palestinian Christian shortly after Socrates's history and using it as one of his sources. Covers from Constantine to about A.D. 425.

Spidlik, Thomas. *Drinking from the Hidden Fountain: A Patristic Breviary.* Kalamazoo, Mich.: Cistercian, 1994. Selections from the Fathers arranged for meditation.

The Liturgy of the Hours According to the Roman Rite. Translated by International Commission on English in the Liturgy. 4 vols. New York: Catholic Book, 1975. The Office of Readings, scattered throughout all four volumes, provides a collection of some of the greatest short readings from the early Church Fathers arranged according to the seasons and feasts of the Church year and the memorials of the saints.

Ward, Benedicta, ed. and trans. *The Sayings of the Desert Fathers: The Alphabetical Collection.* Kalamazoo, Mich.: Cistercian, 1975.

Wiles, Maurice, and Mark Santer, eds. *Documents in Early Christian Thought.* Cambridge: Cambridge University Press, 1977. A worthwhile anthology of patristic texts arranged by subject: Trinity, Christ, Church, etc.

Reference and Secondary Sources

Adam, Karl. *Saint Augustine: The Odyssey of his Soul.* New York: Macmillan, 1932.

Akin, Jimmy. *The Fathers Know Best: Your Essential Guide to the Teachings of the Early Church.* San Diego, Calif.: Catholic Answers, 2010. A very useful handbook.

Aquilina, Mike. *The Fathers of the Church: An Introduction to the First Christian Teachers* (3rd ed.). Huntington, Ind.: Our Sunday Visitor, 2013. A fine popular introduction.

Benedict XVI. *The Fathers* (2 vols.) Huntington, Ind.: Our Sunday Visitor, 2008 and 2010. A collection of his audience talks on the early Christian teachers.

Bercot, David W., ed. *A Dictionary of Early Christian Beliefs: A Reference Guide to More Than 700 Topics Discussed by the Early Church Fathers.* Peabody, Mass.: Hendrickson, 1998.

Bouyer, Louis, et al. *The Spirituality of the New Testament and the Fathers. A History of Christian Spirituality,* vol. 1 New York: Seabury, 1963.

Brown, Peter. *Augustine of Hippo.* University of California Press, 1967. A classic intellectual biography.

Brown, Raymond E., et al., eds. *The New Jerome Biblical Commentary.* Englewood Cliffs, N.J.: Prentice Hall, 1990. Good article on the development of the biblical canon and information as well on the dating of the New Testament books.

Chadwick, Henry. *Early Christian Thought and the Classical Tradition.* New York: Oxford, 1966.

———. *The Early Church* (Pelican History of the Church, vol. 1). New York: Penguin, 1967. Best inexpensive paperback history of the early Church.

Cross, F.J., and E.A. Livingstone, eds. *The Oxford Dictionary of the Christian Church* (2nd ed). Oxford: Oxford University Press, 1974.

Crouzel, Henri. *Origen.* A.S. Worrall, trans. London: T & T Clark, 1984.

Daniélou, Jean. *The Bible and the Liturgy.* Notre Dame, Ind.: Notre Dame University, 1956. A fabulous introduction of the Fathers' use of the Bible.

———. *The Development of Christian Doctrine before the Council of Nicaea.* London: Darton, Longman & Todd, 1964.

———. *Gospel Message and Hellenistic Culture* (History of Early Christian Doctrine Before the Council of Nicaea, vol. 2). Philadelphia: Westminster John Knox, 1973.

———. *The Origins of Latin Christianity* (History of Early Christian Doctrine Before the Council of Nicaea, vol. 3). Philadelphia: Westminster John Knox, 1977.

Davis, Leo Donald. *The First Seven Ecumenical Councils.* Collegeville, Minn.: Liturgical, 1990.

Di Berardino, Angelo, ed. *Encyclopedia of the Early Church* (Institutum Patristicum Augustinianum, 2 vols.). Translated by Adrian Walford. New York: Oxford University Press, 1992. Entries listed alphabetically under names of heresies, persons, places, etc. Great maps and photos.

Di Berardino, Angelo, and Basil Studer, eds. *History of Theology I: The Patristic Period.* Collegeville, Minn.: Liturgical, 1996.

Dvornik, Francis. *The Ecumenical Councils. Twentieth-Century Encyclopedia of Catholicism,* vol. 82. New York: Hawthorn, 1961.

Ferguson, Everett, ed. *Encyclopedia of Early Christianity.* New York: Garland, 1990.

Grant, Michael. *Social History of Greece and Rome.* New York: Scribner, 1992.

Grant, Robert. *The Greek Apologists of the Second Century.* Philadelphia: Westminster John Knox, 1988.

Kelly, J.N.D. *Early Christian Creeds* (3rd ed.). London: Longmans, 1972.

————. *Early Christian Doctrines* (2nd ed.). New York: Harper & Row, 1978. Probably the best detailed account of development of Christology and other theological developments in the early Church.

MacMullen, Ramsay. *Christianizing the Roman Empire.* New Haven, Conn.: Yale University Press, 1984.

Marrou, Henri. *Saint Augustine and His Influence through the Ages.* Translated by Patrick Hepburne-Scott. Texts of St. Augustine translated by Edmund Hill. New York: Harper, 1957.

————. *Paganism in the Roman Empire.* New Haven, Conn.: Yale University Press, 1981.

Meredith, Anthony. *The Cappadocians.* Crestwood, N.Y.: St. Vladimir's Seminary Press, 1996.

Neuner, Josef, S.J., and Dupuis, Jacques, S.J., eds. *The Christian Faith: Doctrinal Documents of the Catholic Church* (6th ed.). New York: Alba, 1996. Contains many of the Catholic Church's doctrinal pronouncements topically organized in English.

New Catholic Encyclopedia. New York: McGraw-Hill, 1967. More updated than the *Catholic Encyclopedia,* which is available online.

Osborn, Eric. *Tertullian, First Theologian of the West.* Cambridge: Cambridge University Press, 1997.

Payne, Robert. *The Holy Fire: The Story of the Fathers of the Eastern Church.* Crestwood, N.Y.: St. Vladimir Seminary Press, 1957. Explores the lives and writings of ten Fathers including Clement of Alexandria, Athanasius, Basil, and John Chrysostom.

Pelikan, Jaroslav. *The Emergence of the Catholic Tradition (100–600)* (Christian Tradition Series, vol. 1). Chicago: University of Chicago Press, 1971. A classic by a Lutheran scholar who is one of the best historical theologians of this century.

Quasten, Johannes. *Patrology* (4 vols.). Westminster, Md.: Newman, 1975. Provides a reliable and extensive introduction to the Fathers of the Church.

Ramsey, Boniface. *Beginning to Read the Fathers.* Mahwah, N.J.: Paulist, 1985. A good introduction to the Fathers and their thought on several key issues.

Schnelmelcher, Wilhelm, and R. Wilson, eds. *New Testament Apocrypha.* Louisville: Westminster, 1991. Another collection of these texts can be found in J.K. Elliott, ed., *The Apocryphal New Testament.* New York: Oxford, 1994.

Simonetti, Manlio. *Biblical Interpretation in the Early Church: An Historical Introduction to Patristic Exegesis.* Edinburgh: T & T Clark, 1994.

Tsirpanlis, Constantine N. *Introduction to Eastern Patristic Thought and Orthodox Theology* (Theology and Life no. 30). Collegeville, Minn.: Liturgical, 1991.

Vallée, Gérard. *The Shaping of Christianity: History and Literature of Its Formative Centuries.* New York: Paulist, 1999.

Van der Meer, F. *Augustine the Bishop.* New York: Harper Torchbooks, 1961.

Van der Meer, F., and Christine Mohrmann. *Atlas of the Early Christian World.* Mary F. Hedlund, et al., trans. New York: Thomas Nelson & Sons, 1959.

Wilken, Robert L. *The Christians as the Romans Saw Them.* New Haven, Conn.: Yale University Press, 1984.

———. *The Spirit of Early Christian Thought: Seeking the Face of God.* New Haven, Conn.: Yale University Press, 2003.